"Devil Dog" Dan Daly

"Devil Dog" Dan Daly
America's Fightin'est Marine

CHARLEY ROBERTS

McFarland & Company, Inc., Publishers
Jefferson, North Carolina

ALSO OF INTEREST

Charles Sweeny, the Man Who Inspired Hemingway
by Charley Roberts and Charles P. Hess (McFarland, 2017)

ISBN (print) 978-1-4766-8676-9
ISBN (ebook) 978-1-4766-4461-5

LIBRARY OF CONGRESS AND BRITISH LIBRARY
CATALOGUING DATA ARE AVAILABLE

Library of Congress Control Number 2021050450

© 2021 Charley Roberts. All rights reserved

No part of this book may be reproduced or transmitted in any form or by any means, electronic or mechanical, including photocopying or recording, or by any information storage and retrieval system, without permission in writing from the publisher.

Front cover image: First Sergeant Dan Daly
wearing his two Medals of Honor
and the Distinguished Service Cross, 1919
(Marine Corps History Division Archive)

Printed in the United States of America

*McFarland & Company, Inc., Publishers
Box 611, Jefferson, North Carolina 28640
www.mcfarlandpub.com*

To Cheryl Romo
my inspiration, conscience,
editor, wife and best friend

Table of Contents

Acknowledgments ix

Preface: Even Heroes Have Heroes 1

ONE—An Epic Moment   5

TWO—The Making of the Man   7

THREE—Marine Recruit   14

FOUR—The Boxer Rebellion   19

FIVE—Peking Siege   27

SIX—Love in War   40

SEVEN—Sea Soldier   47

EIGHT—Vera Cruz   56

NINE—Haiti   71

TEN—Dominican Republic   91

ELEVEN—Over There   103

TWELVE—Chateau Thierry   113

THIRTEEN—Belleau Wood   123

FOURTEEN—The Third Medal of Honor   143

FIFTEEN—Soissons   152

SIXTEEN—St. Mihiel   160

SEVENTEEN—Blanc Mont Ridge   167

EIGHTEEN—Meuse-Argonne   179

Table of Contents

NINETEEN—Final Years   188
TWENTY—Daly's Legacy   199

Sergeant Major Daniel J. Daly's Medals and Citations   205
Chapter Notes   209
Bibliography   223
Index   229

Acknowledgments

I have benefited from the help and support of many persons during my research of this book. I want to pay special thanks to the following individuals and their organizations:

Cheryl Romo for editing this book and providing encouragement throughout the research and writing process.

Eric Daly and Paula Ruehling at Wikitree for helping research Daly's family tree.

Christopher Ellis at the Marine Corps History Division, for providing a copy of Private Oscar Upham's journal from the Peking siege.

Alisa Whitley, branch head and archivist, Historical Resources Branch, Marine Corps History Division, for providing several photos of Daly from the branch's collection.

Annette Amerman, branch head and historian, Historical Reference Branch, Marine Corps History Division, for searching branch databases for records related to Daly.

Tavis Anderson, Bryan McGraw and Cara Moore at the National Personnel Records Center, National Archives, St. Louis, Missouri, for providing me with Daly's military records.

Damani Davis and Mark C. Mollan at the National Archives, Washington, D.C., for helping to identify and locate Navy and Marine Corps records related to Daly's service.

Crystal Reinhardt at the National Archives, College Park, Maryland, for searching Army records pertaining to Daly's service in World War I.

Perone Johnson at the U.S. Department of Veterans Affairs for Daly's military pension records.

Acknowledgments

Anastasia Binkowski at the Library of Congress for searching the files of General John J. Pershing's papers for materials related to the award of the Medal of Honor in World War I.

Carol Stern at the Glen Cove Public Library History Room for checking her files.

Paula Archuleta and Alexandra Pritto at St. Patrick's Catholic Church, Glen Cove, New York, for searching the church's local birth and baptism records for November 1873.

Amy Driscoll at the North Shore Historical Museum, Glen Cove, New York, for searching her files.

Ruth Arnone at the Glen Cove School District for searching district files for Daly's records.

Erin Weinman, manuscript reference librarian, Manuscript Department, Library, New York Historical Society, for searching the archives of Brown Harriman for records related to Daly.

Justin Daly, a cousin of Dan Daly, for sharing Daly family lore about his famous kinsman in interviews with the author. Justin was generous with his time and recollections.

Preface: Even Heroes Have Heroes

As a journalist for 25 years, I met, interviewed and wrote about a wide array of fascinating, sometimes scurrilous and occasionally inspiring personalities. One of my favorite days in that quarter-century of reporting involved one of the least newsworthy events I ever covered: The California Legislature sought to honor home-state heroes who had received this nation's highest military decoration for valor, the Medal of Honor. The lawmakers presented these heroes with a California license plate with the medal's image embossed in the metal at a ceremony at the Capitol.

About 50 honorees attended the event in Sacramento. Among them were several whose exploits were widely known. They included Jimmy Doolittle, leader of the "30 seconds over Tokyo" bombing raid that gave hope to Americans in the dark days after Pearl Harbor, and Gregory "Pappy" Boyington, the Marine Corps flying ace who was almost as famous for his "Black Sheep" behavior as for his aerial victories. There were many more, however, who were well known only to their families and friends.

In talking to a number of these heroes, I learned they have heroes too. One group of honorees, all Marines, told me their heroes were Lewis B. (Chesty) Puller and Daniel J. Daly. Puller never received the Medal of Honor, but he did earn the Navy Cross a record five times. He's been called "the Marines' Marine." Daly is lesser known to the general public today but he is just as revered as Puller by Marines.

More than 40 million Americans have served in the U.S. military during wartime but just over 3,500 have received the Medal of Honor.

Preface: Even Heroes Have Heroes

Of these, only three men have received the medal twice for separate actions since the Civil War, and only Daly was recommended for a third Medal of Honor.

Ironically, Marine Corps Sergeant Major Daly is better known for an action for which he did not receive the medal than for the two for which he did. He received the first medal for singlehandedly holding off enemy attacks during the 55-day siege of the foreign legations in Peking during China's Boxer Rebellion of 1900. He received the second medal for his daring one-man actions during an ambush of his 40-man patrol in Haiti in 1915. Daly was nominated for a third Medal of Honor for his actions in World War I, which included leading a charge against a German stronghold. The charge is now famous as much for what Daly purportedly said that day as for the courage he and his fellow Marines showed in making that assault across open ground in the face of intense enemy fire.

Daly was wounded three times and received both the Army Distinguished Service Cross and the Navy Cross for his heroism in The Great War. One explanation for denying him a third Medal of Honor is that some officials thought it unseemly for anyone to receive three awards of the nation's highest medal for valor. Another explanation is that some officials were embarrassed by the profane language in Daly's battle cry and couldn't imagine repeating it in a citation for the medal. There is also the possibility that inter-service rivalry between the Army and Marines led General John J. Pershing's headquarters to deny Daly a third medal. Regardless of whether it was bureaucracy, profanity or jealousy that cost him this unique honor, Daly's words are now part of Marine Corps lore. They are proudly etched in big, bold letters into the wall of the central gallery of the National Museum of the Marine Corps in Quantico, Virginia, for everyone to see.

Daly's fame and accomplishments made headlines at the time, but today he is largely forgotten by Americans outside the Marine Corps. As a journalist and military historian, I felt Daly deserved better. So I set out to tell his inspiring story in all its dramatic detail, renew public appreciation of this hero, and try to discover the facts behind his famous battle cry and why he never received that third Medal of Honor.

Unfortunately, Daly didn't keep a journal, and any letters he wrote to family or friends, if they still exist, are nowhere to be found. As for interviews by reporters or historians during his lifetime, Daly did his best to avoid any meaningful comment. A 1919 *Recruiter's Bulletin*

Preface: Even Heroes Have Heroes

noted that "trying to get biographical data from Daly about Daly is like quizzing the Sphinx. Both are non-committal."[1] In his obituary, *The New York Times* said he "baffled the efforts of many skilled interviewers to obtain the story of his heroism."[2]

The lack of Daly's version of events has led to a host of stories about this publicity-shy Irish-American. These stories either picture him as the most profane and combative NCO ever to wear the uniform or as a man who hardly ever cursed or brawled; as someone who could be drunk and disorderly or a man who avoided strong drink and displays of his pugilistic skills; a strict, unsmiling disciplinarian or a leader whose concern for the wellbeing of his men was paramount.

Daly was many of these things during his life, but the legend has partially obscured the facts. What follows is a search for the facts behind the legend.

ONE

An Epic Moment

Late on a hot June afternoon in the final months of The Great War, two battalions of U.S. Marines advanced in neatly spaced rows into a vast field of wheat 50 miles northeast of Paris. Before long, German machine guns concealed in a distant forest decimated their ranks. Bullets ripped flesh, broke bones and splattered brains, nourishing the wheat with the blood of the dead and dying. It soon became apparent to the Marines that walking upright toward the wooded German bastion meant almost certain death.

Clearly, this could not continue.

The Marines took refuge in the green wheat that stood knee high around them. The thin stalks couldn't stop a bullet but a man lying flat could at least feel invisible beneath the waving grain. Soon, the salty stench of warm blood and cold sweat wafted through the rippling wheat. German bullets sheared off the tasseled tops, while the Marines hugged the ground below. The symphony of death—the rattle of the machine guns, the shrieks and moans of the wounded, the prayers and curses of those fearing for their lives, and the scraping sound of Marines trying to get a little deeper into the rich French soil—seemed to drone on without end.

The situation was becoming intolerable.

The "crack, crack, crack" of bullets—the sound made when the air is suddenly split apart by a bullet's passage and then violently slapped back together—filled the stifling air above the heads of the Marines. Each sweep of the machine guns mowed the wheat ever shorter, gradually removing the thin veil of illusory protection.

Desperation gripped the men.

Finally, a middle-aged Marine had had enough of waiting for someone to do something. He was not an imposing presence physically, just 5-foot-6 and 132 pounds. But what he lacked in size, he made up for in

"Devil Dog" Dan Daly

grit. His steel-gray eyes, clenched jaw and wiry build conveyed a fierce resolve born of hard experience. In his nearly two decades as a Marine, he had seen far more death than the young men around him and had survived far more clashes with the grim reaper than any one man had a right to expect. It was time someone did something. He decided he was the man to do it.

Placing his hands flat on the ground on either side of him, the old warrior thrust himself upward and stood upright in full view of the German gunners. His leathery face, white hair and the three chevrons above a diamond on his sleeve made him instantly recognizable to the men around him. Brandishing his bayonet-tipped rifle over his head in a sweeping motion toward the deadly forest, First Sergeant Dan Daly roared at the Marines, "COME ON YOU SONS OF BITCHES, DO YOU WANT TO LIVE FOREVER?"

For a few agonizing moments, no one at Daly's feet moved. Then, the electrifying effect of his rallying cry—part plea, part dare—got results. By ones and twos, and then en masse, the Marines rose to their feet. Lashed by German machine guns and pounded by German artillery, the Marines doggedly advanced with Daly toward the *Bois de Belleau*—in English, Belleau Wood.

Where, one wonders, do men like Daly come from?

Two

The Making of the Man

Hard times, like the fires that forge tempered steel, toughen men. The hard times of Daniel Joseph Daly's early years helped make him into America's "fightin'est Marine." This title was conferred on Daly by no less a figure than Major General Smedley Darlington Butler, the only other Marine to earn two Medals of Honor and an eyewitness to some of Daly's heroic acts.

Daly was born November 11, 1873, in Glen Cove, New York, according to his Marine Corps enlistment papers.[1] Glen Cove was then a village within the town of Oyster Bay on the north shore of Long Island. The weather that Tuesday in Glen Cove matched the nation's frigid business climate. The temperature was a little above freezing, and the falling snow, like the prospects for an economic revival, quickly turned to slush.[2]

Despite the date and place in his service record, there is good reason to believe Daly was actually born three years earlier and 3,000 miles eastward. Ireland birth and baptism records show Daniel Daly, son of John Daly and Ellen Donovan Daly, was born November 26, 1870, in Templemartin (Church of St. Martin), County Cork, Ireland, a parish five miles north of Bandon.[3] That record alone would not be persuasive, but U.S. census entries for the Daly family in 1880 and 1892 support the notion that he was born in 1870 in Ireland. The June 1880 U.S. census for Glen Cove lists Daniel as 9 years old for a birth year of 1870 and born in Ireland. The February 1892 New York State census for the Daly family then living in Long Island City lists his age as 22, for a birth year of 1870 as well. However, instead of Ireland as his birthplace, this census lists the United States, making him a U.S. citizen.[4] Thus, both censuses support an 1870 birth year.

Why Daly would have changed not only his birth date but also his country of origin is uncertain. It may be he felt he needed to be younger to enlist in the Marines. As to a different birth date, it is likely November 26 was his baptism date and November 11 was his birth date after all. As for the change in birthplace from Ireland, being a native-born American has always had advantages over being an immigrant. This would have been especially true during the mid- to late 1800s when signs reading "No Irish Need Apply" were commonplace in America.

While the date and place of Daly's birth may be in doubt, one thing is certain: The fall of 1873 was the beginning of one of the bleakest economic periods in U.S. history. The collapse of Jay Cooke's Wall Street investment house in September triggered the Panic of 1873, a severe economic downturn that dragged on for six years. Cooke's firm was a major source of capital for the nation's railroads, and railroad construction was the prime driver of the U.S. economy at the time. When Cooke's firm crashed, the New York Stock Market shut down for 10 days in an unsuccessful attempt to staunch the torrent of red ink. By November, 55 railroads had gone bust, and by the following September, 60 more had folded. During the winter of 1873–74, one in four laborers in New York City was unemployed. More than 18,000 U.S. businesses closed their doors between 1873 and 1875, and by 1876 one out of every seven workers nationwide was unemployed.[5] Labor protests erupted and local, state and federal troops were mobilized to suppress them.

A fresh burst of economic growth and expansion occurred in the 1880s but a second brutal depression struck America in 1893 when international wheat prices suddenly crashed. As a result, the stock market fell into a downward spiral, 500 banks shut their doors, 15,000 companies went out of business and large numbers of farmers went bankrupt. It took the United States four long years to regain its economic footing after the crash of 1893.

The final decades of the 19th century were very hard times indeed.

Daly's parents were a working-class couple who emigrated from County Cork, Ireland, to America during this turbulent period. His father, John J. Daly, was born in 1837, and his mother, Ellen Donovan, in 1844.[6] They had already lived through the most challenging of times in Ireland: the Great Famine (1845–1852) in which a million Irish died of starvation or disease and another million left Ireland in search of enough to eat and a better life. During the famine, Ireland's population shrank by a fourth.

John and Ellen were married on January 28, 1865,[7] in the town of Bandon, located 17 miles southwest of the city of Cork. The Industrial

Two—The Making of the Man

Revolution (1760–1840) and the arrival of railroads had transformed the little market town spanning the River Bandon into a bustling local industrial center with breweries, tanneries, distilleries, cotton mills and corn mills. The marriage apparently met with the approval of the couple's families as the official witnesses at the wedding were the fathers of the groom and bride. Six children would be born to this union. Daniel Joseph Daly was the couple's fourth child.

All but one of Daniel Daly's five siblings was born in County Cork, Ireland, based on Ireland birth records.[8] John and Ellen's first child, Timothy, was born on March 7, 1865, in Kinalea, 19 miles east of Bandon. Their second child, Julia, was born November 25, 1865, in Kilbrittain, seven miles south of Bandon. Both of these children died at an early age. Next came David Nicholas Daly, born March 28, 1868, in Clogagh, 10 miles southwest of Bandon. After Daniel's birth in 1870, the couple had a daughter. The first Julia having died, the couple named their new daughter Julia. She was born April 16, 1873, in South Cork. That's just seven months before Daniel's official birth date, offering further evidence that November 11, 1873, was not his actual birth date. The couple's last child, Mary, was born after the family moved to America. She was born May 27, 1884, in New York City.

Based on the 1880 U.S. census, John and sons David and Daniel arrived in America in the late 1870s, although no record of their arrival appears in any database on Ancestry.com, Familysearch.org or the several sites with passenger lists for that period. Ellen and Julia joined them in June 1880, based on Familysearch.com records. If Daniel's mother did not even arrive in America until nearly seven years after his official birth year that also is evidence he was born in Ireland.

The Daly family had ample cause for moving to America when they did. After the Great Famine, civil strife increased as landlords pushed more and more tenant farmers off the land, adding to the misery in the cities. The failure of the Fenian Rising of 1867, an armed revolt against Britain's iron-fisted rule over Ireland, only deepened the sense of hopelessness. County Cork was one of the poorest areas in Ireland even before the devastating potato famine, and that scourge only intensified the dire straits of its inhabitants. While life and work in America's crowded, unsanitary, crime-ridden immigrant districts, like New York City's infamous Five Points,[9] were hardly an improvement, at least there was hope for something better that did not seem to exist in Ireland.

While Young Daniel and his family experienced privation in

"Devil Dog" Dan Daly

Ireland, the sea voyage to America was hardly a pleasure cruise. During the Great Famine, Irish immigrants were transported to America in the cargo holds of sailing ships reeking of every vile odor imaginable. Crammed together below decks with limited access to food and water, many immigrants fell ill during the four-week crossing and 30 percent perished without ever seeing the New World. By the 1870s, when the Dalys journeyed to America, most immigrants came in the bowels of steamships built to carry passengers. The low-cost quarters in the steerage area were cramped but a marked improvement over the famine-era fleet. The 10-day voyage would have made an indelible impression on Daniel.

Upon arrival at the Port of New York, the Dalys, like every other immigrant of the time, had to pass through Castle Garden, the immigrant reception station near the Battery at the foot of Manhattan.[10] There, inspectors examined them for disease. The Dalys were granted entry to the United States while immigrants with diseases were quarantined on Staten Island or sent back where they came from. This life-altering inspection also would have imprinted itself on Daniel.

The Dalys worked hard in America but making ends meet was never easy, especially with a large family. They settled in Glen Cove, next to the sprawling Duryea Corn Starch Manufacturing Company where Daniel's father was employed as a factory worker by 1880.[11] The presence of corn mills in Bandon, Ireland, may have played a role in the Dalys later settling in Glen Cove.

Established in 1855, the starch works turned locally grown corn into starch, syrup, oil and soap. At its peak the factory occupied 30 acres of land just south of Glen Cove Creek and employed 700 workers.[12] They lived in company-owned tenements, shopped at the company-owned store and read the *Glen Cove Gazette*, which was published on a company-owned printing press and served as the company's advocate. While the factory was a boon to the local economy, it also had a definite downside. "The volume of waste produced by converting corn into corn starch was flushed into Glen Cove Creek, where it settled to form a layer of putrefying, obnoxious-smelling organic detritus."[13] Young Daniel Daly lived close-by the polluted pond and the stench, which was pervasive throughout the south side of the village, would have been a constant irritant. One wonders if he ever got that smell out of his nostrils.

Glen Cove was a microcosm of America's harsh realities and pleasant possibilities. While the south side of Glen Cove was dominated by

Two—The Making of the Man

factories and tenements, the north side was home to some of America's wealthiest and most powerful citizens. After the Long Island Railroad extended its tracks to Glen Cove in 1867, many of New York City's elite built lavish estates there along Long Island Sound. They included Wall Street tycoon J.P. Morgan, retail titan F.W. Woolworth and oil baron Charles Pratt. Glen Cove became the center of Long Island's famed Gold Coast. Some of these luminaries even ditched the train in favor of sailing their yachts to their offices in Manhattan. It was the Gilded Age, after all, and lush living was flaunted.

Daniel attended the public school in Glen Cove. Built in 1857 north of the creek at the southeast corner of Highland Road and School Street, it served the community for nearly half a century.[14] While the 1880 U.S. census lists 9-year-old Daniel and his 12-year-old brother David as "at school," it is unclear how much schooling Daniel received before he quit to join the workforce. The Glen Cove School District has no student records for the 1800s. However, Daniel apparently attended long enough to be able to read and write and do math.

The Daly family worshipped at St. Patrick's Catholic Church, a small wood-frame structure located on a hilltop north of the creek near the corner of Glen Street and Pearsall Avenue. It was erected the same year as the school, 1857, to accommodate the growing number of Irish immigrants who were employed at the starch works. It stood until 1900 when it was replaced by a handsome new structure in the style of a classic Irish Gothic cathedral that still stands.[15] St. Patrick's has birth and baptism records for 1873, but there is no record for Daly.

Daniel's father died when the younger Daly was still in his teens. The 1892 New York State Census shows Ellen, but not John, living with her children—Daniel, David, Julia and Mary—in the gritty Hunter's Point section of Long Island City, across the East River from Manhattan, between today's 59th Street Bridge and Queens' Newtown Creek.[16] The area was a warren of factories and tenements. Once again, Daniel would have been confronted by the shabby surroundings, discordant sounds and foul smells that made up the world of the working poor.

Tenements of the day in Hunter's Point, like those throughout New York City, tended to be poorly constructed, multi-story buildings operated by landlords whose sole concern was profit. The tenements frequently were unsafe, unsanitary, and prone to fire and collapse. Clean air and clean drinking water generally were in short supply. Crime was commonplace, overcrowding was rampant, and rats, lice and disease added to the miserable conditions of the impoverished tenants. Complaints to the landlords about these conditions were generally met by either silence or eviction. One report detailing conditions in New York City's tenements of this period described them as "overcrowded, unventilated, without adequate water supply and reeking of every abomination."[17]

Growing up on these mean streets could have led young Daniel into a life of crime. However, his innate integrity, tenacity and decency, which would be noted later in his life, steered him toward more positive pursuits.

Beginning at age 12, Daniel Daly worked as a New York City newsboy in Manhattan.[18] At the time the city's newspapers were clustered along Park Row, a major thoroughfare in lower Manhattan near the Courthouse, City Hall and the terminus of the Brooklyn Bridge. Being a newsboy was more than a job; it was a daily struggle for survival. Newsboys purchased their papers from the newspaper publishers. The publishers would not buy back any unsold papers, so the newsboys had an added incentive to be aggressive salesmen. The newsboys hustled all day to recoup their investment and earn enough money to buy food and lodging that night. The lucky ones were able to rent a nightly bed and buy a meal at one of the newsboys' lodging houses started by the Children's Aid Society. The unlucky ones spent the night wherever they could find a little cover from the weather and something to eat.

"A newsboy's typical day began at four or five in the morning, when he would rise from his night's shelter in the loft of a stable or under a ragman's cart and hurry to the back doors of the *Sun*, *Herald* or *Times* to be at the front of the line to get papers," wrote historian Stephen O'Connor.[19] "The first boys on the street not only sold their papers faster, and thus had more time for making money by other means, but were less likely to get stuck with unsold papers." The newsboys paid one-and-a-half cents apiece for the papers and sold them for two cents. The sale of 56 papers, an average load, would net the newsboy 28 cents. By 9 a.m., the papers were all sold and the newsboy would buy breakfast for nine cents before launching into other money-making ventures. For example, carrying steamship passengers' bags could bring in another 15 to 20 cents. The newsboy would then spend six cents for lunch before heading back to Park Row to purchase the evening papers. Hawking them on the street would hopefully earn another 28 cents. Twelve cents went to buy dinner and 25 cents rented a bed for the night. If the newsboy had any money left over, he might buy a theater ticket or spend the evening drinking or gambling. It was a grueling life and one that O'Connor said the English author Charles Dickens considered "the quintessence of American ambition, drive and depravity."[20]

Newsboys fought, quite literally, for the best locations because those boys strategically situated could sell more papers faster and earn more money. If Daly wasn't already handy with his fists, this is where he would have acquired some of his early combat training. Although short in stature, Daly gained a reputation as a boxer and fought in local sporting clubs for money.[21]

When he grew to manhood, Daly sought out more secure employment. In the 1890s he worked at the large Devoe Manufacturing Co. factory,[22] located in Hunter's Point along Newtown Creek, which separates the boroughs of Queens and Brooklyn. The Devoe plant manufactured, filled and packed cans of various petroleum products, including Devoe's Brilliant, a leading global brand of kerosene. The plant also canned paints, varnishes, lubricants and polishes.[23]

The noise and smells inside the factory must have been intense. Unfortunately, there was no relief outside. During Daly's time, Newtown Creek was a major industrial center, with more ship traffic than the Mississippi River.[24] In addition to the Devoe refinery and cannery, the area along the 3½-mile-long creek was home to an estimated 500 enterprises, including such smelly industries as glue factories, smelters and fat-rendering plants. In addition to the industrial wastes from these activities, in 1856 the city began dumping raw sewage into the creek.[25] This pungent concoction produced a toxic sludge that must have made Daly's eyes water and his nostrils burn.

By his mid–20s, Daly concluded that he wanted more out of life. World events soon offered him an opportunity to change his life, and he leapt at it.

Three

Marine Recruit

The same year as Daniel Daly's official birth date, 1873, writer and humorist Mark Twain published a novel, *The Gilded Age: A Tale of Today*, that satirized the corruption and greed in the United States in the years after the Civil War. The title of the book became the title given to the era that stretched from the late 1860s to the late 1890s. The Gilded Age was one of rapid industrial development in the Northeast and Midwest and settlement of the far West. Despite periodic cataclysms like the Panic of 1873, industrialists and financiers became fabulously rich and delighted in showcasing their enormous fortunes with opulent mansions, private railroad cars and luxurious yachts. Meanwhile, immigrants streamed into the United States from all over the world to compete for jobs with native-born Americans, which led to friction and strife.

In addition to putting down labor uprisings in the East during this period, the U.S. Army fought many small wars against Native American tribes who resisted being pushed off their ancestral lands by the westward tide of settlers. Daly was a child when the Indians defeated General George Armstrong Custer at the Little Big Horn in 1876, and on the cusp of adulthood when the Indian Wars came to an end at Wounded Knee in 1890. That same year, the director of the U.S. Census declared that, due to rising population density in the West, "the frontier" was now history. Americans seeking fresh starts, like Daniel Daly, would have to look elsewhere.

While the concept of Manifest Destiny had propelled the United States to add continental territories that would become states, the country had shied away from acquiring colonies that U.S. officials never intended to grant statehood. Doing so would have required giving full U.S. citizenship to these colonies' non-white, native populations.

However, by 1890, this anti-colonial attitude had begun to change.

Three—Marine Recruit

The United States had become the world leader in industrial production and per capita income, but the nation's business leaders were worried about sustaining their place atop the world's economic pyramid. As other industrialized nations raced to emulate Great Britain and build a network of colonies to provide raw materials and secure global markets, U.S. executives and politicians feared America would be left behind. Adding to this growing U.S. interest in foreign affairs, naval strategist Alfred Thayer Mahan published his seminal work, *The Influence of Sea Power on History, 1660–1783*, which asserted that a nation's prosperity depended on a strong navy to ensure unfettered access to the sea lanes. The final push to join the scramble for colonies came from the notion that developed nations had a duty to bring the benefits of European civilization to peoples of underdeveloped regions. This notion allowed colonizers to portray their self-interest as a selfless, noble cause, which Rudyard Kipling labeled "The White Man's Burden."

Driven by these dynamics, the United States cast aside President George Washington's warning about foreign entanglements and began to reshape its foreign policy. In the 1880s, the United States set about building a modern, steel-hulled navy to protect its interests and project its influence overseas. As its military capability increased, U.S. officials began to consider where and how to use it. Small-scale military actions in the 1880s and 1890s included landing U.S. Marines during uprisings in Samoa, Haiti, Hawaii, China, Korea and Nicaragua, ostensibly to protect American citizens.

In the late 1890s, a circulation battle between New York newspaper barons William Randolph Heart and Joseph Pulitzer had a dramatic impact on the course of U.S. history and the life of Daniel Daly. The "yellow journalism" practiced by Hearst's *New York Journal* and Pulitzer's *New York World* turned Cuba's long struggle for independence from Spain into a major political issue in the United States. Finally goaded into action by lurid stories of Spanish atrocities, some of which were true, President William McKinley sent an armored cruiser, the U.S.S. *Maine*, to Cuba to ensure the safety of American lives and business interests there, particularly tobacco and sugar cane plantations and factories. On the night of February 15, 1898, a thunderous explosion sent the *Maine* to the bottom of Havana harbor with the loss of 70 percent of her crew. Six weeks later, a U.S. Navy investigation concluded that an underwater mine had set off the ship's gunpowder magazine. Spain, however, claimed an internal explosion in a coal bunker next to the

"Devil Dog" Dan Daly

Maine's powder magazine was responsible for the disaster. Opinions as to the cause differ to this day.

Whatever the facts, the Hearst and Pulitzer papers wasted no time in pointing an accusing finger at Spain and demanding a declaration of war with the battle cry "Remember the *Maine*." Congress obliged on April 25. U.S. naval forces won easy and decisive victories over the obsolete Spanish squadrons based in Cuba and the Philippine Islands, and U.S. ground forces landed and soon defeated Spanish troops ashore.

The fighting ended August 13, 1898, with Spain's capitulation less than four months after the war began. The Treaty of Paris, formally ending the war, was signed December 10, 1898, and the U.S. Senate ratified it on February 6, 1899. It compelled Spain to hand over control of Cuba and ownership of the Philippines Islands, Guam and Puerto Rico. The United States had suddenly become a major player on the world stage with global interests to defend, and Daniel Joseph Daly was about to discover his calling.

Daly enlisted in the U.S. Marine Corps on January 10, 1899.[1] Why he didn't enlist during the brief but popular Spanish-American War is unclear. The same is true of his choice of the Marines over the larger military branches—the Army and Navy. It may be that he wanted to avoid being assigned to one of the Army's dreary, isolated forts in the American West or languishing aboard a Navy ship at sea, chipping paint and swabbing decks. It may be that he was moved to join the Marines by the news reports of their daring adventures in exotic foreign lands.

Although the Spanish-American War had effectively ended four months before Daly enlisted, the period of American expansionism had just begun. Instead of granting independence to the former Spanish possessions now under their control, U.S. political and business leaders elected to hold on to them. Publicly, they claimed that the natives in these territories weren't ready for self-government and needed to be educated and civilized. Privately, they stated that the United States needed to become an imperial power to compete with other major industrial nations. These colonies, for that is what they were, would provide raw materials for U.S. industries and a captive market for finished goods. Some U.S. officials also argued that it was the white man's destiny to rule darker races.

All of this meant that U.S. military forces would be needed to protect the nation's interests from foreign intervention as well as internal revolt, and to project U.S. power abroad. The need for military action

Three—Marine Recruit

quickly became apparent in the Philippine Islands. Filipinos had been waging a war for independence from Spain since 1896. When the United States defeated Spain, the Filipinos had expected to be granted independence like the Cubans. When they were denied it, Filipino insurgents revolted against U.S. rule.

The Philippine-American War, also known as the Philippine Insurrection, lasted from February 1899 to July 1902. The fighting was savage, and both sides committed atrocities as barbaric as any the Spanish were ever accused of committing. The Filipinos engaged in guerrilla warfare, ambushing American patrols. Captured troops and natives suspected of aiding the Americans were often tortured to death. U.S. forces responded with search-and-clear missions that laid waste to entire districts and put the civilians into giant concentration camps that bred disease. Deaths among combatants—4,300 Americans and at least 20,000 Filipinos—exceeded the total for the Spanish-American War. Estimates of civilian deaths range from 100,000 to 250,000.

After signing his enlistment papers, Daly reported to the Brooklyn Navy Yard for basic training. There were no Marine Corps recruit training depots, like Parris Island or Camp Pendleton, in those days. New recruits were trained at the nearest Navy yard by Marine Corps non-commissioned officers stationed there. Daly spent two months at the Brooklyn Navy Yard engaged in physical

Private Daly at around the time of the Peking siege, 1900.

conditioning and learning the rudiments of being a Marine: military discipline, close-order drill, personal combat and marksmanship.

Years of hard labor and fisticuffs had toughened Daly's body and mind. Consequently, the physical part of Marine basic training presented no challenge to him. The same could not be said for his acceptance of the strict discipline of the Marine Corps. Based on later incidents in his service record, it would take a decade in uniform for Daly to become a good fit in the corps.

As a newly minted Marine private, Daly's annual pay was $166.[2] (Adjusted for inflation, $166 would be the equivalent of about $5,000 today.) By comparison, a white male factory worker in 1900 earned about $500 annually. However, it is worth noting that Daly received free room and board from the Marine Corps while the factory worker needed about $600 a year to make ends meet. That dynamic helps to explain why children worked in factories to help support their family, albeit for only a third of what an adult earned.[3] So, what would $166 a year buy in 1900? In the United States, a man's suit cost $7–$16; a five-pound bag of flour, 12 cents; a dozen eggs, 21 cents; a pound of butter, 26 cents; and a 10-pound bag of potatoes, 14 cents.[4] A bottle of whiskey cost a princely sum of $2.[5]

On March 22, 1899, Private Daly joined the Marine detachment aboard the U.S.S. *Newark*, a protected cruiser armed with 12 six-inch guns that had participated in the destruction of the Spanish squadron off Santiago, Cuba, the year before. The ship left New York the next day and sailed around South America, stopping at Port Low, Chile for three weeks to cut wood for fuel. It arrived at San Francisco Bay on September 4 and moored at the Mare Island Navy Yard at Vallejo. A month later, the *Newark* sailed for the Philippines, with a stop in Hawaii. It arrived at the Cavite navy base on the south shore of Manila Bay on November 25. The Marine detachment, under Lieutenant Newt H. Hall, spent the next six months based at Cavite performing various ship and shore duties, including landing troops and escorting ships.[6]

Hall was about the same age as Daly but he was a much more experienced Marine. A Texas native, he had graduated from the U.S. Naval Academy in 1895 and been commissioned a Marine second lieutenant in 1897. Hall had seen action at Guantanamo Bay, Cuba, with Company B, 1st Marine Battalion during the Spanish-American War.[7]

In August 1899, a new crisis arose that would provide the first real test of Daly as a Marine.

Four

The Boxer Rebellion

On May 20, 1900, the U.S.S. *Newark*, with Daly aboard, sailed out of Manila Bay bound for China with orders to rush its Marine detachment to the defense of the American legation in Peking. A violent peasant cult—calling itself "the Righteous and Harmonious Fists," but referred to by Westerners as "the Boxers"—was rampaging across China, murdering Christian missionaries by the hundreds, their Chinese converts by the tens of thousands, and seeking to drive all foreigners out of China.

The Boxer Rebellion had begun in August 1899, but the uprising was decades in the making. Several European nations had established zones of influence within China, essentially dividing portions of the country into de facto colonies for the economic benefit of those European nations. The imperial government of China was too weak to resist these assaults on its sovereignty.

A severe drought followed by massive floods in the late 1890s created widespread misery in northern China. These conditions combined with antipathy toward Christian missionary activity to fuel an anti-foreigner movement in rural Shantung province north of Peking, China's capital city. The cult-like Righteous and Harmonious Fists practiced martial arts and its followers came to believe they could not be harmed by the foreigners' bullets.

The rebellion began with attacks on local Christian missions, which had been allowed to proliferate and proselytize across China under the treaty with Great Britain and France that ended the Second Opium War in 1860. By the time large numbers of Boxers entered Peking in the spring of 1900, the rebellion had the tacit support of the dowager empress, Cixi, who held her nephew, the emperor, under house arrest at the time and was in control of the government. This meant Chinese army forces would not stop the Boxers, and in many instances imperial troops actively aided in their attacks.

"Devil Dog" Dan Daly

Seven European nations, as well as Japan and the United States, had diplomatic missions in Peking, and the heads of these legations sent urgent appeals to their governments for troops to protect the diplomats, their families and staff from possible massacre by the Boxers. Warships from eight nations—Austria-Hungary, Britain, France, Germany, Italy, Japan, Russia and the United States—began assembling in the waters off Tientsin, the Chinese port nearest Peking, which is 80 miles inland from Tientsin. Ultimately, 54 ships and 50,000 troops would be involved.

The *Newark* was one of the early arrivals. It reached Tientsin on May 27. Standing on the deck of the *Newark*, Daly counted 16 other allied warships gathered 12 miles offshore.[1] After only 16 months in the Marine Corps, Daly was still a rookie, untested by combat. Not much of a talker at this point, he likely kept his mixed emotions of anticipation and apprehension to himself.

En route to China, the *Newark*'s landing force of 24 Marines, led by Captain Hall, had been augmented at Nagasaki, Japan, by 26 Marines from the U.S.S. *Oregon*, led by Captain John Twiggs Myers. Six sailors from the *Newark* also were assigned to the detachment, bringing the total to 56. As the more senior captain, Myers assumed overall command of the combined force.[2] Myers was a 28-year-old graduate of the U.S. Naval Academy, class of 1892. Nicknamed "Handsome Jack," he sported a large handlebar mustache during the Boxer Rebellion. Both his father, Abraham Myers, and his maternal grandfather, David Twiggs, were career U.S. Army officers who became Confederate generals during the U.S. Civil War. Prior to the Boxer Rebellion, Myers participated in the capture of Guam during the Spanish-American War and led several amphibious assaults during the early days of the Philippine-American War.

Tientsin is located 40 miles up the Peiho River from Taku. To reach Tientsin from the open ocean, ships had to pass under the artillery batteries of the coastal forts at Taku at the mouth of the Peiho River. The forts were constructed of wood and brick, with a two-foot thick outer layer of cement to help absorb the impact from artillery shells. The walls, which ranged in height from 30 to 50 feet above the surrounding flatlands, were studded with artillery pieces of varying calibers.

At 4:30 p.m. on May 29, Admiral Louis Kempff, the ranking U.S. naval officer, received a message from Edwin Conger, the head of the U.S. legation in Peking, instructing him to land a Marine detachment in Tientsin and await further orders. An hour later, Daly and the Marine

Four—The Boxer Rebellion

detachment, plus about 75 sailors and a 3-inch field piece, with Navy Captain Bowman McCalla in overall command, boarded tugboats and headed toward Tientsin. The men remained hidden below decks while the tugboats passed under the guns of the Taku forts.[3] The foul odors of decayed fish, machine oil, and sweat in that confined space likely reminded him of his days in the kerosene plant on New Creek.

About six miles in, the tugs grounded on a sandbar and the passengers transferred to sampans to continue. Later, the landing force transferred to a steamer before arriving in Taku. They then marched to the railroad depot but no trains were available. So they marched back to the harbor, boarded an old scow, and were finally towed the last leg upriver to Tientsin.[4]

Marching from the port to the Tientsin railroad depot on the morning of May 31, the landing force commandeered a train and arrived at the rail terminal in Peking at about 6 p.m. The train also carried military detachments from Britain, France, Italy, Japan and Russia. Altogether this body totaled about 350 officers and men. The detachment formed a column with the Americans at the front, and Myers gave his Marines the order to "fix bayonets." The sharp metallic clang of that savage weapon clicking into place would have energized Daly and every other Marine. The entire detachment then marched at a rapid pace seven miles into the heart of the city, with each nation's contingent vying to be the first to arrive at the legations.

The Marines were armed with Lee Navy model 1895 rifles. These straight-pull bolt-action rifles fired a .236 cartridge using smokeless powder and weighed eight-and-one-third pounds without its clip of five cartridges. With its bayonet attached, the rifle was about as long as Daly was tall, but it would soon prove to be in very capable hands.

Peking at the time had a population of about one million. It was divided into a number of walled cities. The so-called Chinese City, located on the south side of Peking nearest the rail terminal, was surrounded by walls 30 feet high and over 20 feet thick. Adjoining the Chinese City on the north, the Tartar City was surrounded by even more impressive walls, over 40 feet high, 50 feet wide at the top and 60 feet wide at the bottom.[5] That's the height of a four-story building and wide enough at the top to park four modern automobiles side by side. On the legation side of the Tartar Wall, large, wide ramps led up to the top of the wall near either end of the area that held the legations. There were three large gates in the wall between the Chinese City and the Tartar

City, three large gates each in the western and eastern walls and two gates in the northern wall of the Tartar City. "Within the Tartar City lay the Imperial City, a complex of palaces, temples, public offices, and pleasure gardens. And within the Imperial City was the Forbidden City," the home of the emperor.[6]

The legations—walled compounds where foreign diplomats, their families and staffs resided—were clustered together in the Tartar City, just inside the wall adjoining the Chinese City and just outside the southeast corner of the wall of the Imperial City. The Legation Quarter, as it was called, was roughly a square three-quarters of a mile in length on each side. That's the equivalent of 72 U.S. city blocks or 360 football fields, roughly half the size of New York City's Central Park or three times the size of Disneyland in California.

Eleven nations had legations in the quarter: Austria, Belgium, Britain, France, Germany, Holland, Italy, Japan, Russia, Spain, and the United States. There also were civilians within the quarter who acted as the diplomatic representative of additional foreign nations, such as the Swiss proprietor of the Pekin Hotel who represented Switzerland.

Between the legations were lavish homes of wealthy Chinese, local shops, foreign banks and business offices as well as the dwellings of ordinary Chinese. The Legation Quarter was split into left and right halves by a stinking open sewer of a canal, euphemistically named the Jade River. It flowed south through the Legation Quarter and out through a sluice gate in the wall between the Tartar and Chinese cities, and into a moat on the Chinese City side of that wall. The quarter also was sliced into large blocks by two tree-lined avenues. One avenue ran north to south in the middle of the right side of the quarter. The other and more important avenue, Legation Street, ran east to west and crossed the Jade River over a stone bridge. These large blocks were further divided by narrow streets and alleys.

The British Legation compound was located in the upper left quadrant of the quarter and abutted the Jade River. It was the largest and grandest, and occupied about three acres. The somewhat smaller American Legation compound was located in the lower left quadrant on the south side of Legation Street. The Russian Legation compound sat across Legation Street from the American compound. The Dutch Legation compound was a short distance west of the American. All of the other legation compounds were located on the right or east side of the Jade River. Most of these legations were located along Legation Street.

Four—The Boxer Rebellion

For Daly, the Legation Quarter was his most exotic locale yet, with its babel of foreign languages, fancily dressed diplomats and gaily costumed local lords surrounded by throngs of working-class Chinese.

Given the many formidable walls of Peking and the large number of Boxers in the city, it would have been possible for the Chinese to prevent the combined landing force from reaching the Legation Quarter. This certainly occurred to the leader of the American landing force. Fearing the Chinese would close the gates to block their way, McCalla had his men double time the last 300 yards through the Chienmen Gate in the center of the Tartar City wall. Turning right, the Marines quickly arrived at the legations. Marine Private Oscar Upham described this as a "grandstand rush." In any event, McCalla's action enabled the Americans to be the first contingent through the gate.[7] To everyone's surprise, the "dense mass of Chinese that thronged the roadway" made no attempt to prevent the foreign forces' arrival. Captain Myers considered their presence more ominous than hostile.[8] Daly sensed the hatred.

Once again, Daly's senses were assailed by fetid conditions. The heat and humidity in Peking were oppressive. His woolen uniform shirt, soaked in sweat, clung to his body, while the pungent odors of the cooking fires mixed with the reek from open sewers, clawed at his nostrils.

Marching into the Legation Quarter late on the final day of May, Daly and the other Marines were met by cheers from the foreign residents.. "Thank God you have come," exclaimed the head of the U.S. legation, Edwin Conger, as he rushed to up to the Marines. "Now we are safe."[9] The next several weeks would prove him terribly wrong.

Myers quickly established three defensive posts and Daly and his fellow Marines settled into a routine. They built barricades, dug trenches and set up checkpoints. If there was going to be a fight, the Marines wanted to be ready for it. The first week of June was relatively quiet while the Boxers tightened their cordon around the Legation Quarter and the trapped residents waited anxiously for the arrival of a much larger relief force that was supposed to be on its way.

On June 10, a detachment of 10 Marines from the Legation Quarter was sent to guard the American Mission, a missionary compound about the size of three football fields surrounded by 12-foot-high walls. Located about three-quarters of a mile outside the Legation Quarter, it contained a church, a hospital, two schools for Chinese children, and many dwellings. The following day, an additional 10 Marines were dispatched to the American Mission as the behavior of the Boxers became more threatening to the missionaries.[10]

The situation became more intense starting on June 13 when German marines killed 10 Boxers in the Chinese City by firing on them from the Tartar City wall. Captain Hall took a small detachment of Marines down to the Hatamen Gate in the Tartar Wall, at the east end of the Legation Quarter. There, he relieved the keeper of the key to the gate so that he could not let the Boxers enter the quarter. A Marine guard was then posted at the gate. Over the next three days, the Boxers set fire to shops in the city selling foreign goods. An estimated 4,000 shops and their wares were reduced to ashes, creating a dense pall of smoke over the city. The fires also badly damaged the tall, ornate archery tower atop the Chienmen Gate in the center of the Tartar Wall. The Chienmen Gate guarded the main route from the Chinese City to the Imperial City.[11]

With each passing day, Daly witnessed rivers of refugees pouring into the Legation Quarter seeking sanctuary from marauding bands of Boxers. He took stock of their scant possessions, furtive glances and excited chatter. As the crowding increased, so did the anxiety among the teeming humanity in the quarter. Adding to the tension, Chinese imperial troops supposedly sent to guard foreign property now joined Boxers in looting these places.

To mock the foreigners in the quarter, on June 13 a lone Boxer seated himself on a cart on Legation Street and began sharpening a large carving knife on his boot, daring anyone to stop him. The challenge proved too much for the hot-tempered head of the German legation. Charging into the street, he bludgeoned the Boxer with his walking-stick before having him hauled into the German Legation as a prisoner. Bands of Boxers swiftly responded with a bloody rampage through western parts of the city. Christian cathedrals were set ablaze and those Chinese converts not consumed in the flames were hacked to death by vengeful Boxers.[12]

Daly and his fellow Marines began to wonder what they were expected to do against the hordes of rampaging Boxers that seemed to grow in number and boldness with each passing day. The Alamo and Custer's Last Stand were celebrated moments of bravery in the face of insurmountable odds, but they did not end well for the badly outnumbered combatants.

In response to the Boxers' depredations, 10 U.S. Marines and 20 Russian troops were dispatched to South Church, located outside the

Four—The Boxer Rebellion

quarter and adjacent to the Tartar Wall. There they killed about 50 Boxers who were killing and torturing Chinese Christians and rescued about 300 of them. Another clash occurred the following day. A force of American, British and Japanese troops engaged a group of Boxers in a temple near the Russian Legation who were doing their exercises and chants, and killed 58 of them without any allied losses.[13]

In the midst of this mayhem, the Chinese government received a message from the foreign military forces on its coast that it viewed as an insulting ultimatum. It stated that the foreign powers planned to seize the Taku forts the next day. The dowager empress erupted in rage at what she saw as an act of war.

On June 19, the Chinese government issued an edict that all foreigners in the Legation Quarter leave Peking within 24 hours. There were then 473 foreign civilians from 18 nations within the quarter, plus 409 military personnel from eight countries. There also were about 3,000 Chinese Christian converts in the quarter. Most of the foreign civilians were billeted in very crowded conditions within the British compound. Many of the converts were housed in a large, palatial compound known as the Fu that belonged to a wealthy Chinese courtier.[14]

After six hours of heated debate among the chief diplomats, the legations informed the Chinese government that they would leave, but they needed more time to prepare. When no response was received by the next day, June 20, the head of the German legation set out in a sedan chair for the Chinese foreign ministry about a mile away to demand an answer. He ignored suggestions that he take along a contingent of guards. He didn't get far. A Chinese army officer, in full uniform with a mandarin's hat and a button and blue feather, stepped up to the sedan chair on the street. Leveling his rifle at point-blank range, he shot the German diplomat once in the head.[15] Daly and a small force of allied troops rushed out to try to rescue the German or retrieve his body, but they were quickly driven back by a screaming horde of Boxers armed with rifles and spears.[16]

Daly had no illusion about what he and the others in the Legation Quarter could expect in the way of mercy if the Chinese decided to attack in overwhelming numbers.

Conger, the chief American diplomat, sent an urgent message to a Methodist mission a half mile outside the quarter: "Come at once within the Legation lines and bring your Chinese with you." Soon a pitiful parade of several hundred was on the move, wending its way through

"Devil Dog" Dan Daly

suddenly deserted streets. Captain Hall and his Marines, including Daly, provided a security cordon along the route, rifles with fixed bayonets at the ready to repel any assault. Daly and the others put on a brave face, but they all knew the score. Much to Daly's surprise and everyone else's, no attack occurred. One of the missionaries, Mary Gamewell, later described the surreal scene: "A great hush seemed to have settled upon the city, as if in awe of the enormity of the crime committed, or holding its breath for an expected explosion."[17]

Five

Peking Siege

Any thought of the legations leaving Peking died with the German diplomat. The legations' leaders concluded that the dowager empress had decided to openly support the Boxers in their purge of foreigners. Any attempt to leave now could end in a massacre. Thus, June 20 marked the beginning of what became a 55-day siege of the legations as they fended off daily attacks and waited with mounting desperation for their nations to come to their rescue. A relief column had been repeatedly reported to be on its way to Peking from Tientsin. But day after day it failed to arrive. The legation's roughly 400 military defenders now faced a combined force of about 50,000 Boxers and Imperial Army troops.[1]

In addition to being badly outnumbered, the legation defenders faced other challenges. First, they did not all speak a common language so communication among the fighting forces was difficult and often time-consuming. Second, they had an inadequate supply of ammunition to sustain a lengthy siege. Third, each nation's military force used a different type of rifle, so they could not share even their limited supply of bullets. Fourth, they also had a similar supply problem with their heavier weapons: an Italian one-pounder artillery piece, and three machine guns—an American Colt, an Austrian Maxim and a British Nordenfelt. And fifth, they had a great many mouths to feed and too little food for such a multitude. A search of Chinese warehouses in the quarter added substantial amounts of wheat and rice to the legations' own supplies. In time, the many horses stabled in the quarter became a source of meat as did the many stray dogs and cats. Rationing helped stretch the food supply further but it also left the defenders progressively weaker and short-tempered.

In addition, the legations had too large an area to adequately defend. However, the defensive perimeter soon shrank significantly. The Austrian, Belgian, Dutch and Italian compounds on the edges of the quarter were abandoned when they proved too difficult to hold against large-scale Boxer attacks. As a result, the size and shape of the quarter changed from a large square to a lopsided rectangle roughly half the original area. It stretched 700 yards from the Russian and American compounds on the west to the French compound on the east, and 750 yards from the British compound and the Fu on the north to the Tartar Wall on the south. Bunched together along Legation Street within these boundaries were the German, Japanese and Spanish compounds, as well as the Hotel Pekin and its Swiss proprietor, Switzerland's resident diplomat.[2]

Chinese forces began the siege in earnest with an attack on the British and Russian legations on June 21, while Boxers burned and looted some of the outlying missionary compounds. The next day, Boxers looted the abandoned Dutch legation located 300 yards outside the defensive perimeter. On June 23, Chinese troops and Boxers combined to attack the opposite side of the Legation Quarter. Chinese soldiers also began firing into the quarter from the top of the Tartar Wall with rifles and a three-inch field piece.[3] In addition, Chinese troops breached the wall of the Fu, the mansion across the Jade River from the British compound where many of the Chinese converts were lodged. Despite being badly outnumbered, Japanese soldiers drove the invaders back.

While a few Marines had been slightly wounded up to this point, June 24 marked the first fatality. Private Charles B. King died instantly when shot through the head by a sniper. The Germans responded by mounting the Tartar Wall, using the ramp behind their compound, and driving the Chinese sharpshooters back. Captain Myers and a detachment of Marines, including Daly, then continued that advance along the wall to within 500 yards of the Chienmen Gate. Coming under increasingly heavy fire, the Marines descended the wide ramp behind the American compound. Three hours later, the Marines returned to the top of the wall, now supported by a Colt model 1895 light machine gun. Mounted on wheels or a tripod, the air-cooled, belt-fed gun could fire 400 rounds per minute. It fired a .236-caliber bullet, the same as the Marines' Lee Navy model 1895 rifles. Catching the Chinese by surprise, they drove them back along the wall.

Before long the Marines had erected a barricade four feet high across about two-thirds of the 50-foot-wide top of the wall near the west end of the quarter. With bugles blaring, the Chinese launched an attack on the Marine barricade. Fierce fighting ensued but when it ended the

Five—Peking Siege

Marines were still in possession of the barricade.[4] Daly fought well, dispatching many Chinese, first with his rifle and then with his rifle butt and bayonet.[5]

At the outset of the siege, buildings bordering the legations' defensive perimeter were torn down to deprive any attacking Chinese of cover from allied fire. In addition, a trench 14 feet deep was dug along the defensive perimeter and barricades were erected, using rubble from the demolished buildings, to block streets leading into the quarter. Loopholes were created in the barricades so defenders could fire at attackers without having to show themselves. Chinese converts worked alongside foreign civilians and military personnel to build the barricades. Sand bags also were used, especially atop the Tartar Wall, to build barricades. Over the course of the siege, an estimated 100,000 sandbags were used. To make so many bags, the women in the legations sewed cloth taken from wherever it could be found. This included satin curtains, monogrammed linen sheets, brocades and tapestries from the Fu.

"Those Legation ladies were wonderful," Daly later recalled. "They ripped up all their ballroom dresses to sew up sand bags for us, all kinds of colors. I never saw such fancy sand bags. Some of 'em were even trimmed in lace."[6]

One Legation diarist wrote of the sand bags: "There was no doubt that the sky-blue, blood-red, yellow and many other colored sandbags made the most colorful barricades and breastworks in the history of warfare."[7]

On average, the Marines stationed 15 men at the barricade on the Tartar Wall, six more stood guard at a barricade at the foot of the ramp behind the American compound, and another eight manned a barricade on Legation Street, adjacent to the compound. Owing to the danger from Chinese snipers, the Marines atop the wall could only be relieved or resupplied at night.[8]

Battling over the barricade continued through the following days, with charges and counter-charges, and mounting casualties. On June 27, about 200 Boxers, prodded to attack by Chinese army bayonets at their back, surged toward the Marine barricade. Daly emptied his rifle into the attackers before climbing over the barricade to club and bayonet several more, including two he knocked off the wall. Unable to dislodge the Marines, the Chinese erected their own barricade atop the wall, about 100 yards from the Marines.[9]

The drought that had fueled the rebellion ended with a mighty downpour on June 30. The rain came down so hard that Daly couldn't see more than a few feet in front of him. Marines left the security of the barricade to dance on the wall, assuming that if they could not see the enemy, Chinese sharpshooters couldn't see them. The assumption apparently proved correct.

On July 1, the Germans were driven from their own barricade on the Tartar Wall on the east end of the quarter behind their compound. This left the Marines at their barricade exposed to rifle fire from their rear as well as their front. So Captain Myers ordered the Marines off the wall. Reinforced by 20 British Marines, the Americans charged up the ramp to the top of the wall and began building a second barricade to deal with the threat from the rear. Overnight the Chinese erected a new barricade closer to the new allied barricade. The Chinese were now literally only a stone's throw from the Americans, as the Chinese began lobbing rocks at the Marines.[10]

Adding to the misery of the American defenders, Chinese sharpshooters could now keep the Marines pinned down, making it especially hazardous for them to leave the wall to get any rest. Captain Myers sent a scribbled note down to Edwin Conger lamenting that "it is slow sure death to remain here…. The men all feel that they are in a trap and simply await the hour of execution."[11] Despite such despair, neither Daly nor any other Marine gave any thought to surrender. If die they must, all preferred to meet death on their feet, not their knees.

As if things couldn't seem to get any worse, by early morning of July 3, the Chinese had erected a tower as part of their barricade and begun heaving larger stones into the Marine position. In response, Captain Myers organized his forces—15 Americans, 15 British and seven Russians—for an attack on the enemy works. Sandbags were removed from either end of the allied barricade to allow passage. At 2:30 a.m., Myers launched his assault. Two files of attackers, including Daly who was at the head of one of the files, quietly advanced, one on either side of the wall's 50-foot-wide top. As they drew close, they were detected and the Chinese fired blindly down the center of the wall, missing the Marines along the edges as Myers had hoped would happen. The allied attackers returned fire but the assault momentarily stalled. However, two Marine privates, R. Turner and R.E. Thomas, managed to work their way to the rear of the Chinese barricade and took the defenders under fire. Daly and other Marines rushed forward and a general melee of firing, clubbing and bayoneting ensued before the Chinese took flight.[12]

Five—Peking Siege

The defenders reported 50–60 Chinese were killed in the brief but fierce fight. Casualties among the 37 allied troops were comparatively light. Three were killed, including both Turner and Thomas, and six were wounded, but one of those was quite consequential. Captain Myers received a serious spear wound in the thigh, and while recovering in the quarter he contracted typhoid that put him out of action for the remainder of the siege. The bodies of the dead Chinese were unceremoniously thrown off the wall into the Chinese City below. The reek of their putrefying corpses and the garbage rotting in the street added to the nausea experienced by Daly and some of his fellow Marines. The bodies of Turner and Thomas were reverently laid to rest in the Russian compound. They were the fifth and sixth Marines killed so far in the siege. Myers was the seventh Marine to be wounded.[13]

The skirmish at the barricade seemed to take some of the fight out of the Chinese for a couple of days. The Marines celebrated the Fourth of July while standing guard atop the wall with a drink supplied by a retired British Army officer. The Chinese provided some fireworks in the form of a few rifle shots that succeeded in wounding one Marine and knocking down the American flag posted on the barricade.

Despite the momentary lull in the fighting, conditions atop the wall and inside the quarter were becoming intolerable. Daly and the other defenders rarely left the top of the wall during this period. As a result, they had little opportunity to bathe, and in the searing summer heat and humidity, reaching 110 degrees in the shade if one could find any, the body odor of the troops packed together atop the wall began to rival the stench from the piles of corpses, garbage and sewage in the street below. Adding to the misery and tensions, the defenders had to contend with diarrhea from a disgusting diet of horse meat and rice, a dwindling supply of ammunition, and a declining hope of rescue, despite repeated assurances that help would arrive soon. While it was true that help was on the way, one relief column had already been driven back and a larger second column was engaged in fierce fighting between Tientsin and Peking.

On July 6, one of the Chinese converts inside the quarter made a discovery that proved a great blessing for the defenders. "The Chinks had artillery," Daly later recalled, "but all we had to come back at them with was rifle fire. At last we got us a cannon."[14] The Chinese convert unearthed the barrel of an old smooth-bore, three-inch, muzzle-loading cannon barrel in a deserted foundry. A resourceful 23-year-old U.S.

"Devil Dog" Dan Daly

Navy gunner's mate first class, Joseph Mitchell, mounted the barrel on a large beam attached to a set of wheels from an Italian gun carriage. "Mitchell, a seaman named Axel Westermark, a Marine from Oregon, Brigham Young, and a couple of other Marines had her ready to go inside one day," recalled Daly. Given his familiarity with this process, Daly was probably one of the other Marines he mentioned.

Next, they dismantled a store of ammunition for a Russian nine-pounder artillery piece that had been discarded in Tientsen, poured the propellant into the barrel and rammed home a Russian shell. The contraption delivered an ear-splitting blast and a lethal punch. Mitchell quickly put it to work in support of Japanese troops defending the quarter's northeast border, the Fu, from a serious attack by Chinese troops supported by a Krupp gun.[15]

"She was a good gun," Daly recalled. "We used Russian powder, Japanese fuses and some English shells. Mostly we used bags of nails as grape-shot. We called her 'Betsy' and 'Old International.' The Limeys called her 'The Old Crock.' Some Legation fellow named her 'Empress Dowager.' We used her first against a Chink barricade—running her up close while some German sailors covered us with rifle fire. We touched her off, and those Chinks were silent for hours."[16]

In the ensuing days, the Chinese army forces mounted artillery pieces on the Imperial City wall and shelled the British Legation. The Marines did their best to discourage this activity. They placed their Colt machine guns in such a way that whenever the Chinese troops tried to reload their cannons, they came under fire. The Chinese gunners also proved to be poor shots. The majority of their shells flew over the quarter and landed in the Chinese City beyond.[17]

It was during this period that the Japanese troops scored a coup of their own. Chinese troops were building a barricade adjacent to the north wall of the Fu. Seeing the Chinese troops' rifles stacked against the wall, the Japanese defenders quietly gathered up the rifles and returned to the Fu before they were discovered. This act not only bolstered allied morale but also increased the supply of weapons and ammunition.

On July 13, a force of about 500 Chinese attempted to storm the east side of the quarter. They charged down the ramp behind the German compound and advanced along the street next to the Tartar Wall. They were met by a fusillade of rifle fire from the German troops and ultimately driven back by sharpshooting American Marines atop the wall.

Five—Peking Siege

That night, an attack on the French compound on the north side of Legation Street began when the Chinese detonated a mine in a tunnel dug under two buildings. The blast destroyed the buildings and killed two Frenchmen but the attack was repulsed. Ironically, the Chinese suffered far greater casualties in the initial blast. Misjudging the force of the explosion, about 30 Chinese stood too close and died in the blast.[18]

Overnight, the Marines built a makeshift barricade on the Tartar Wall about 200 yards east of the allied barricade. This new barricade extended two-thirds of the way across the top of the wall. Later that day, however, Captain Hall, who had assumed command of the Marines from the bed-ridden Myers, concluded that this new position would have to be strengthened to withstand attack.

After dark on July 14, Hall and Daly slipped around the makeshift barricade and crept quietly forward about 100 yards. There they took cover in a bastion, a fortified extension of the wall. After surveying the situation, Hall told Daly he needed a volunteer to stay at the bastion and repel any Chinese while he went back down into the quarter to bring up more men and sandbags. "I won't order you to stay out here," Hall whispered to Daly. "But if you can hold them back tonight, they'll never drive us back tomorrow." Daly didn't hesitate. "I'll stay," he whispered back, nonchalantly adding, "See you in the morning, Captain." Hall handed Daly several bandoliers of ammunition, squeezed his arm, and disappeared into the darkness.[19]

At such moments, legends are born. Daly piled the ammunition in front of him inside the bastion and waited. He could hear chattering voices speaking Chinese nearby. Before long, two Chinese loomed out of the night. Daly put a bullet in the head of each man. Having alerted the Chinese to his presence, he now expected them to rush him. Instead, the Chinese cautiously approached in small groups, apparently unsure of where or how many defenders awaited them. The light of fires at the base of the wall provided enough illumination for Daly to take careful aim and put a bullet in each of the attackers.

When a group of four Chinese suddenly rushed him, Daly coolly worked his rifle bolt to chamber and fire three quick shots that dropped three of the attackers. However, one of them wasn't finished yet and he charged again. Daly didn't have time to work his rifle bolt this time, so he thrust his bayonet into the man's chest. Yanking the bloody blade out, Daly turned just in time to miss being struck by the fourth man's slashing sword stroke. Continuing to pivot, Daly slammed his rifle butt into the man, knocking him off the wall.[20]

Other Chinese began firing in Daly's general direction, based on the report of his rifle. In the darkness, however, they couldn't see him inside the bastion. Once again, small groups of Chinese advanced slowly toward him, and once again he dispatched them with single shots.[21] Several times during the night, the Chinese angrily yelled a racial epithet at him that can best be translated as "very bad devil."[22] This would not be the last time an enemy called Daly a "devil."

Alone, armed with only his rifle, bayonet and a shrinking supply of bullets, Daly steadfastly held off attackers while waiting anxiously for daylight and hoped-for reinforcements.

In the early morning hours of July 15, when his fellow Marines reached Daly, they found him still at his post, now surrounded by heaps of enemy dead. No one bothered to count the corpses as they rolled them off the wall. Legend has it that there were as many as 200. While that number is undoubtedly an exaggeration, it was a very long night and the body count was high enough to impress Daly's fellow Marines.

Captain Hall sent three Marines and 23 Chinese workers carrying sandbags to erect yet another new barricade on the wall. This one was about 200 yards farther east of the latest barricade. The purpose of the new barricade was to provide access to the Jade River's sluice gate in the event of either the need to provide an escape route from the quarter or to link up with any rescue force trying to enter through the gate.[23]

The Chinese responded by moving their barricades closer to the allied barricades at either end of the Tartar Wall above the Legation Quarter. By the end of July 15, the Chinese were 300 yards from the allies' eastern barricade and 30 yards from the allies' western barricade.

At this point, the situation took a somewhat surreal turn. The Chinese allowed a message from U.S. Secretary of State John Hay to be delivered to Edwin Conger, the head of the American legation in Peking. It proposed a truce. The Chinese sent a delegation into the quarter to discuss the matter and a truce was arranged. During this period, the Chinese removed the bodies of their dead on the wall. "It's about time as they have been lying there under our noses for near three weeks," Marine Private Oscar Upham noted in his journal. "As they lower them off the wall in straw matting we can see heads and limbs fall out.... We are very thankful to them for removing their dead as the stench has been something awful for a dead chinaman has a peculiar odor all his own. Some of the bodies were lying within 3 or 4 feet of our barricade and were quite an inducement to the flies and I think all of the flies in Peking were here."[24]

On July 18, the legations received their first reliable piece of news from the outside world about the prospect of rescue. A messenger sent by the Japanese legation to Tientsin managed to slip back into the quarter with word that a relief force of 11,000 allied troops had captured that city and was expected to reach Peking in two days. However, the arrival of this good news coincided with the Chinese beginning work on a new barricade in violation of the truce. The allies warned them to stop, and when they didn't, the International Gun was used to knock down the barricade. The construction stopped and all firing ceased.[25]

The truce came to an abrupt end on July 29. As Upham recorded in his journal, "The war is on again in earnest. The Chinese started it by picking off some of our coolies. We retaliated by picking a few of them off their roost. This brought a general engagement. We feel better having something to do than we did during the truce."

Upham also related an incident involving a Chinese army colonel that occurred during the truce. At a meeting with allied officials, the colonel "eagerly asked who those men were that wore the big hats. On being told they were American Marines, he shook his head and said, 'I don't understand them at all. They don't shoot very often, but when they do I lose a man. My men are afraid of them.'"[26]

On August 2, with no sign yet of a relief force, a messenger slipped into the quarter from Tientsin with word that a relief force would leave Tientsin for Peking on July 28 or 29. While this was more than a week later than expected, it still heartened the defenders. The following day, the diplomats received another message that a relief force of 10,000 men would leave Tientsin on August 1, and more troops would follow. On August 10, yet another messenger reached the quarter with news that the relief force was expected in Peking on August 13 or 14.[27]

If these seemingly conflicting messages confounded the defenders in Peking, they would have been even more perplexed by the news appearing in European newspapers during this period. Several of the papers reported the massacre of all the besieged foreigners, complete with lurid details of their horrible demise at the bloody hands of the Boxers. The false reports were started by an unscrupulous stringer for one paper and repeated with embellishments by many others. As a result, the fate of the besieged gained even greater public attention worldwide.[28]

Meanwhile, as the relief force inched toward Peking through a series of engagements, the legations came under increasing pressure from the Chinese forces in the capital. It became clear the Chinese hoped to capture the quarter before its inhabitants could be saved. The east side of the quarter came under fire for the first time since July 16, while the Chinese erected a tower about 30 feet high on the west side to bring more of the quarter under fire.[29]

On August 12, the Chinese near the Hatamen Gate on the east side of the quarter opened fire with a smooth-bore cannon. A few well-placed rifle shots from the allies sent the Chinese gunners scurrying for cover. However, they returned to the gun that night and began a bombardment of the German legation with solid shot.

Early the next morning, the Marines and their Russian counterparts installed an American flag and a Russian flag atop the wall at the east and west ends of the quarter, respectively. The hope was the flags would help a relief force approaching Peking locate the legation quarter within the sprawling metropolis. The hoisting of the flags proved timely. In the wee hours of the very next day, August 14, Private Upham recorded in his journal that "the boom of artillery ... and the steady crack of Maxim gun fire" could be heard outside the east side of city. Rescue was nearly at hand.[30]

However, the Chinese firing and shelling of the legations intensified during the hours of pre-dawn darkness. The Chinese also launched a series of determined assaults through the Mongol Marketplace on the west side of the quarter in what one survivor of the siege later described as "a last desperate attempt to kill us all before the arrival of the relief force."[31]

With the first glow of daylight on August 14, the defenders could see shells from the relief force outside the east walls bursting over the Imperial City.[32] At 2:15 p.m., the Marines on the Tartar Wall had their first sighting of their rescuers. A British detachment, led by Sikhs, forced their way through the Shawomen Gate on the east side of the Chinese City. Advancing through the streets of the Chinese City, the Sikhs made their way northwest toward the Tartar Wall and the American and Russian flags. A Marine atop the Tartar Wall used blue-and-white semaphore flags to signal in Morse code: "Come in by sewer." The Marines then pointed at the water gate directly below them. As the Sikhs

Five—Peking Siege

approached, they found a seven-foot-tall tunnel through the Tartar Wall. While the Sikhs waded through the stinking Jade River toward the legations, American Marines inside the quarter rushed to remove the obstacles and rotten iron grille from the water gate to allow the Sikhs to enter.[33] Upon emerging from the tunnel, the Sikhs were met with wild jubilation by the residents. American troops arrived in the quarter soon after. Led by the 14th U.S. Infantry Regiment,[34] they had scaled the Tartar Wall east of the quarter near the Tungpienmen Gate. At that point, the Chinese at the Chienmen Gate west of the quarter retreated westward, and the Marines and Russians within the quarter rushed forward and drove the Chinese manning barricades on Legation Street several hundred yards westward.[35]

Up on the Tartar Wall, the Marines also charged forward, driving the Chinese from their barricade on the west side of the quarter. Daly was the first to reach the enemy barricade. Although he found it now abandoned, he could see swarms of Chinese ahead. Once again, Daly led a surge toward the towering charred hulk of the Chienmen Gate. He and his fellow Marines soon swept the retreating Chinese from the wall.[36]

While the legations had been rescued, there was still the matter of subduing the Chinese forces within Peking. Four large steel-covered gates barred the way into the Imperial City and the Forbidden City. A battery of the 5th U.S. Artillery Regiment quickly set to work breaching the gates while the allied troops exchanged rifle fire with the Chinese defenders. The fighting proved brief but fierce. When allied troops entered the palace grounds of the Forbidden City on August 15, they found the dowager empress had fled the city with the emperor in tow.

A total of 66 foreigners were killed during the siege and 150 were wounded. In addition, two adults died of illness and six infants died for want of suitable food.[37]

Of the 50 Marines from the *Newark* and the *Oregon* who had deployed to Peking, eight died during the 55-day siege and nine suffered wounds but recovered.[38]

A total of 33 Medals of Honor were awarded to U.S. Marines for actions during the Boxer Rebellion. Of these, 18 went to enlisted Marines from the *Newark* and the *Oregon* in Peking, including Daniel Daly and Oscar Upham.[39] In addition, two sailors from the *Newark*, Gunner's Mate First Class Joseph A. Mitchell, who constructed and manned the International Gun, and Chief Machinist Mate Carl E. Petersen, received the Medal of Honor.

"Devil Dog" Dan Daly

In his letter recommending Daly for the medal, Captain Hall wrote: "I respectfully invite your attention to the courage and fidelity of Private Dan Daly, U.S. Marine Corps, at all times, and to his conduct on the night of July 15, 1900, when he volunteered to remain alone in the bastion under fire of the enemy while I returned to the barracks for laborers."[40]

Daly's Medal of Honor citation is a masterpiece of understatement. It reads: "In the presence of the enemy during the battle of Peking, China, 14 August 1900, Daly distinguished himself by meritorious conduct." That's all of it. While devoid of thrilling details, which later became common in citations for the medal, the sparse wording is consistent with most other Marine citations of that period. The date on the citation is the date the relief force arrived, not necessarily the date of Daly's heroic actions during the siege.[41]

Marine officers were ineligible to receive the Medal of Honor at the time of the Boxer Rebellion. However, seven officers who participated in the siege or relief expedition received brevet promotions in lieu of the medal. Captains Hall and Myers each received brevet promotions of one rank to major.[42] Hall ultimately attained the rank of colonel, while Myers retired as a major general. Years later, Myers was elevated to the rank of lieutenant general.

Shortly after the siege was lifted, Edwin Conger, the head of the American Legation, wrote to U.S. Secretary of State John Hay praising the Marines for holding "the most difficult and dangerous position of the defense by reason of our proximity to the great city wall and the main city gates over which the large guns were planted."

A group of American missionaries adopted a resolution of thanks to the Marines. "The Americans who have been besieged in Peking desire to express their hearty appreciation of the courage, fidelity and patriotism of the American Marines, to whom we so largely owe our salvation,." adding that "by their bravery in holding an almost untenable position on the city wall in the face of overwhelming numbers, and in cooperating in driving the Chinese from a position of great strength, they made all foreigners in Peking their debtors, and have gained themselves an honorable name among the heroes of our country."[43]

Forever modest about his heroism, even years later, Daly made light of it. Once, when asked about his heroic acts in Peking, he replied, "They thought they ought to give someone a medal, so they handed it

FIVE—Peking Siege

to me."⁴⁴ Another time when asked, he shot back, "Oh hell, twenty-two Marines and sailors got the Medal of Honor during that scrap. Why pick on me?"⁴⁵

In late September 1900, Daly and his fellow Marines, including Hall, set sail for Manila Bay aboard the *Newark*.

Six

Love in War

How Dan Daly found time during the siege of Peking for a love affair is a bit of a mystery, given his role in the defense of the legations. However, according to Daly family lore, that is exactly what he did.

The object of his affection, or at least his attention, was Annie Chamot, the spirited and attractive 28-year-old American-born wife of the 33-year-old Swiss proprietor of the Hotel Pekin, Auguste Chamot. She was born Annie Elizabeth McCarthy in 1871 in San Francisco, the daughter of an Irish immigrant who became a local real estate magnate, and his Massachusetts-born wife. Growing up, she rebelled against lady-like activities in favor of athletic pursuits such as riding, shooting and sailing. In 1891, the McCarthy family was wealthy enough to send 20-year-old Annie and her mother on an extended tour of Europe. A passport application for that journey described Annie as 5-feet-7-inches tall, with blue eyes, brown hair, fair complexion and a dimple in her chin.[1] A photo[2] of her around this time shows a tall, slender woman with perceptive eyes, a straight nose, small mouth and square jaw. Her expression suggests a don't-mess-with-me attitude.

Auguste and Annie met in 1894 while she and her mother were staying at the Hotel Pekin. They married in San Francisco on May 15, 1895, and then returned to China.[3] Like her father, Annie's husband was an enterprising businessman. Born near Lausanne, Switzerland, in the town of Pentraz where his father was the mayor, Auguste Francois Chamot II first arrived in Peking in 1883 with little money but a winning personality and a determination to succeed. He went to work for his sister's husband, who was then the proprietor of the Hotel Pekin, a luxurious 400-room Western-style hotel. In due course, he became the proprietor. A photo of Auguste in the mid–1890s shows a good-looking young man with dark hair and eyes, a trim mustache and a look of absolute self-assurance. Later, news articles described him as "debonair" and "dashing."

Six—Love in War

The Chamots proved a formidable pair during the siege and they emerged from the shell-shattered Legation Quarter as international celebrities for their gallantry. At the outset of the siege, dressed as Chinese peasants and accompanied by faithful servants, Auguste and Anne rounded up as much flour and other food as they could find in the buildings outside the quarter. They then established a bakery in the hotel, with Chinese staff grinding grain and baking bread to feed the besieged foreigners. They also ground grain to help feed the Chinese converts, who did not share equally with the Europeans in the food rations and otherwise would have starved.[4] Dr. Robert Coltman later recalled, "After some shells had burst in the bakery and killed one and severely wounded others of the Chinese bakers, Mrs. Chamot, rifle in hand, held the coolies to their work while her husband served with the guards."[5]

Annie Chamot, the American-born wife of the Swiss consul in Peking and Daly's love interest during the siege (from Robert Coltman's *Beleaguered in Peking*, F.A. Davis Company, 1901).

Annie and Auguste also came under fire daily as they crossed the stone bridge over the Jade River to deliver freshly baked bread from the hotel to the British legation, where most of the foreign civilians had taken refuge. "Their route was via Legation Street," Dr. George E. Morrison, an Australian medical doctor, adventurer and *Times* of London correspondent, later wrote. "Annie Chamot sat in the cart, rifle in hand, Monsieur Chamot on the shafts, guiding the mule, the two of them untroubled by the bullets and shells passing a few feet over their heads."[6]

Annie Chamot earned the admiration of virtually everyone for her pluckiness, according to Robert Coltman, an American professor of surgery at the Imperial University in Peking and a correspondent for the *Chicago Record*. "When every other woman in Peking left her home and repaired to the British legation, Mrs. Chamot remained by her husband, with a rifle in her hand, and took her regular hours of watching at the loopholes in the barricade erected on Legation street, between the Hotel de Peking and the German legation."[7]

It is likely that Daly first encountered Annie Chamot while they were standing guard at one of the street barricades leading into the Legation Quarter. It may be that any assignations occurred during these times.

The Hotel Pekin was an imposing structure at the outset of the siege, but by the end it was a total wreck. "There is no building left standing in Peking that has as many shell-holes in it as the northern two-story building of this hotel," wrote Coltman. "Anyone visiting the hotel immediately after the relief, and before the debris had been at all cleared, would scarcely believe that a brave American woman had lived there for sixty days unharmed. Her hairbreadth escapes were every-day occurrences."[8]

However, both Auguste and Annie took even greater risks, far greater than most foreign civilians within the quarter during the siege. As historian Peter Fleming, brother of James Bond creator Ian Fleming, wrote in *The Siege at Peking, The Boxer Rebellion*, "The diplomats showed few signs of derring-do, but on 29 May a small unofficial rescue-party, armed with rifles and revolvers, set out on ponies through the unquiet countryside."[9]

Their goal was to rescue a party of 16 Belgian engineers and their families, cut off and under attack by 300 Boxers, 16 miles outside Peking at Changsintien. The engineers were there to build a railway link between Peking and Hankow. According to historian Diana Preston, "(T)hey set out heavily armed with carts, spare animals and provisions. They met no resistance and succeeded in plucking a party of some seven children, nine women and about a dozen men from danger in the very nick of time. As they retreated northward toward Peking, the refugees could see their houses and compound going up in smoke. Chinese soldiers sent to protect them joined the Boxers in looting."[10]

Six—Love in War

"This prompt and daring rescue was one of the best incidents of the Siege," Dr. Morrison later wrote in *The Times*.[11]

Not content to rest on their laurels, the Chamots made another daring foray two weeks later. On the night of June 13, "a party of volunteers, led by a young Frenchman and accompanied by the brave Chamots, rode out to the South Cathedral and brought back to safety all the Catholic missionaries there, including five sisters of charity and twenty Chinese nuns. They had hardly left the Cathedral ... when it was fired. It burnt for many hours, while in the surrounding streets—the centre of the Catholic community in Peking—hundreds, perhaps thousands of Christians were butchered.... Peking had become a charnel house."[12]

During this daring expedition, Annie Chamot witnessed some of the most gruesome acts imaginable. "Women and children hacked to pieces, men trussed like fowls, with noses and ears cut off and eyes gouged out," wrote Dr. Morrison. Lancelot Giles, a young British student interpreter, recalled, "Many were found roasted alive, and so massacred and cut up as to be unrecognizable." Bertram Lenox Simpson, an employee of the British Customs Service, wrote that "the stench of human blood in the hot June air was almost intolerable and the sights more than we could bear."[13] There is no record that Annie Chamot ever asked for or accepted special consideration on account of her gender. She was as brave and daring as Daly, a quality that may have brought them together.

History is filled with examples of how shared danger forges strong emotional bonds between strangers, and how, with human carnage all around them, they seek out sex as a way to feel alive. This may have been the case with Annie Chamot and Dan Daly, two young people facing the prospect of sudden death drawn to a life-affirming experience in each others' arms.

After the siege, Auguste Chamot claimed that he and his wife had personally dispatched 700 Boxers and Chinese troops with their rifles, a gross exaggeration.[14] Auguste also claimed to have been wounded seven times and his wife four times, although observers later reported only that Auguste had sustained a spear wound in his hand during fighting at one of the barricades.

The Chamots left Peking after the siege and arrived in San Francisco via the transpacific steamship *City of Peking* in January 1901. There they were feted as heroes. The following year, they were showered with honors from a host of European powers; For Annie, these included the

"Devil Dog" Dan Daly

French Legion of Honor, the Belgian Double Eagle of King Leopold, the Russian Order of Stanislaus, and the Spanish Order of Isabella. Auguste received similar honors, plus the Order of Gregorius from Pope Leo XIII.

More importantly to the newly homeless couple, newspapers at the time reported that the foreign powers, whose legations the Chamots had helped defend, deluged them with monetary rewards totaling $420,000. Auguste also had a claim against the Chinese government for the loss of his various business holdings in Peking, including the hotel, a silk factory, a carpet factory and a store for selling foreign goods. All were destroyed in the siege. His claim came to $513,000, and had the support of nine foreign governments.

Nor was that the end of the Chamots' good fortune. As soon as the shooting stopped, the looting began. Allied troops, diplomats and foreign civilians raced into the palaces and temples of the Imperial City and the innermost sanctum of the emperor, the Forbidden City, to haul off as many treasures as they could carry. The Chamots joined in this frenzy, although with more business savvy than most. In fact, they proved "the most shameless and successful of them all."[15] They "acquired many of the best treasures at bargain prices looted by the eager-for-cash soldiers during the occupation."[16]

Years later, Auguste's attending physician told how his patient did it. "Standing at the exit of the palace, he accosted soldiers or drunken sailors, saying, 'What are you carrying there? You will never arrive in Europe with this trinket ... or you will lose it on the way. Me, I will give you ten (or twenty) dollars, gold and pay cash.' The others, ignorant to the value of these treasures, accepted without haggling. This is how Chamot acquired, for a piece of bread, an imperial tiara ... later valued at five thousand dollars."[17]

By the time the Chamots left Peking, they were laden with jewelry, art objects, ornate furnishings and elegant items of apparel. A March 11, 1907, a *Washington Post* article described many of these "Chinese curios" that were then on display at the American Art Galleries in New York City. They included a "bonnet" belonging to the dowager empress and "presented to Mrs. Chamot by the international troops in recognition of her services at that time." The headdress was "covered with butterflies, flowers and ornaments encrusted with 1,600 pearls, sapphires, uncut rubies and tourmaline." Other items included the solid-gold imperial seal of Prince Li, the throne chair of Emperor Chien Lung

(1711–1799) made of reindeer antlers with gold mounts, enameled panels from the imperial palace with birds and flowers carved in ivory jade and mother of pearl, two fans belonging to the dowager empress—one with a compass in the handle and the other with a clock—and a priest's scepter made of gold and jade. In 1907, Auguste Chamot put the value of these historical objects at over $100,000.[18]

Using the mountain of cash they had acquired, the Chamots "built two magnificent houses, set up a private menagerie of pythons, bears, panthers and monkeys, and bought a sailing yacht."[19] One home was on Stockton Street in a fashionable part of San Francisco. The other was a four-story mansion in rural Inverness, overlooking Marin County's scenic Tomales Bay.

Unfortunately, the Chamot's sweet run of luck soon soured. In addition to their expensive homes, they spent freely and entertained lavishly; Auguste began drinking and gambling; then the great San Francisco earthquake and fire in April 1906 destroyed both of their homes as well as their investment properties in the city. The Chamots barely survived the pre-dawn quake. They awoke to find their Inverness mansion thrust 30 feet off its foundation, and the first-floor kitchen stove sticking up through the floor of their third-floor bedroom.[20]

Compounding these losses, Annie's brother, who managed their real estate holdings, had failed to buy insurance on their properties, which might have recouped their losses and paid off their creditors. By early 1907 the Chamots were in bankruptcy.

In February 1908, Annie sued Auguste for divorce in a sensational case of "affinity." She accused him of living as husband and wife with one Betsy Dollar in Marin County, north of San Francisco. Auguste met Dollar, a manicurist at the Fifth Avenue Hotel in New York City, while there the previous year arranging for the sale of the Chamots' celebrated collection of Chinese curios to raise cash to live on. He brought Dollar back with him to San Francisco as his "nurse," a subterfuge that fooled no one, least of all Annie.

Auguste offered equally scandalous charges in his countersuit. He accused Annie of having a clandestine meeting with one Arnold Renold at the Trocadero—a lively roadhouse in the city offering gambling and dancing—shortly before he and Annie left for Peking, and that she had admitted as much in front of her own mother. He also accused Annie of hiring what she described as two "lovely" chauffeurs, one of whom—Charles McCord—she had taken with her to New York City. Auguste admitted that he and Dollar were living together but not as man and wife. While he said he could prove his charges against his wife, he added he was prepared to grant her a divorce if she would withdraw her allegations that he furnished Dollar with large sums of money and spent lavishly on clothes for her.[21]

After a brief court hearing in which Annie testified but Auguste did not, nor did he offer any defense, the court granted Annie a divorce on the grounds of mental cruelty in May 1908.[22]

Daly's name did not appear in the court papers or news accounts. Perhaps Auguste didn't know about whatever happened in Peking between Annie and Daniel.

Auguste married Betsy Dollar on his deathbed in Marin County in September 1909, and died a few days later of pulmonary tuberculosis. He left his new bride his last 15 cents.[23]

As soon as her divorce from Auguste was final, Annie remarried in June 1909. Her new husband, Gustave L. Renstrom, was a Swedish immigrant 14 years her junior. She met him at a car dealership where he worked. He taught her to drive and she hired him to be her chauffeur.[24] The marriage didn't last but Annie did. She lived on in San Francisco, dying at age 79 in 1951.

Whatever happened between Annie Chamot and Dan Daly in Peking, he never married. The fact that his family learned of this affair from an intensely private man suggests it was of some importance to him. Late in life, when asked why he never married, Daly replied simply, "I can't see how a single man could spend his time better than in the Marines."

Seven

Sea Soldier

Daly and the *Newark* arrived in Manila Bay in September 1900. While he was out of imminent danger, at least for now, it did not take long for him to find a new kind of trouble. On October 29, Daly's service record states he was put on report for failing to return on time from leave in the Philippines. It would not be the last time he ran afoul of the strict discipline in the Marine Corps. Daly had demonstrated his courage and proficiency as a fighting man in Peking, but it would be some time before he showed a similar capacity for the firm self-control that would mark his later years.

In mid–April 1901, the *Newark*, with Daly aboard, sailed out of Manila Bay bound for the United States. Daly was appointed an acting corporal for this trip, no doubt because of his exceptional conduct during the Peking siege. En route, the ship completed Daly's circumnavigation of the globe, making port calls at Hong Kong, Ceylon (now Sri Lanka) and Suez, before sailing through the Mediterranean Sea and across the Atlantic Ocean, arriving at Boston in late July. At that time Daly was on restriction for 30 days for being "10 hours over leave." It was his fourth such offense in 10 months. Upon arrival in Boston, he reverted to the rank of private and took his place in the Marine Barracks detachment at the Boston Navy Yard.

After two years at sea and abroad, Daly was now a combat veteran but he still had much to learn about being a Marine. Assigned to the Marine detachment at the Boston Navy Yard, he quickly found himself in serious trouble. According to his service records, on August 23, 1901, a summary court-martial convicted him of being under the influence of alcohol while on post. The court sentenced him to "solitary confinement, in single irons, on bread and water, for 30 days with a full ration every third day," and forfeiture of three months' pay, totaling $42.

While Daly was in the brig, an event occurred that would

forever alter the course of American history. On September 6, 1901, a Polish-American anarchist shot President McKinley while he was greeting visitors to the Pan-American Exposition in Buffalo, New York. McKinley died eight days later and Vice President Theodore Roosevelt became president. Where McKinley had been a reluctant expansionist, Roosevelt was an ardent one. A case in point was the addition of the Roosevelt Corollary to the Monroe Doctrine. In 1904, several Caribbean and Central American governments were in default on massive loans and foreign investors were clamoring for intervention to secure payment. The Monroe Doctrine barred European powers from intervening in the Western Hemisphere. So Roosevelt announced that from now on the United States would act as an international policeman in the Americas, allocating to itself sole authority to intervene with force if necessary to build up economic stability and put down insurrections.

As a result, Daly and his fellow Marines were thrust with increasing frequency into the affairs of other nations. This was especially true of the so-called "Banana Wars" of the Caribbean and Central and South America between 1900 and 1940. Some interventions lasted a few days or weeks, while others continued for decades. The Marines occupied Nicaragua from 1912 to 1933, Haiti from 1915 to 1934, and the Dominican Republican from 1916 to 1934.

To meet these added demands on its personnel, the Marine Corps doubled in size between the end of the Spanish-American War in 1899, when Daly enlisted, to 10,000 by 1912. By the end of World War I, just six years later, the corps would balloon to 73,000. Veterans like Daly would be crucial to training, leading and inspiring this sudden crush of new Marines.

Less than three weeks after being released from the brig for the August offense, Daly was in trouble again. According to his service record, a summary court-martial on October 17 found him guilty of drunkenness in the barracks as well as "using obscene, threatening and abusive language toward a sergeant of the guard." Once again he was sent to the brig for 30 days on bread and water with a full ration only every fifth day. He also forfeited three months' pay.

Daly's succession of offenses marked a low point in his Marine Corps career, although it was soon followed by one of his many high points. On December 11, 1901, less than a month after his latest release from the brig, he was formally presented with the Medal of Honor for his one-man stand atop the wall during the Boxer siege in Peking.

Seven—Sea Soldier

While Daly was now officially a hero, he was not Superman. In late December 1901, he was hospitalized with catarrhal gastritis, an acute inflammation of the stomach lining resulting in nausea, loss of appetite and discomfort after eating. He spent 25 days in the hospital. This condition proved chronic, and he experienced frequent flare-ups, including "persistent vomiting," requiring occasional hospitalization over the course of his career. The condition's origin was listed in his medical records as "in line of duty, incident to service." The cause is not specified, but it seems likely that the intense and prolonged stress of the siege in Peking took its toll on him. Daly tended to bottle up his emotions, but behind that unflappable exterior he was in turmoil. By 1916, his medical records indicate doctors suspected Daly had developed a stomach ulcer. Despite this serious ailment, he was able to return to duty after each episode and rise to any new challenge. This makes Daly an even greater man. A hero isn't someone who knows no fear or pain; a hero is someone who experiences fear or pain but doesn't let it stop him.

Once out of the hospital, Daly resumed the routine of a Marine stationed at the Boston Navy Yard: guard duty, training, drill and occasional ceremonial functions. Unfortunately, he also found time to break the rules again. In late April 1902, he went absent without leave (AWOL) for two days and was placed on 30 days restriction. In September, he overstayed a liberty by a day and was disciplined again with loss of liberty privileges for 30 days.

That fall, Daly joined a battalion of Marines dispatched aboard the U.S.S. *Prairie* to the Caribbean Sea. This was the first of several voyages he made aboard the *Prairie,* a former ocean liner purchased by the U.S. Navy in 1898 and commissioned first as an auxiliary cruiser and then as a training ship and transport. Daly was assigned to Company B, First Battalion, Marine Provisional Regiment and stationed at Camp Roosevelt on Culebra, an island half the size of Manhattan 17 miles east of mainland Puerto Rico. Over the next several months, the battalion participated in maneuvers designed to discourage European nations from seeking to establish footholds in the Caribbean in the turbulent period after the Spanish-American War. During this time, Daly got into trouble for being drunk and AWOL. He was placed on restriction for six days in January, again in February, and given 30 days confinement in April. In December, he was an hour late returning from liberty and assigned a day of extra duty.

His discipline issues continued into 1903. In early January, he was confined for six days for being under the influence of alcohol upon returning from liberty, and later that month he was given 10 days of extra duty for leaving the camp without permission. In late April, he was deprived of liberty for 28 days for being two hours late returning from liberty. He spent part of July and most of August assigned to kitchen detail as a cook.

In July 1903, Daly and the battalion left Culebra aboard the U.S.S. *Panther* for maneuvers off the coast of Maine. The *Panther* had been a commercial freighter until the Navy purchased it in 1898 and commissioned it as an auxiliary cruiser before refitting it as a training ship in 1902. In September, the *Panther* delivered the Marines to the Philadelphia Navy Yard. Daly was detached from the battalion at that point and sent to the Marine Barracks at the Boston Navy Yard. There, his first four-year enlistment ended on January 11, 1904, and he was discharged with a character rating of "good." Given his many infractions, his rating suggests the Marine Corps thought he was worth keeping. Two days later, he began his second four-year enlistment.

On February 17, 1904, Daly joined the Marine detachment on the U.S.S. *Marietta*, a schooner-rigged gunboat commissioned in 1897. Three weeks later, the ship sailed for Panama. There it operated along the coast of Central America during the U.S.-backed revolt in Panama that led to the isthmus becoming independent of Colombia. Officially, the ship and its Marines were there to protect American citizens and interests in Panama. Unofficially, it was there to help prevent Colombia from retaking Panama, so the United States could build the Panama Canal.

Once tensions there eased, the *Marietta* sailed across the Atlantic Ocean, arriving at Gibraltar in June. In addition to his regular duties as a Marine aboard ship, Daly served as mail orderly during each of the port calls between March and December 1904. This assignment was a mark of distinction. Only those who demonstrated the highest degree of trustworthiness and integrity were entrusted with going ashore to collect the ship's mail. The ship served with the South Atlantic Squadron until December when it arrived at the Philadelphia Navy Yard. There, Daly was sent to the Marine Barracks at the Boston Navy Yard. On May 12, 1905, Daly received two weeks of restriction for being drunk on guard mount and smuggling in liquor.

On March 23, 1906, he was promoted to corporal, and in May he joined the Marine detachment on the U.S.S. *Cleveland*, a Denver-class

Seven—Sea Soldier

protected cruiser commissioned in 1903. The ship sailed to the West Indies and Cuba before returning to Boston in late May. Daly performed well aboard ship but once again got into trouble ashore. He overstayed a liberty by two hours in June and drew a week's restriction, and was 14 hours late in November and was given 14 days restriction. He remained in Boston and stayed out of trouble through 1907. He completed his second enlistment while in Boston on January 12, 1908, and was discharged with the rank of corporal. Despite his occasional offenses, his character was listed as "excellent."

Three weeks before Daly's second enlistment ended, the Great White Fleet of 16 U.S. Navy battleships began its historic around-the-world cruise. The 14-month cruise, which ended in February 1909, conveyed President Theodore Roosevelt's blunt message to military and economic rivals that the United States was now a global force to be reckoned with. It was fully capable of protecting overseas territories, enforcing treaties and influencing world events. As the size and importance of the U.S. Navy grew, so too did the Marine Corps.

As this new chapter in the nation's and the corps' history opened, Daly began his third four-year enlistment at the Marine Barracks in the Philadelphia Navy Yard on January 31, 1908, with the rank of corporal. The physical description of Daly that accompanied his reenlistment papers includes a list of scars on his left arm, left wrist, right wrist, left middle finger, left breast, lower lip and left shin. The document doesn't explain where, when or how he obtained these. It seems likely some or all were acquired during his many instances of close combat in Peking.[1]

Eight days after reenlisting, he was awarded a Good Conduct Medal. Ten days after that, however, Daly was again in trouble. His service record contains only a single-word description: "offense." There is no mention of the punishment, which suggests it was minor. Given past incidents, this latest one probably involved drink or being late returning from liberty.

At the end of March 1908, Daly was assigned to the Marine detachment on the U.S.S. *Mississippi*, a newly commissioned pre-dreadnaught battleship. On July 1, the ship began its shake-down cruise along the east coast of the United States, visiting numerous ports there before returning to Philadelphia in September for repairs. There, Daly once again boarded the *Prairie*. The next day, December 22, the *Prairie* sailed for Puerto Rico, where the 57 Marines aboard were delivered to the San Juan Naval Station for a two-year assignment as a ready-reaction force for the

51

"Devil Dog" Dan Daly

Caribbean. Daly's performance, both on and off duty, was excellent during this period. He was made an acting sergeant in February 1909 and permanently appointed to that rank on August 24, 1909, a decade after first joining the corps. During his time on the *Prairie*, Daly served as a police sergeant from December 1910 to April 1911.

While Marine expeditionary forces saw action in Central America during this period, it was a relatively quiet time for Daly. That changed briefly on March 3, 1911. A gasoline fire broke out aboard the *Springfield*, a four-masted wooden cargo-hauling schooner berthed at the San Juan Naval Station. Daly and six Marine privates[2] risked their lives to extinguish the flames before its cargo of gasoline could blow up the ship. The action earned all seven Marines letters of commendation from Major General Commandant William P. Biddle and Secretary of the Navy George Meyer. Biddle wrote in part: "While it is believed that the coolness and disregard of personal injury exhibited by these men on the occasion mentioned was only such as was to be expected from all enlisted men of the Marine Corps, this office

Sergeant Daly sometime between 1909 and 1915. It was during this period he saw action in Vera Cruz and Haiti (Marine Corps History Division Archive).

52

Seven—*Sea Soldier*

desires to express its appreciation of the promptness and efficiency displayed in subduing this dangerous fire."

Daly sailed to New York in May 1911 where he joined the Marine detachment aboard the U.S.S. *Ohio*, a Maine-class pre-dreadnaught battleship commissioned in 1904. The ship served with the Atlantic Fleet and engaged in routine training during Daly's time aboard. While aboard, he served as the acting first sergeant of the Marine detachment. He also served as a police sergeant.

He returned to the Marine detachment at the Boston Navy Yard in September. He spent a week in the naval hospital at Chelsea before being assigned in November 1911 to police and guard duties at the Portsmouth Naval Prison in Maine. There, his third enlistment ended January 30, 1912, and he was discharged with the rank of sergeant and a character rating of "excellent" again. He also received his second Good Conduct Medal. It seems that, as Daly would say years later, he was "getting the hang of" being a Marine.

Daly began his fourth four-year enlistment on January 31, 1912, with the rank of sergeant. In March, however, he was given two weeks' restriction for "making an insolent remark to his C.O." His service record doesn't say what prompted his comment or what he said.

On May 25, he joined Company A, Second Provisional Regiment, and the following day reported aboard the U.S.S. *Minnesota*, a Connecticut-class pre-dreadnaught battleship commissioned in 1907. In June, the Second Regiment was sent to Cuba to help put down an uprising by Afro-Cuban former slaves who had fought against Spain in the war for independence. An agreement between the United States and Cuba gave the former the right to intervene in the latter to preserve order. The Second Regiment was comprised of three battalions under the overall command of Lieutenant Colonel Franklin J. Moses.

Slavery in Cuba had been abolished in 1886, but the former slaves were still mistreated. After the war for independence, the Afro-Cubans formed the Partidio Independiente de Color (Independent Party of Color) to seek better treatment from the post-war government. However, in 1908, a newly elected Cuban government abolished parties based on race, effectively shutting Afro-Cubans out of the nation's political system. The Afro-Cubans, who had fought and died in far greater numbers than other Cubans in the war, were outraged. As a result, they launched an armed revolt in Oriente Province, the eastern part of Cuba where most Afro-Cubans were employed in the sugar mills owned by foreign investors who were buying up land aided by corrupt local officials. The province is home to Guantanamo Bay, the port city of Santiago, and the birthplace of Fidel Castro. The Afro-Cuban rebels looted and burned businesses and property belonging to foreign investors. In response, the Cuban government sent in the army with orders to stamp out all resistance. The troops burned the Afro-Cubans' property and slaughtered many of them with machine guns fired into unresisting villages. An estimated 3,000 to 6,000 Afro-Cubans were killed. The revolt was suppressed by late July, and the Afro-Cubans subjugated.

The United States dispatched 10 warships to Cuba with two regiments totaling 2,100 Marines to protect American lives and property, which included sugar plantations, copper mines, and trains. The Second Provisional Regiment was commanded by Colonel James E. Mahoney.[3] Daly and the Marines from the *Minnesota* landed at Guantanamo Bay on June 7. A battalion landed at Havana on June 10, and a detachment from the *Mississippi* landed at El Cuero on June 19. According to historian George B. Clark, the Marines' only fight with Afro-Cubans occurred at El Cuero. There, the rebels were driven away without fatalities on either side. There is no indication from Daly's service record that he saw any combat during this operation.

(Within two years of the Oriente Province revolt being suppressed, half of the sugar mills in the province were owned by Americans. The intolerable conditions that led to the revolt of 1912 became unbearable and a new uprising occurred in early 1917. Once again U.S. Marines were called in to protect U.S. commercial interests with results similar to those in 1912.)

In August 1912, Daly was assigned to the permanent garrison at Guantanamo Bay. He remained there until January 1, 1913, when he returned to police and guard duty at Portsmouth Naval Prison following 10 days of restriction for being late returning from liberty. This infraction may be why he was reassigned to Portsmouth, or it may reflect his unhappiness at this reassignment.

While Daly was stationed at the naval prison, Woodrow Wilson succeeded William Howard Taft in the White House. As president, Wilson viewed his predecessors' foreign policy as imperialistic and sought to foster more democratic, less paternalistic approaches. However, this did not restrain him from repeatedly sending the Marines into Latin American hotspots.

Daly earned the sharpshooter medal in September 1913, according

SEVEN—Sea Soldier

to his service record, and in November he joined Company A, Second Advance Division Base Regiment aboard the *Prairie*. In January 1914, the *Prairie* and Daly sailed for Puerto Rico. On March 1, while stationed at Culebra, Company A was redesignated the 15th Company.

While many Marines had spent the past decade engaged in expeditionary actions large and small around the globe, Daly had seen relatively little action. However, world events were about to change that. Daly's mostly peaceful interlude was about to come to a tumultuous end.

Eight

Vera Cruz

The year 1914 would mark the start of three armed clashes—each more cataclysmic than the one before—that would directly impact Daly and ultimately make him a living legend.

The first of these began April 9, 1914, in Mexico with what became known as the Tampico Affair. The Mexican Revolution was in its fourth year. After 35 years in power, the dictator, Porfirio Diaz, had been forced into exile by revolutionary forces loyal to Francisco Madero, an idealistic reformer who wanted to redistribute land to the peasants. After Madero was deposed by a military coup and shot "while attempting to escape," General Victoriano Huerta made himself president. This re-ignited the civil war, with three rebel factions—led by Pancho Villa, Emiliano Zapata and Venustiano Carranza—battling federal troops to oust Huerta.

Adding to the turmoil, tensions between the United States and Mexico were near the breaking point. The United States had repeatedly intervened in Mexico's internal affairs to protect the interests of American investors. In 1906, U.S. soldiers and Arizona rangers crossed the border to put down a labor strike at an American-owned mine in Cananea, Sonora, by Mexican miners who were protesting slave-like conditions. In 1912, the U.S. ambassador to Mexico, Henry Lane Wilson, conspired with Huerta and others to bring about the coup against Madero and install a conservative government more friendly to U.S. business interests.

While it was standard U.S. practice to recognize a regime in power, the ambassador's boss, President Woodrow Wilson, was appalled by Madero's murder and adamantly refused to "recognize a government of butchers."[1] In a rebuke to his ambassador's efforts and Huerta's undemocratic junta, President Wilson announced that the United States would observe strict neutrality between the competing factions in Mexico.

EIGHT—Vera Cruz

This meant the United States would refuse to recognize any faction as the legitimate government. This, in turn, prolonged the bloody civil war by imposing an arms embargo on all of the factions. Had Wilson recognized one of the factions as the legitimate government, that faction would have been eligible to obtain arms and ammunition from foreign suppliers, while its opponents would have been barred such support.[2]

By August 1913, Wilson had grown weary of waiting for the Mexicans to end the fighting. He proposed his own terms for settlement: an immediate cease-fire, free and fair elections that fall, and a pledge by Huerta not to run for president in the election. Huerta rejected Wilson's terms and in October he had 110 dissident members of the Mexican Congress arrested, shut down that institution and made himself dictator. Fed up with Huerta, Wilson reversed himself in February 1914 and lifted the arms embargo in an effort to help Carranza oust Huerta.

The stage was now set for the Tampico Affair, which triggered a diplomatic break between the United States and Mexico and an armed intervention at the major gulf coast port of Vera Cruz by U.S. sailors and Marines, including Daly.

Carranza's forces had laid siege to Huerta's troops in Tampico, a gulf coast port with thousands of American residents owing to heavy U.S. investment in the oil industry there. To protect these interests, the U.S. Navy had dispatched warships to Tampico, including the gunboat *Dolphin*. On April 9, 1914, the *Dolphin*'s commander sent a whaleboat with nine unarmed sailors ashore to purchase 440 gallons of gasoline and deliver them to the ship. The gasoline warehouse was located near a key defensive position in the siege, the Iturbide Bridge. It was held by Huerta's troops, who had come under fire in recent days and expected an attack by Carranza's forces at any time.

The *Dolphin*'s whaleboat, flying the U.S. flag at both the bow and stern, landed at the Iturbide Bridge. As the sailors were loading the gasoline aboard, they were taken prisoner by Mexican soldiers and marched to a military headquarters for questioning. Less than 90 minutes later, Huerta's port commander ordered the sailors released. This was followed by an apology from the commander as well as a note of regret from Huerta.

Huerta had previously imposed martial law in Tampico and ordered that no one be allowed to land at the bridge. The *Dolphin*'s commander was unaware of this when he sent the sailors ashore, while the Mexican soldiers at the bridge were just carrying out Huerta's order.

"Devil Dog" Dan Daly

This misunderstanding could have ended there, but Rear Admiral Henry T. Mayo, the pugnacious commander of the U.S. naval squadron at Tampico, considered the arrest of the sailors an affront to American honor.[3] Without consulting his superiors, he demanded a more formal apology and a ceremonial salute from the Mexicans. Huerta was willing to fire a 21-gun salute to the American flag, but he insisted on a return salute to the Mexican flag, with the guns of the two nations firing alternately.

President Wilson rejected Huerta's counteroffer. He saw the incident as an opportunity to justify intervention and asked Congress for authorization to use military force if necessary to obtain from Huerta "the fullest recognition of the rights and dignity of the United States." A pacifist, Wilson convinced himself that his objective could be achieved without armed conflict.[4] After some debate, Congress approved Wilson's request by a vote of 337 to 37 on April 22.

By then, however, events in Mexico had overtaken events in Washington, D.C. Rear Admiral Frank F. Fletcher, commanding U.S. naval forces at Vera Cruz, had received word from the U.S. consul there that the German steamship *Ypiranga* was due to arrive in the port on April 21 with a cargo of 200 machine guns and 15 million rounds of ammunition for Huerta.[5] An American businessman with substantial investments in Mexico had purchased the arms in the United States from the Remington Arms Co. and shipped them via Hamburg, Germany, in an effort to evade the U.S. arms embargo of Huerta.

As a result of the arms shipment, plans to land U.S. forces at Tampico were swiftly abandoned in favor of a landing at Vera Cruz. Stopping the arms from reaching Huerta was a higher priority than demanding the salute at Tampico, and Vera Cruz was the bigger prize: It had the best harbor on Mexico's gulf coast. Historically, it had been the starting point for invasions aimed at Mexico City from the days of Hernán Cortés (1519) to the U.S. war with Mexico (1846–1848).

Fletcher had the battleships *Florida* and *Utah* and the troop transport *Prairie* at Vera Cruz. Aboard these ships were 1,200 Navy "bluejacket" riflemen and Marines, including Daly and the *Prairie*'s 325 men of the First Provisional Battalion, Second Advance Base Regiment, commanded by Lieutenant Colonel Wendell C. Neville.[6]

Acting on orders from President Wilson to "Take Vera Cruz at once," Fletcher dispatched the sailors and Marines into Vera Cruz on the morning of April 21. His orders from Wilson were to take control

EIGHT—Vera Cruz

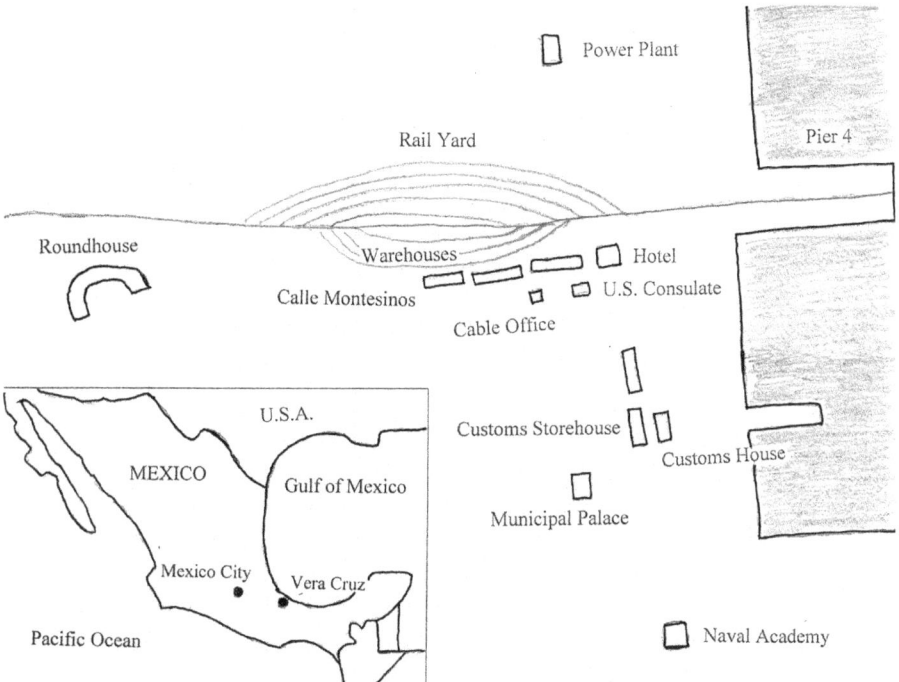

Map of Vera Cruz showing key locations during the Marine landing in 1914. Pier 4 on the upper right is where the Marines landed. The Customs House is in the middle right. The Naval Academy is in the bottom right. Calle Montesinos, the street where much of Daly's action occurred, runs from the rail yard roundhouse on the left to the hotel on the wharf on the right. (author's map).

of the customs house, impound the arms shipment, assist any Americans in distress, and treat the Mexican population with respect. "No two of these purposes were wholly compatible," concluded historian Jack Sweetman. "Attempting to combine all four was like trying to make an omelette without breaking any eggs."[7]

Neither Wilson nor Fletcher expected any resistance from the Mexican forces. They were badly mistaken. The landing kicked over a hornet's nest, and Daly was right in the midst of it.

Standing on the roof of the consulate, U.S. Consul William W. Canada watched the first boatload of Marines leave the *Prairie* and noted the time, 11:12 a.m. The consulate was a two-story building with a clear view of the rail terminal across the street as well as the customs house a few blocks away and Pier Four, where the Marines and bluejackets were to land. Canada then phoned General Gustavo Maas, the local military commander, to tell him U.S. troops were coming ashore. He said the troops would confine their activities to the waterfront to avoid a clash with Mexican forces. Canada also phoned the top customs official and the chief of police.[8]

Canada expected Maas to withdraw his troops from the waterfront. To Canada's surprise, Maas sent about 100 men to "repel the invasion," deployed a battalion to defend their barracks, released prisoners in the jail and gave them rifles, and armed civilian militia members.[9]

Maas then received an order from Mexico City telling him to pull out of Vera Cruz and set up a defensive position 10 miles inland. While Maas could withdraw the battalion at the barracks, it was already too late to stop the soldiers and civilians swarming along Avenida Independencia toward the customs house and waterfront to confront the Americans.[10] In addition, cadets at the Vera Cruz Naval Academy had taken up arms to resist the invasion.

While the Mexicans were arming, the American landing party was heading for shore. The landing party was made up of two regiments hastily cobbled together. The Marine regiment, led by Neville, comprised his battalion aboard the *Prairie* plus the Fleet Marines aboard the battleships, a total of 22 officers and 578 men. A seaman regiment, led by *Florida's* Lieutenant Commander Allen Buchanan, had 30 officers and 570 men from the battleships.

The Marines wore khaki fatigues, broad-brimmed campaign hats and knapsack rolls. The Navy bluejackets wore white V-necked shirts with haversacks on their backs and bell-bottom pants tucked into canvas leggings. Both sailors and Marines carried bolt-action M1903 Springfield rifles, while naval officers wore white high-collar tunics and sidearms.[11]

The Marines approached the shore in whaleboats towed by motor launches. Daly and the 15th Marine Company were in the first wave. The younger Marines in his platoon were reassured by Daly's steady demeanor as they headed toward a hostile shore. They also were intimidated by their company commander, 33-year-old Captain John Arthur Hughes. After failing the entrance exam for West Point, Hughes had enlisted in the Marine Corps as a private in late 1900. He so impressed his superiors that a year later he was commissioned a second lieutenant. Over the next dozen years, he served in the Philippines, Cuba and

Eight—Vera Cruz

Panama. Along the way he acquired the nickname "Johnny the Hard" for his hard-charging attitude, demanding standards and mercurial temper. He inspired fear, awe and exasperation in subordinates and superiors alike.[12]

Pulling alongside Pier Four at about 11:40 a.m., Hughes barked the order to disembark. Daly led his platoon up the stone steps, down the length of the wide pier and across a grassy area toward the entrance to Calle Montesinos, the east-west street that ran inland between the rail terminal and the consulate. Most of the civilians who saw Daly and his men quickly disappeared. The waterfront took on an eerie quiet, like a darkening sky before a thunderstorm. Not a shot had been fired. The only sound was the clang of church bells calling parishioners to services. The bells reminded Daly it was a Sunday.[13]

Vera Cruz at the time was a city of about 40,000 residents. The homes and businesses that lined the narrow grid-pattern streets retained their old Spanish colonial character. The pastel-colored buildings were two and three stories tall with wooden balconies and wrought-iron railings. However, the city's beauty was best viewed from a distance, wrote historian Jack Sweetman. "At close quarters, Vera Cruz was filthy, foul-smelling and incredibly ill-kept."[14]

After Peking, the sights and smells of Vera Cruz were no big deal for Daly. He was becoming inured to the squalor, stench and hardship he encountered in each new war zone.

To accomplish the mission, Fletcher had divided Vera Cruz into two parts with Navy Captain William R. Rush in overall command of the two regiments ashore.

The Navy landing party was given the southern part. The bluejacket riflemen would have the honor of seizing the prime objective, the customs house, a large stone and marble structure four blocks south of Pier Four. Their other objectives were the post office and telegraph, located between the consulate and the customs house. Rush set up his headquarters at the Hotel Terminal, a two-story stone building at the foot of the rail terminal facing Pier Four.

Neville and his Marines were assigned the northern part with the goal of securing the rail terminal, rail yard, roundhouse, cable office and power plant. The roundhouse was located about 10 blocks east of the waterfront at the foot of the rail yard. The power plant was located north of the rail yard, the equivalent of about four blocks from the rail terminal. The cable office stood one block east of the consulate.[15]

"Devil Dog" Dan Daly

The Marines' advance guard occupied the rail terminal without incident. They were disappointed to find no locomotives to seize, just box cars. Maas had already taken the trains to remove his barracks battalion from the city. The Marines then moved into positions to control the approaches to the rail yard. The power plant and the cable office were seized without opposition. The Marines began moving inland along Calle Montesinos, with the rail yard on their right flank.

Meanwhile, the 100 soldiers sent by Maas to "repel the invasion" as well as armed civilians began taking up fighting positions near the waterfront. Other than the machine gunners, who positioned themselves to fire down some of the larger streets, there was no strategic plan or coordination among the Mexicans.

The first shot came from a municipal policeman who fired at bluejackets on Calle Morelos, a north-south street along the waterfront near the customs house. The Navy riflemen took cover in alcoves and returned fire. The policeman became the first fatality of the landing, cut down by several bluejacket bullets.[16] That exchange broke the creepy calm. Suddenly, the waterfront buzzed with bullets from all directions. Captain Rush came out of the Hotel Terminal to see what was happening and was shot through the calf. After tying a large handkerchief over the wound, he carried on.

All along Calle Morelos, bluejackets moving toward the customs house came under rifle and machine gun fire. Ordering the rest of his men to provide covering fire, an ensign led five volunteers into an alley between the customs house and the adjacent warehouse. There they came under fire from a machine gun on a balcony of the Oriente Hotel. Returning fire, they killed the gunner, but one bluejacket was mortally wounded. They then broke out a window and crawled into the customs house. The Mexicans inside threw down their weapons without a fight. The ensign sent a runner back to tell Rush the landing's prime objective was in U.S. hands.[17]

Meanwhile, the Marines who had been working their way inland on Calle Montesinos began taking fire as their lead element approached Avenida Bravo, about six blocks east of the consulate. Mexicans with rifles fired down from rooftops all along the street.

Captain Hughes ordered Daly and the men of the 15th Marine Company to find cover and return fire. Daly led his men into the rail yard warehouses on the north side of the street. Knocking firing loopholes in the walls, the Marines began picking off the Mexican snipers.

EIGHT—Vera Cruz

Once covering fire had been established, the Marines shifted back to offense. Neville sent Marine skirmishers into the nearby streets to begin clearing the buildings while Marine sharpshooters climbed onto rooftops to provide cover moving forward. The skirmishers soon cleared the immediate area of snipers. At that point, Neville received orders from Rush for the Marines to "fall back to the original positions."[18]

At 12:30 p.m., Rush advised Fletcher that the landing party was facing an estimated one thousand men with rifles and machine guns. He asked the admiral to send in the reserve bluejacket battalion of 17 officers and 367 men. The battalion was on its way at 1:12 p.m.[19]

While this was happening, the *Ysiranga* came into view. She stopped next to the *Utah*, and her captain was informed that the customs house had been seized and he would not be allowed to leave without landing the arms. The captain opted to anchor with his cargo still aboard and await further developments.

At 1 p.m., Rush became concerned about a new source of Mexican fire that had begun to rain down on Pier Four. He assigned Chief Boatswain's Mate John McCloy to find the source. McCloy had received the Medal of Honor as part of the Boxer Rebellion relief expedition. He was about to win a second award of the medal, making him one of only three men to win two for separate actions since the Civil War. The other two are Smedley Darlington Butler and Daly.

McCloy took three steam-powered launches, each with a one-pound cannon mounted in the bow, and set off from Pier Four along the waterfront. As he approached the naval academy, each boat fired a shot into the academy. The response was immediate. One-pound cannons at academy windows and riflemen in a scow anchored nearby pelted McCloy and his men with cannon balls and bullets. The torrent of fire punched holes in the launches and wounded several crewmembers, including McCloy, shot in the thigh. Having provoked the Mexicans into revealing their positions, McCloy's tiny flotilla high-tailed it back to Pier Four while the *Prairie*'s 3-inch guns scattered the Mexican riflemen and drove the cadets from their cannons.[20]

At 1:40 p.m., the reserve bluejacket battalion that Rush had requested landed at Pier Four and came under rifle fire. A company of these reinforcements was immediately sent to relieve the Navy riflemen under fire and taking casualties around the customs house. Other units were dispatched to support the Marines and fill in gaps in the defensive line.

Newly arrived bluejackets battered down the door to the warehouse next to the customs house. Inside, they found bales of cotton and other goods. They loaded them onto hand carts and pushed them out into the streets where they were used as mobile breastworks.

Assessing the situation, historian Jack Sweetman wrote: "The first day at Vera Cruz was strictly a small-unit fight: the junior officers were on their own. Once a section had been sent to the front, the nature of the action and lack of communication made it impossible for brigade headquarters to exert more than a vague influence on its operations. A company advancing down one block had no idea what was happening to the company a block away."[21]

During the afternoon, bluejackets worked their way block by block deeper into the city's center, sometimes clearing buildings floor by floor. Mexican snipers continued to take a toll. As firing in the city slackened around 3 p.m., Admiral Fletcher sent a message to Secretary of the Navy Josephus Daniels advising him that the customs house and all of the other objectives had been seized, and the delivery of the arms had been prevented. U.S. casualties were four dead and 20 wounded.[22] Now what?

While the casualties so far were relatively light, the fight wasn't over. The bluejackets and Marines ashore were still being shot at from boats, rooftops and the naval academy. The size and intention of the Mexican forces was uncertain.

When Fletcher's cable reached Washington, D.C., in mid-afternoon, President Wilson was shocked to learn that the landing had triggered a fierce firefight. He and his advisors had not expected any resistance. Equally troubling was word that the captain of the *Ypiranga* had been told he could not leave Vera Cruz without first offloading his shipment of arms. This was a violation of international maritime law and could lead to conflict with Germany, which was already in a war-like mood in Europe. Suddenly, a minor crisis had ballooned into a major one.

Meanwhile, the Americans in Vera Cruz faced a more immediate concern. Daylight was waning and darkness would hand the Mexicans a tactical advantage. They knew the city far better than the Americans. Fletcher and Rush shifted to a defensive posture for the night. Daly and his Marines manned firing loopholes in the rail terminal warehouses and barricades along Calle Montesinos. Similarly, the bluejackets hunkered down around the objectives they had seized. To prevent the Mexicans from bringing artillery pieces into place to shell the U.S. ships in

EIGHT—Vera Cruz

the harbor, searchlights on the ships were trained on the shore to detect and deter any such attempt.

Overnight, Fletcher's forces at Vera Cruz were augmented by the arrival of Rear Admiral Charles J. Badger's squadron of ships with more Marines and bluejackets. A battalion from the mine depot ship *San Francisco* came ashore during the pre-dawn hours and joined the bluejackets around the customs house. A battalion from the scout cruiser *Chester* also landed and its bluejackets were posted at the power plant. The *Chester*'s battalion included a company of Marines, plus Major Smedley Darlington Butler. Lieutenant Colonel Neville sent the Marines to the railroad roundhouse and put Butler, an old friend from Boxer Rebellion days, in charge there.

With the arrival of Badger's five battleships, the added personnel were organized into composite units. One battleship's battalion was added to the seaman regiment already ashore, while a 1,200-man second seaman regiment was created with the battalions from the other four battleships. The 300 Marines from these ships were formed into a battalion led by Major Albertus W. Catlin and added to Neville's Marine regiment already ashore.

During the night, Fletcher tried to arrange a cease-fire, but no one in authority on the Mexican side could be located. Consequently, at around 8 a.m. he directed the U.S. forces ashore to begin moving out to secure the city. The seaman battalions were directed to push toward the city center. Neville's Marines were assigned to search and clear the streets inland between Calles Montesinos and Calle Benito Juarez to the sand hills, an area of about 21 blocks parallel to the rail yard.

The renewed offensive began badly for the bluejackets. A battalion led by a Navy captain with long sea service but no land-fighting experience marched inland down Calle Francisco Canal near the customs house in parade-ground formation. Raked by rifle, machine gun and cannon fire, the stunned bluejackets bolted back to the waterfront. Several U.S. warships in the harbor responded by shelling the naval academy and other buildings from which the Mexicans were firing on the hapless battalion. This silenced the fire. Buoyed by this support, the battalion advanced as skirmishers and occupied the shattered naval academy.[23] Other battalions used better judgment in the way they advanced and achieved results with fewer casualties.

While this was happening, the Marines began expanding their perimeter. Neville sent two battalions north across the rail yard and one battalion southwest from Calle Montesinos. Unlike the bluejackets, who marched down the streets taking fire from the rooftops, the Marines advanced from house to house by breaking through the adobe walls. They also climbed the interior stairs to the rooftops to drive the snipers there ahead of them.

At one point, Daly and his men became pinned down in a steep-walled gully by rifle fire from the windows of a house. Attempts to move close enough to rush the house were beaten back. After one of his men was shot in the head, Daly ordered his men to remain in the gully while he crawled along it looking for a way to flank the house. He eventually found one. Continuing to crawl, he worked his way around to the back of the house. There he discovered a door. It was unguarded. Forcing his way through the door, Daly confronted seven armed but startled Mexicans. Thinking faster than his foes, Daly repeatedly fired and worked the bolt of his rifle to kill five of them. Having emptied his five-round clip, Daly charged at the other two Mexicans and killed them both with bayonet thrusts. He then returned to his men and carried on with the mission.[24]

Butler, leading one of the battalions north of the rail yard, later described what he saw of the fighting. "Since the Mexicans were using the houses as fortresses, the Marines rushed from home to home, kicking in the doors and searching for snipers. Just as two of my men were smashing through one door, they were mysteriously shot to the stomach from below. The house was deserted, but from the angle of the bullets, the Mexicans were obviously under the floor. We poured a volley through the floor and then ripped up the boards. There they were, two dead Mexicans, dangling between the cross beams. Our fire had caught them."[25]

The arrival of the Navy transport *Hancock* delivered a second Marine regiment to Vera Cruz. Led by Colonel John J. Lejeune, the regiment landed around 11 a.m. Lejeune took charge of the improvised Marine brigade ashore, while Neville retained command of the first regiment.

By the third day, April 23, the firing had slackened enough for the U.S. troops to begin burying or burning the bodies of the Mexican dead to prevent the spread of disease. The dead had lain in the sun for two sweltering days. The smell of rotting corpses was terrible, but the reek from burning bodies was something many men there later said they could never forget. These smells were likely a sharp reminder for Daly of what he had endured during the siege in Peking.

EIGHT—Vera Cruz

No accurate count of the Mexican casualties was ever obtained. Estimates of the dead range from 320 to nearly 450, and many more wounded. U.S. casualties were 17 killed and 63 wounded.[26] This disparity suggests two things: The Americans were much better shots, and U.S. weapons, tactics and organization were far superior to that of the Mexicans.

Daly was raised Catholic and his faith was an important part of his life. After the shooting stopped, he attended a funeral for some of the Mexicans killed in the fighting. It was the kind of respect a warrior would give to worthy opponents. It was who Daly was. He didn't fight out of hate for his foe but out of love for his country, his corps and his men.

With resistance reduced to an occasional shot, Fletcher now faced a new challenge: None of the Mexican officials would agree to resume their duties. A Mexican law adopted after the French invasion in 1862 made it a crime to serve under a foreign occupying force. It appeared the Americans would have to administer Vera Cruz for as long they remained in the city.

Meanwhile, news of the landing led to rioting in several Mexican cities. General Huerta ordered the U.S. consulate in Mexico City closed but provided safe escort for the consul and his staff to Vera Cruz. Flagrantly false reports in local newspapers inflamed the situation by claiming several U.S. battleships had been sunk and Mexican military forces had invaded Texas.

While Mexicans boiled with patriotic fervor, so did many Americans. Demonstrations endorsed the landing, and some journalists and politicians pushed to extend the intervention to annexation. However, the Democratic majority in the U.S. Senate blocked such a move by adopting a resolution restricting U.S. action to the limits in Wilson's original request. Republican Senator Elihu Root, Teddy Roosevelt's former secretary of state, decried the Senate action, saying it deprived the United States of an opportunity to protect American lives and property in Mexico. Nevertheless, the House followed the Senate's lead. As historian Jack Sweetman later wrote: "Brought face to face with the realities of war, the legislators were considerably less exuberant than they had been when Wilson had addressed them four days earlier."[27]

The foreign ministers of the so-called ABC Powers—Argentina, Brazil and Chile—now stepped forward to offer to mediate the dispute, and President Wilson accepted immediately. At about the same time, Fletcher solved his administrative headache in Vera Cruz. After he threatened to install a new municipal government that "would probably not suit them as well as their own," the Mexican officials agreed to resume their posts and administer the city.[28]

The ABC Powers tried but failed to find a settlement acceptable to Wilson, Huerta and Carranza, and in late June they gave up. Two weeks later, however, Huerta broke the impasse. On July 15, he resigned and went into exile in the face of a new offensive by Carranza's forces. With Huerta gone, Wilson's justification for intervention ended. He informed Carranza the troops would leave Vera Cruz, which they did on November 23.

While the Navy bluejackets returned to their ships shortly after the city was secured, Daly and his Marine battalion were retained there, serving as an occupying force with an Army brigade under Brigadier General Frederick Funston. Daly and the Marines finally departed Vera Cruz aboard the steamship *City of Memphis* on the final day of the occupation, November 23.[29]

In the wake of the Vera Cruz intervention, Congress changed the law to make officers of the Navy, Marine Corps and Coast Guard eligible to receive the Navy Medal of Honor.[30] Previously, only enlisted personnel of these service branches had been eligible. However, the Marine Corps opted at that time to exclude its enlisted men from eligibility, concluding that the medal should recognize distinguished service in a command position. This reversed the earlier situation during the Boxer Rebellion when enlisted men, but not officers, could receive the medal.

Nine Marine officers received the Medal of Honor for Vera Cruz. They included one lieutenant colonel (Neville), four majors (Butler, Catlin and two other battalion commanders), and four captains (including Hughes). No Marine below the rank of captain received the medal.

Butler received his first Medal of Honor for his actions on the second day of the landing: "Major Butler was eminent and conspicuous in command of his battalion. He exhibited courage and skill in leading his men through the action of the 22d and in the final occupation of the city."

Forever a rock in the shoe of his superiors, Butler returned his medal explaining, "I had done nothing which entitled me to this supreme decoration." In response, he said, "The Navy Department sent the medal back to me with the order that I should not only keep it this time, but wear it also."[31]

EIGHT—Vera Cruz

In an August 3, 1916, letter, Secretary of the Navy Daniels told Butler that granting his request would "detract from the merit of the Medal awarded to other officers [for services] performed during the same action. It would also establish a precedent which might prove an embarrassment to the department" by questioning its prior decisions on the medal.[32]

The wording of Catlin's Vera Cruz citation is identical to Butler's. The wording of the citations for the other two battalion commanders is nearly the same, as is Captain Hughes' citation.

Neville's award covered the period from noon the first day, when he landed, to noon the second day, when the fighting slackened: "His duties required him to be at points of great danger in directing his officers and men, and he exhibited conspicuous courage, coolness and skill in his conduct of the fighting. Upon his courage and skill depended, in great measure, success or failure. His responsibilities were great and he met them in a manner worthy of commendation."[33]

The Navy awarded 46 Medals of Honor for Vera Cruz to Navy personnel. Of these, 16 went to enlisted men and 29 to officers, including nine senior officers: Admiral Fletcher, Captain Rush, two other captains, three commanders and two lieutenant commanders. This distribution was more equitable than that of the Marines but still tended to favor officers over enlisted.

None of this commentary is meant to diminish the courage of those who received the medal. However, the number of Medals of Honor awarded for Vera Cruz has proven controversial. Fifty-five medals were awarded for the 24-hour firefight at Vera Cruz compared to 59 for the two-month Peking siege and relief expedition. Were all of them justified? It is difficult to judge the merits of most of the Vera Cruz medals because so many of the citations are devoid of details.

So, what about Daly's daring one-man attack on the house? Catlin stated in his memoir that "Daly inspired his men to limitless daring and for this he was recommended for a third medal [of honor]."[34] If enlisted Marines had been eligible to receive the Medal of Honor for Vera Cruz, should he have received one? Once again, the limited details in the citations make it difficult to impossible to make such a determination. Although his obituary in the *New York Times*[35] said he was cited for heroism at Vera Cruz, there is nothing in Daly's service record to indicate he received even a commendation letter for that action.

Based on historian Jack Sweetman's thorough account of the Vera

Cruz landing, there is one action that offers a clue to how to evaluate Daly's action if he had been eligible. The medal was awarded to the ensign who burst into the customs house with five volunteers to confront the Mexican defenders there. A volunteer who aided the wounded sailor also received the medal. That suggests Daly could have received his second Medal of Honor at Vera Cruz instead of later.

History is full of tantalizing what-ifs. Whether Daly should have received the Medal of Honor for his actions at Vera Cruz will have to remain one of those unknowables.

Nine

Haiti

The second of the three armed clashes that would make Daly a Marine Corps legend occurred in the troubled Caribbean nation of Haiti.

A former French colony that shares the island of Hispaniola with the Dominican Republic, Haiti sits at a chokepoint on a major sea lane between the Atlantic Ocean and the Panama Canal, which opened in August 1914. This event increased the importance of Haiti to U.S. military and economic interests in the region. Consequently, the United States paid close attention to a European military power potentially inserting itself into such a sensitive location.

In 1914, Haiti was an economic house of cards on the verge of collapse. The Haitian government was deep in debt to France, Germany and the United States due to mismanagement and corruption, both foreign and homegrown. When a bellicose Germany pressed Haiti for full repayment of its loans and threatened to intervene there if its demands were not met, the United States became alarmed. Citing the Monroe Doctrine and the Roosevelt Corollary, the United States warned that such action would invite a U.S. military response.

However, America was already poised to intervene in Haiti. U.S. officials regarded the Caribbean as the "backyard" of its empire, and were simply looking for a "just cause" to take action. Racism also played a role. Most Haitians were descendants of former African slaves. As such, they were regarded with the same scorn as blacks in the Jim Crow America of that time.[1]

These attitudes, put into practice by President Theodore Roosevelt's Big Stick policy, served to protect American commercial interests in Latin America at the expense of the peoples living there. U.S. companies made large loans at high interest rates to these nations, claiming that the risks of nonpayment justified the high rates. However, the

"Devil Dog" Dan Daly

risk was a fantasy. As a practical matter, if a nation fell behind on its payments, it faced the threat of U.S. military intervention. Thus, nations like Haiti went out of their way to stay current. If, however, a nation did actually fall behind, the United States would intervene and force the debtor nation to accept draconian U.S. controls as well as the sale of many of its assets to Americans at fire-sale prices.

After he retired from the Marine Corps in 1931, Smedley Butler spoke out about these practices: "I spent most of my time [in the Marine Corps] being a high-class muscle-man for Big Business, for Wall Street and for the Bankers. In short, I was a racketeer, a gangster for capitalism.... I helped make Mexico ... safe for American oil interests in 1914. I helped make Haiti and Cuba a decent place for the National City Bank boys to collect revenues in. I helped in the raping of half a dozen Central American republics for the benefits of Wall Street.... I helped purify Nicaragua for the international banking house of Brown Brothers.... I brought light to the Dominican Republic for American sugar interests in 1916. In China I helped to see to it that Standard Oil went its way unmolested."[2]

By the summer of 1914, the U.S. Navy had drawn up detailed plans for the invasion of Haiti. This was before the situation there provided any justification for U.S. intervention. Although Haiti had large outstanding loans to foreign interests, prior to U.S. intervention Haiti was current on its payments. In fact, Haiti had committed 80 percent of its revenue to paying its debts, and had a better payment record than most nations in Latin America at the time.[3]

A more pressing issue for the United States than Haiti's debt was its refusal to sell land at Môle-Saint-Nicolas to the U.S. Navy for a base there to monitor the vital passageway between Haiti and Cuba.[4] Despite Haiti's constitutional prohibition on selling land to foreigners, the U.S. departments of State and Navy feared Germans on the island might prevail upon that nation's government to allow Germany to establish a naval base there and challenge U.S. supremacy in the region. German residents of Haiti controlled 80 percent of the foreign trade.[5]

While taking steps to discourage foreign intervention, the U.S. government took other steps to pave the way for its own. First, it arranged in 1910 for a group of American investors, led by the National City Bank of New York, to acquire a controlling interest in Haiti's sole commercial bank, which doubled as the nation's treasury. Then, in December 1914 it had a U.S. Marine detachment enter Haiti and transport the nation's

Nine—Haiti

gold reserve, valued at $500,000, to the New York City vault of National City Bank for "safe-keeping." Supposedly this was to prevent Germany or France from seizing the gold to secure payment, or to prevent Haitian politicians from looting it. However, U.S. officials used their possession of the Haitian treasury to pressure Haiti to hand over control of its finances to the United States.[6]

Besides being an economic basket-case in 1914, Haiti also was a political powder keg. Five Haitian presidents in a row between 1908 and 1914 had been overthrown or killed, leaving the country on the edge of outright anarchy, Early in 1915, a sixth president was driven out of office.

A Haitian general, Jean Vibrun Guillaume Sam, had played a role in some of these violent events. In 1908, a revolt toppled President Pierre Nord Alexis. This was followed by a revolt in 1911 led by Sam that replaced President Francois Antoine Simon with Cincinnatus Leconte. One year later, a huge mysterious explosion at the national palace killed Leconte and a couple of hundred soldiers. Michel Oriente succeeded him as president in 1913 but a revolt led by wealthy landowners in early 1914 replaced him with one of their own, Oreste Zamor. General Joseph Davilmar Theodore then led a revolt by cacao farmers and bandit/mercenaries (called *cacos*) that forced Zamor out in late 1914. However, Theodore was driven from office just four months later when he failed to pay the *cacos* as promised for ousting Zamor. By some accounts, Sam precipitated Theodore's demise by cutting off the funds Theodore needed to pay the *cacos*.

No longer willing to let others rule, on March 4, 1915, Sam had himself proclaimed president. A revolt against him soon began. It was led by Dr. Rosalvo Bobo, a politician opposed to Sam forming closer economic ties with the United States. To retain his grip on power, Sam, an Afro-Haitian, cracked down on his opponents, who tended to be educated and wealthy mulattoes.

The political powder keg exploded on July 27, 1915. Sam had imprisoned 175 political opponents—generals, doctors, lawyers, merchants, and politicians—in Port-au-Prince's cramped city jail. Before dawn on the 27th, a group of armed rebels attempted to storm the national palace in order to free the prisoners. The guards fought back but rebels within their ranks turned the guards' machine guns on the guards. The rebel attack failed when Sam and the remaining guards barricaded themselves in the palace. However, fighting continued at points around the city.

Sensing the end, Sam sent a note to the jail commander, telling him: "If in the morning I am unable to hold the Palace, do at once what you have promised me you would do." When Sam fled the palace over a garden wall into the neighboring French embassy seeking asylum, the jail commander did what he had promised. He and five of his jailors "worked their way from cell to cell cutting, stabbing as they went, ahead of them the frantic cries of the unfortunates who heard their butchers coming, behind them a sodden silence." They viciously murdered 168 of the 175 defenseless prisoners, recalled Robert Beale Davis, Jr., the U.S. chargé d'affaires. "Six managed to escape in the melee and one, shamming death, lived to tell the horror which had gone on over his body."[7]

After personally seeing the butchered bodies in the jail, Davis ran back to the U.S. legation and sent a cable to Rear Admiral William B. Caperton, aboard the armored cruiser *Washington* at Cap Haitien on Haiti's north shore, urging him to sail at once to Port-au-Prince.

Caperton then cabled President Woodrow Wilson, who ordered him to send in the Marines. Wilson's stated purpose was two-fold. He wanted to prevent Sam's anti–American rival, Bobo, from seizing power, and he wanted to keep Germany from using the unrest as an excuse to invade Haiti. The bloodshed also served as the justification he needed to extend U.S. control over the island.

Sam spent the night of the 27th in the French legation, hoping the rebels would honor the sanctuary granted him by the French. However, nothing could have enraged the rebels more than what had happened to their families, friends and colleagues at the jail. On the 28th, the rebel leaders battered their way into the legation, beat Sam mercilessly, and tossed him over the legation's wrought-iron fence. There, an angry mob literally hacked Sam to pieces and paraded the bloody parts through the city. The entire country then convulsed into two weeks of chaos.[8]

An hour after Sam met his horrific end, the *Washington* dropped anchor in Port-au-Prince harbor. That afternoon, the 12th Marine Company and three companies of bluejackets, about 340 men total, came ashore and marched into the city. Marines would remain in Haiti for the next 19 years.[9] The Marines in their khakis and campaign hats and the sailors in their white uniforms did not come in with bugles blaring. Instead, they slipped quietly into the city with bayonets fixed, ready for a fight. As evening settled in, detachments took positions at key points around the city. By 9 p.m., the Marines were in control of Port-au-Prince. Only one Haitian tried to resist the landing. He was shot and killed by a Marine.

NINE—Haiti

On July 28, the same day that Sam died and the first Marines landed at Port-au-Prince, Daly and the 15th Marine Company sailed from Philadelphia aboard the battleship *Connecticut*, destination Haiti. Daly was now a gunnery sergeant, having been appointed on April 5, 1915. He and his fellow Marines of the 2nd Marine Regiment arrived in Haiti five days later, August 4, to join the occupation force. The regimental commander was Colonel Eli K. Cole, an 1888 Naval Academy graduate who had seen action in the Philippines and Panama.[10]

Later that month, the armored cruiser *Tennessee* delivered the First Brigade Headquarters and the First Marine Regiment to Haiti. The 1st Marine Regiment was commanded by Colonel Theodore P. Kent. Among the regiment's battalion commanders were Daly's old Peking commander, Major Newt C. Hall, and Major Smedley Darlington Butler, who had earned a brevet medal with the Peking relief expedition and the Medal of Honor at Vera Cruz.

Colonel Littleton T. Waller, a veteran of the Spanish-American War, the Peking relief expedition, the Philippines and Vera Cruz, arrived on the *Tennessee* to command the brigade. He came from a distinguished old-line Virginia family. His ancestors had been slave owners and several Waller family members were among the whites savagely murdered in Nat Turner's 1831 slave revolt. As a result, Waller was openly racist toward blacks of any nation, which influenced his treatment of Haitians.

While the Marines disarmed the rebels in Port-au-Prince, fighting among competing Haitian factions vying for power continued in the northern part of the country. To quell the violence, the gunboats *Nashville* and *Eagle* landed Marine detachments at Cap Haitien. The Marines prevented that city from being seized by rebel forces. Waller decided to bolster his northern forces by sending Cole and a battalion of four companies commanded by Butler to Cap Haitien, the largest city on Haiti's north coast.

Over the next six weeks, Marine detachments took charge of Haiti's major ports while other detachments set up camps in towns in the interior and patrolled the paths in the hills. The U.S. military ruled Haiti for the next nine months, until April 1916. During this time, U.S. officials extended their control to include the customs houses, banks and national treasury. Having Haiti's finances firmly within their grasp, they allocated 40 percent of the nation's income to repay foreign debts.

To keep Bobo from becoming president, U.S. officials offered the post to several other Haitians but they all turned it down. Finally, Philippe Sudré Dartiguenave, the mulatto president of the Senate, agreed to serve as president, a figurehead under U.S. control. The Haitian Congress dutifully elected him to the post on August 12 under the watchful eyes of Marines standing in the aisles with fixed bayonets.[11] This was a classic example of the United States imposing its will on a foreign nation for the benefit of American business interests rather than the local populace. As a Marine NCO, Daly was just a pawn in U.S. foreign affairs and had no say in such actions. However, it's likely he found it troubling to be used in this way.

U.S. Assistant Secretary of the Navy Franklin Delano Roosevelt then supervised the drafting of a new Haitian constitution. While it included some liberal reforms, one provision outraged the populace. It allowed foreigners to buy land in Haiti. When the Haitian legislature refused to adopt the constitution with this provision, Dartiguenave dissolved the body at the insistence of the Marines. The constitution was finally approved by voters in 1918. Only five percent of the electorate cast ballots in this plebiscite. The vote was suspiciously lop-sided, 98,225 to 768. The largely illiterate electorate voted for whichever side held power. In this case, it was the Marines.

Dartiguenave's government also "negotiated" a treaty that gave the United States effective control of Haiti for the next 10 years. Signed September 15, it created a national constabulary staffed by Haitians but led by Americans. It also gave U.S. officials veto power over government decisions, and installed Navy and Marine Corps officers as administrators in government departments.

The national constabulary, the Gendarmerie de Haiti, became the principal means of U.S. control over Haiti, and the Marines played a major role in that force. It consisted of 250 officers and 2,500 men. Marine officers, sergeants and corporals held officer rank in the constabulary.

The task of tamping down uprisings and maintaining order in as fractious a place as Haiti was compounded by its size. Haiti is over 400 miles long from east to west and 160 to 170 miles wide from north to south. It has about 900 miles of coastline, creating plenty of opportunities for smuggling of goods to avoid customs duties and arms to launch uprisings. Encompassing 10,700 square miles, Haiti is larger than the state of New Jersey, with a population at the time of about 2.5 million. The Afro-Haitian population tended to be poor and illiterate. The mulatto population was better educated and wealthier, and looked down on their darker-skinned countrymen.

One of the challenges faced by the Marines in subduing Haiti was the lack of modern roads in the interior. In 1915, Haiti had just three miles of roads outside of towns that were usable by motor vehicles. In response, the Marines and the constabulary began in an intense road-building program. Money was in short supply, so the Marines improvised. Smedley Butler dusted off an 1864 Haitian law that required the local populace to work on the roads if they could not pay a road tax. By 1918, 470 miles of modern roads had been built. However, this forced-labor program also stoked anger and resentment among rural Haitians who felt abused, disrespected and, ultimately, enslaved.

The *cacos* in the north around Cap Haitien were soon in open revolt against the new rulers of Haiti. Their name is derived from a native bird of prey whose cry sounds like "Kaaa-ko." By some accounts, the name refers to the bird's practice of hiding under leaves to ambush its prey. Butler later claimed the name refers to a bird that "lives off weaker birds,"[12] As the revolt grew, the *cacos* ambushed Marine patrols, attacked outposts and besieged towns. Waller attempted to broker a deal with the *cacos* to support Dartiguenave, the American puppet president, but the *cacos* remained committed to Bobo.

Upon learning that 100 Marines stationed at Gonaives were besieged by an estimated 800 *cacos*, Waller directed Butler to take a detachment and relieve the outpost. The town, located on Haiti's west coast, has special significance to Haitians. The Battle of Ravine-à-Couleuvres, also known as the Battle of Snake Gully, was fought near there in 1802 in the Haitians' fight for independence from France. Losses on both sides were in the hundreds. Gonaives also is where Haiti declared its independence in 1804.

On September 20, Butler arrived at Gonaives with 108 men. Learning that General Pierre Rameau and his *cacos* were nearby, the Marines drove them off.[13] Early the next morning, Butler headed out with 50 Marines to find the insurgents. Arriving at the village of Poteau, they found about 450 *cacos* preparing to flee. Butler instructed his men to yell out General Rameau's name, and the general soon appeared. Walking up to Rameau, a "wizened old Negro on a horse," Butler ordered Rameau to dismount. When the general refused, Butler yanked him out of the saddle and dumped him unceremoniously on the ground. "This was more humiliating to him than defeat in battle," said Butler. "His prestige with his men was destroyed, and he was no longer a great general."[14] The next day, Butler and a patrol found six *cacos* robbing a woman. They shot three of them. The others fled and the *cacos* in the area disbanded.[15]

In October, Colonel Waller ordered Butler to lead an expedition into the mountains to find a *cacos* stronghold known as Fort Capois. Butler's regimental commander, Colonel Cole, had 700 men at Cap Haitien but he told Waller it would require 3,000 men to invade the rugged *cacos* territory. At the time, there were 2,500 Marines in all of Haiti. No military force of white men had dared venture into the mountains of northern Haiti since the French had departed in 1804. Butler proposed to undertake the mission by stealth with a single platoon.

The mission began on October 22, 1915, at Fort Liberté, an old stone fort on the northeast coast of Haiti, near the Dominican Republic border. Built by the French in 1731, the fort sat at the tip of a crooked finger of land jutting into a large bay. The Marines used it as a base camp. The 40-man patrol, comprised of Butler, three other officers, 35 enlisted Marines and a medical aid man,[16] set out south from Fort Liberté mounted on ponies with a dozen pack animals to carry food, ammunition and a machine gun. Butler chose his men carefully for this mission. He selected a close friend, Captain William P. Upshur, as his second in command, and Gunnery Sergeant Daly as his "top kick," or first sergeant. Butler later described Daly as "the fightin'est man I ever knew.... When the relief column in which I was marching reached Peking, everyone was talking of Fighting Dan Daly."[17]

Recalling that time in Haiti, Butler said of Daly, "His hair was grey even then, and he looked like Lon Chaney. He was smooth faced, with skin like leather. Hard-boiled as the devil, but fine clear through.... I admired his courage and modesty and became very much attached to him."[18]

On the third day, October 24, the detachment came across a "hideous, ungainly brute" of a Haitian man. Butler persuaded him to lead them to the *cacos* fort by giving him a choice: five dollars in Haitian money or a bullet. The man chose the money. That afternoon, the man pointed out the location, "a mountain about a mile away, towering about one thousand feet above us," Butler later recalled. "The cone-shaped peak was surrounded by rough stone walls and trenches. Every detail was outlined distinctly in the afternoon sunlight. Through my field glasses I saw men crawling over the ramparts and the thatched roofs of the huts inside the walls."[19]

NINE—Haiti

Sizing up the situation, Butler realized he would need a lot more men to attack this fort. Heading for a town he believed to be about five miles away, Butler figured that if they were attacked they could barricade themselves in the church. After several hours of riding through a drizzling rain, they arrived on the banks of a swift-running river, the Grande-Rivière-du-Nord. Gingerly, the men led their horses down the steep slope in the growing darkness. The river proved too deep to wade across. The horses had to swim across with the men holding on to their tails. Suddenly, bullets splashed and zinged all around them. Their conscripted guide had led them into a trap by an estimated 400 *cacos*. By some stroke of luck, all 40 Marines made it across the river. However, 12 of the horses were lost in the crossing. The *cacos* were poor marksmen but horses are a much bigger target than a man.

Crawling on hands and knees, and leading their horses behind them, the Marines reached high ground several hundred yards from the river. They found a shallow pond and formed a circle around it with the horses in the center.

"Better set up the machine gun, Daly," Butler said.

"It was lost in the river," Daly replied, matter of factly.

"Well," said Butler after a long pause, "we'll have to do the best we can without it."

At that point, Butler recalled that Daly disappeared. An hour or so later, Daly reappeared and calmly informed Butler that he had set up the machine gun. Daly had crawled all the way back to the river through the underbrush with *cacos* bullets kicking up dirt and clipping leaves around him. Diving repeatedly into the cold murky torrent in the dark, Daly's searching hands had found one dead horse after another until he finally located the machine gun still tied to the dead pack animal. He had cut the gun lose and hauled it to the river bank. Strapping the machine gun to his back, he had crawled back through the gantlet of enemy fire to the encircled Marines. Some accounts say he killed several *cacos* with a knife during that journey.[20]

"I wouldn't have had the courage to do that," recalled Butler, who was famous for courage under fire. "Remember, he went back on his own initiative without a hint or suggestion from me. For this amazing stunt I recommended him for the Medal of Honor. And that's how Fighting Dan Daly got his second Congressional medal."[21]

As Butler later said, it was lucky the Marines now had the machine gun. They were surrounded and outnumbered about 10 to one.

"Devil Dog" Dan Daly

Throughout the night, machete-wielding men rushed at them out of the darkness, only to be felled by Marine bullets and bayonets. The Marines shivered, chilled to the bone by the cold water in the river and the menacing screams of the *cacos* surrounding them. "All the men were praying," said Butler, who was raised by Quakers. "Even hard-boiled Marines pray when they feel helplessly snared in a death trap." No doubt Daly, who was raised Catholic, found time to cross himself and say a prayer that night.

Just before dawn, October 25, Butler divided his men into three squads, with Captain Upshur, First Lieutenant Edward A. Ostermann and Daly each leading a squad. "Just go for those devils as soon as it's light," he told them. "Move straight forward and shoot everyone you see."[22] At a signal from Butler, the three squads charged in three different directions. The sudden attack surprised the *cacos*, who fled with Marines in hot pursuit. Eight *cacos* were killed in this attack and 10 were wounded. First Lieutenant Adolph Miller fired 60 rounds from the machine gun and accounted for 18 more dead or wounded *cacos*, according to Butler's report.[23]

"It is true," wrote Butler, "that these men were in pitch darkness, surrounded by ten times their number and fighting for their lives, but the manner in which they fought during that long night[,] the steady, cool, discipline that prevented demoralization is remarkable. Had one squad failed not one man of the party would have lived to tell the story."[24]

Some of the *cacos* took refuge in a fort 300 to 400 yards away and resumed firing. The Marines charged again, this time bursting into the fort. In the ensuing melee, they reportedly killed about 75 of the defenders. The rest ran into the hills. The Marines then burned the walled compound to the ground. They later learned it was known as Fort Dipitie.

Surprisingly, all 40 Marines were still alive. Only one man, Private Russell Fredericks, was injured. He had a flesh wound to the left arm.[25] Unfortunately, they were still deep in *cacos* country and a long way from any reinforcements. Sleepless, exhausted and hungry, they began following the river toward what they figured would be the sea. At one point, they entered a canyon, with high, steep walls. Working their way along a ledge about six feet above the river, they continued walking. A downpour began and the river rose above the ledge. Men were swept off the ledge by the rushing water and a human chain had to pull the men back up. Finally, they arrived at a village where they were able to get some food and rest. Early the next morning, the detachment set out

NINE—*Haiti*

again. It was a 30-mile trek over the mountains back to their base at Fort Libertè, but they made it.[26]

Butler summarized this mission in an October 31 letter to his father: "In a nutshell, we marched 120 miles in 5 days 10½ hours ..., fought one continuous fight with over 300 devilish *Cacos* for 21 hours, crossed four mountain ranges, passed through a flood that made us sit up in trees all night and reached Fort Liberté again without losing a man."[27]

In addition to recommending Daly for the Medal of Honor, Butler also recommended Captain Upshur and Lieutenant Ostermann. All three received the medal. After some criticism for restricting the medal to Marine officers at Vera Cruz, the Marine Corps changed its policy to once again make enlisted Marines eligible to receive the medal. Both Upshur and Ostermann went on to become major generals.

Having now discovered the location of Fort Capois—located halfway between the towns of Bahon and Grande-Rivière[28]—Butler led a force of 600 men to capture this citadel of the *cacos*. The two-week campaign began on November 1. Daly was part of this fighting force along with 33 other men from the 15th Marine Company, once again led by Captain Upshur. (Upshur became a two-star general in World War II before dying in a plane crash in 1943.)

En route to Fort Capois, Daly engaged in combat with hostile *cacos* at Le Trou and the Cross Roads of Crucifixion, both on November 2. As the expedition closed in on Fort Capois, Daly and Second Lieutenant Allen H. Turnage led the advance guard that battled *cacos* at St. Susanne on November 4.[29] St. Susanne is located seven miles north of the fort.[30]

"It was my good fortune," said Turnage, "to have Gunnery Sergeant Dan Daly as second in command of my platoon throughout the operations against the *cacos* in north Haiti in 1915. I consider Dan Daly a superior Marine not only for the fact that he won two Medals of Honor during his career, but because of his intense devotion to the Marine Corps and his country."[31]

In a letter to the regimental commander, Captain Upshur singled out Daly and three other men for their "meritorious conduct" during these actions. He commended Daly for "exceptional coolness and leadership of the men under fire at Dipitre, Le Trou, and the Cross Roads of Crucifixion and the advance guard action in the advance to St. Susanne."[32]

When the expedition reached Fort Capois on November 5, most accounts say the Marines found the fort deserted.[33] However, Marine

"Devil Dog" Dan Daly

Major Samuel M. Harrington, writing in 1922 in the *United States Naval Institute Proceedings,* said eight *cacos* were killed in the capture of the fort.[34] As many as 150 *cacos* were seen fleeing Fort Capois just ahead of the approaching Marine expedition. Despite the fort's strong natural defensive position, the *cacos* had apparently had enough of confronting the Marines in a pitched battle. The Marines' superior marksmanship more than made up for the cacos' superior numbers in these head-on clashes.

Three days later, as the expedition headed northeast back toward Fort Liberté, they captured Fort Selon and Fort Berthol, located near Vallieres.[35] Once again, the *cacos* had abandoned these forts without a fight.[36]

Upon his return to Fort Liberté, Butler was summoned to Cap Haitian to plan a campaign to destroy the *cacos* last major stronghold in the north at Fort Rivière. The fort was a square structure of brick and stone with thick walls 15–25 feet high around a courtyard about 200 feet long on each side. At each corner a bastion jutted out with indentations in the wall. These features allowed defenders to fire down on anyone close to the walls without having to expose themselves. It was built by the French on Montagne Noire, "a hogback ridge about a quarter-mile long," according to a report written by Franklin D. Roosevelt in 1917 after a guided tour of it by Butler.[37] A hogback ridge is narrow at the top with steep sides like the back of a pig. The top of the ridge is about 4,000 feet above sea level, near the Grande-Rivière-du-Nord, about 20 miles south of Cap Haitien.

Once again Colonel Cole expressed the view that a large body of men would be needed to capture the fort. And once again Butler persuaded Waller and Cole that he could do it with far less. He proposed to approach by stealth with four columns from all sides in a coordinated attack.

In mid–November, Butler and Daly headed south from Cap Haitien with three 24-man companies from the 5th, 13th and 23rd Marine companies and small detachments of Marines and Navy bluejackets from the *Connecticut.* They also brought along two .30 caliber Model 1909 Benét-Mercié Machine Rifles. These gas-operated, air-cooled, 30-round-clip or belt-fed machine guns could fire up to 400 rounds per minute. They weighed 27 pounds, light enough to hold and fire while standing. They also had a bipod to support the barrel when fired from the prone position.

NINE—Haiti

Traveling first to the towns of Grande-Rivière and then Le Coupe, where they met up with the bluejacket contingent from the *Connecticut*, the Marines moved to within striking distance of the fort by November 16. There they waited for first light the next day to surround the fort. At 7:40 a.m. on November 17, Butler, Daly and four squads of the 5th Marine Company, reached a position 800 yards southwest of the fort. A second unit from the 13th Marine Company and the Marines from the *Connecticut* arrived at a position 800 yards southeast of the fort. Butler then advanced to within 500 yards, where he placed a machine gun to cover the advance.

Moving across open ground, Butler and one company of Marines advanced toward the fort. The gate was on the north side of the fort but it was blocked with bricks and stones. It would have taken artillery to break through the gate. However, the Marines located a small drainage tunnel in the south wall that led into the courtyard, according to Roosevelt's recounting of what he learned from Butler. The tunnel was about 2½ feet high and 2 feet wide. Butler was about to lead the 26 men with him into the tunnel when Sergeant Ross Lindsey Iams of the 5th company stopped him. "Sorry, sir," Iams said. "I was in the Marines before you were and this is my privilege." After a brief hesitation, Butler stepped aside and Iams led the way, followed by Private Samuel Gross of the 23rd company and then Butler.

"On coming to the end within the courtyard, he [Iams] saw the shadows of the legs of two cacos armed with machetes guarding the hole," Roosevelt wrote. "He took off his hat, put it on his revolver, pushed it through, felt the two machetes descend on it, and jumped forward into the daylight. With a right and a left he got both *Cacos*, stood up and dropped two or three others while his companions, headed by Smedley Butler, got through and onto their feet. Then ensued a killing, the news of which put down insurrections we hope for all time to come. There were about 300 *cacos* within the wall and Butler and his 18 companions, including Daly, killed about 200 of them, others jumping over the wall and falling prisoner to the rest of the force of Marines which encircled the mountain."

Once Butler, Daly and their men entered the fort, the other Marines and sailors outside the walls attacked. The fighting, which included hand-to-hand combat, lasted 10 to 15 minutes. Accounts of the number of *cacos* engaged in the action and the number killed vary. One account says there were 60 rebels in the fort, 50 of whom were killed before the others escaped. It states that more than 20 rebels were killed fleeing the fort. No prisoners were taken. The Navy secretary later put the *cacos'* dead at 29 inside the fort and 22 more killed after jumping over the walls.

The only U.S. casualty was a lieutenant who lost two teeth when he was struck in the mouth by a rock.[38] Many of the *cacos*, although armed with rifles, resorted to more familiar weapons—rocks, knives and machetes—in close combat.

Whatever the numbers in this particular engagement, the crushing defeat of the *cacos* that day ended the rebellion in the north, at least for some time. Officially, the first *caco* rebellion ended with three Marines killed and 18 wounded. The number of rebels killed is estimated at 200.[39] This number is surprisingly low given the much larger numbers claimed in after-action reports by the Marines. It is likely the combatants over-stated the number of enemy killed. It is also possible the U.S. government purposely under-reported the number of Haitian dead because the lopsided totals might make the fight look more like a turkey shoot than a battle.

Butler recommended both Iams and Gross for the Medal of Honor for their courage in leading the way into the bastion. Both received the medal. Butler, too, received the medal. Like Daly, it was his second award. Following the Fort Rivière action, Iams was promoted to first sergeant and Gross to corporal. During World War I, Iams served in France as a captain and retired from the Marine Corps at that rank in 1932. Sadly, Gross didn't fare as well. He developed epilepsy soon after this fight and spent much of the remainder of his life in a veterans' hospital.

Butler also commended Daly for his "conspicuous" conduct during the capture of Fort Rivière. The ever-colorful Butler added a special tribute: "Daly is a real red-blooded marine and it was an object lesson to have served with him."[40]

In adding his endorsement of these Medal of Honor recommendations, Marine Commandant George Barnett added a note that Daly was the "most conspicuous figure among the enlisted personnel" during the operations in the vicinity of Fort Rivière. Secretary of the Navy Daniels concurred, commending Daly for his "conspicuous gallantry" at both Fort Dipitie and Fort Rivière. Although Daly's Medal of Honor citation for Haiti only cites his heroism at Fort Dipitie, the Navy secretary wrote that Daly's Medal of Honor was for his "heroic actions" at both forts.[41]

While Daly departed Haiti for a new assignment in January 1916,

NINE—Haiti

Butler was promoted to lieutenant colonel and put in command of the constabulary with a rank in that organization of major general. He remained in Haiti until March 1918. Together with 114 Marines he trained over 2,500 Haitians to serve as a combination army and police force. "It was an attractive assignment for Marines like Butler because they received a higher rank in the gendarmerie and a second salary to supplement their corps paycheck."[42] The constabulary essentially ran the country and its officers operated like sovereign lords, controlling government funds and dispensing justice.

Occasional skirmishes continued for a time and a second *caco* rebellion erupted in late 1918. The new revolt stemmed from the brutal and corrupt actions of constabulary units in the north administered by Marine Major Clarke H. Wells, particularly in the use of conscripts from nearby towns and villages to build roads. Following a personal inspection tour by Brigadier General Albertus W. Catlin, the new Marine commander in Haiti in March 1919, Wells was relieved of his command and sent back to the United States. A court-martial was ordered but in November 1920, after a court of inquiry headed by Rear Admiral Henry Mayo found insufficient evidence to proceed.[43] Clarke, the grandson and namesake of a rear admiral, resumed his Marine Corps career and retired as a full colonel.[44]

Nor were the actions surrounding road-building the only provocation. The departure of the best Marines from Haiti to fight in France resulted in a sharp rise in violent crimes by the Marines who remained in Haiti.[45] This created an environment where the shooting of prisoners by Marines was condoned, which further inflamed the Haitian populace. Investigations by the Navy Department in 1920 and by a Senate Select Committee in 1921–1922 concluded that, while a few extra-judicial killings had occurred, overall the Marines had done "a splendid job" in Haiti.

As for the *caco* uprising begun in 1918, it quickly overwhelmed the capacity of the constabulary to contain it and a large force of Marines was landed to deal with the emergency. U.S. military aircraft also were employed. Most of the fighting took place in the rugged interior of the country. Both sides engaged in harsh treatment of combatants, and sometimes of civilians. The *cacos*, whose numbers have been estimated at 5,000 full-time fighters and perhaps 15,000 part-time, achieved some initial success, and in 1919, their leader, Charlemagne Péralte, declared a provisional government in northern Haiti.

"Devil Dog" Dan Daly

In October of that year, he led a bold attack on Port-au-Prince, but the rebels were ultimately driven off. Later that month, Péralte was killed by a Marine when one of his own men, Jean-Baptiste Conze, betrayed him for a $2,000 reward. On the night of October 31, 1919, Conze's assistant led Sergeant Herman H. Hanneken, Corporal William R. Button and a constabulary detachment disguised as *cacos* to the rebel leader's camp up in the hills near the town of Grande-Rivière. Hanneken knew from Conze that the *cacos* planned to attack the town, which meant that most of Péralte's 1,200 men would be away from the rebel camp. Hanneken reinforced the town's defenses and gambled that they would be able to fend off the attack while he went after Péralte. About a hundred *cacos* remained in the rebel leader's camp.

"With 16 hand-picked gendarmes, Hanneken and Button went through six caco outposts undetected. They were inspected by flashlight at each point, but incredibly enough, they were able to disguise their skin by the use of black cork coloring. They made it through each outpost undetected, white men 'dressed' in *caco* skin. When they arrived at the main rebel base, Conze silently pointed out Charlemagne hovering near the light of a small campfire. The American [Hanneken] pumped two .45 caliber slugs into the betrayed leader, killing him instantly. The bodyguard was instantly felled by automatic rifle fire."[46]

A wild shootout followed in the camp. The *cacos* were killed or driven off. Hanneken and Button then tied Péralte's body to a mule and returned to Grande-Rivière-du-Nord, which had withstood the attack. To prove the rebel leader had been killed, photos of the body tied upright to a door were distributed. The attempt to intimidate the rebels backfired, however. The position of Péralte's body in the photo evoked the crucifixion of Christ, and that, together with the treatment of the body, generated sympathy for the cause and anger at the occupiers. Péralte is still revered in Haiti as a freedom fighter and his image has appeared on a Haitian coin.[47]

Five months later, Hanneken killed another rebel leader, Osiris Joseph, in another daring raid. Both Hanneken and Button received the Medal of Honor for their raid on Péralte's camp, and Hanneken received the Navy Cross for the other raid. He also was commissioned a second lieutenant. During World War II, he commanded a battalion on Guadalcanal and retired as a brigadier general. Button was promoted to sergeant but died of malaria less than two years later.

The second *caco* rebellion resumed with the selection of

NINE—Haiti

Benoît Batraville to succeed the martyred Péralte. Batraville led an attack Port-au-Prince in January 1920 with disastrous results for the rebels. About 300 were killed and 3,200 more were soon captured.

The Marines took the fight to a new level with tactics learned in the just-concluded First World War. They employed seven seaplanes and six biplanes to scout the rebel forces and drop bombs on them. They also divided the ground into districts and methodically drove the rebels back time after time with heavy losses. The Marines were aided by improved machine guns for use by troops on the ground and aircraft strafing from above. The Lewis gun was a gas-operated, air-cooled, drum-magazine-fed, bipod-mounted, shoulder-fire weapon. It weighed 28 pounds and fired a .30-06 cartridge, the same as the 1903 Springfield rifle carried by the Marines.

In May 1920, Batraville was captured when his base camp was overrun and he was executed. The death of the rebels' leaders, coupled with offers of amnesty, ended the rebellion. The second *caco* rebellion was bloodier than the first. The official death count was 28 Americans and 70 constabulary members killed, and more than 2,000 rebels dead.[48]

The U.S. occupation finally began to draw to a close after an incident in December 1929 at Les Cayes. U.S. Marines shot and killed 10 Haitians who were among marchers protesting economic conditions. President Herbert Hoover appointed two commissions to investigate conditions and they criticized the exclusion of Haitians from leadership positions in the government and constabulary. Hoover began the process of dismantling the occupation and this work was completed by President Franklin D. Roosevelt, who as assistant secretary of the Navy had presided over the writing of the Haitian constitution. The occupation officially ended in 1934 when the last U.S. Marines left Haiti, although the United States continued to supervise the country's external finances until 1947.[49]

Daly was long gone from Haiti by then, having returned to the United States in January 1916. In April of that year, he received a letter of commendation from Secretary of the Navy Josephus Daniels.[50] Dated March 30, it begins by quoting from Smedley Butler's report of the October 1915 reconnaissance patrol, ambush at the river and capture of Fort Dipitie: "Gunnery Sergeant Daniel Daly, 15th Marine Company, during the operations was the most conspicuous figure among the enlisted personnel. Daly is a real red-blooded marine and it was an object lesson to have served with him."

"Devil Dog" Dan Daly

The Navy secretary's letter concluded: "The Department is pleased to note that your conduct and bearing while engaged on hazardous duty was such as to call forth the praise of your superior officers, particularly so when all reports show that every man was not only willing but anxious to do his full duty and to meet any and all hardships without complaint."

In an accompanying transmittal note, Major General Commandant George Barnett, added, "Your conduct reflects much credit upon yourself, and fully upholds the best traditions of the Marine Corps."[51]

This was followed on May 14, 1917, by a letter and attachments from Barnett to the chief of the Bureau of Naval Personnel recommending the award of the Medal of Honor to six Marines, based on the Military Operations Report for Northern Haiti, December 5, 1915. The six were Daly, Upshur and Ostermann from the October 24–25 fight at Fort Dipitie, and Butler, Iams and Gross for the November 17 Fort Rivière attack.

The attachments included the Navy regulation and act of Congress regarding the Navy Medal of Honor approved March 5, 1915, Butler's operations report, Colonel Cole's report, Colonel Waller's endorsements, Admiral Caperton's comments, and an exchange of letters between Barnett and Caperton, related to the proposed awards.

After briefly recounting the October ambush at the river, Barnett quoted from Colonel Waller's endorsement letter:

> The action of the thirty-five men in the attack made upon them during the night of October 24th cannot be commended too highly. It is true that these men were in pitch darkness, surrounded by ten times their number and fighting for their lives, but the manner in which they fought during that long night, the steady, calm, discipline that prevented demoralization is remarkable. Had one squad failed not one man of the party would have lived to tell the story. The actual assault upon the enemy, made in three different directions and beginning as soon as the light permitted them to see, was splendid. It meant success or utter annihilation. It succeeded, thanks to the splendid examples given by the officers and noncommissioned officers supported by the men. I believe therefore that Captain William P. Upshur, First Lieutenant Edward A. Ostermann and Gunnery Sergeant Daniel Daly should be given medals of honor for this particular engagement and the work that followed that day.

Next, Barnett briefly described the November 17 attack on Fort Rivière. He then cited the endorsements of Butler for Iams and Gross, as well as for Daly for the earlier action; the endorsement of Colonel Cole; and Colonel Waller's concurring endorsement for Iams and Gross.

NINE—Haiti

Waller also recommended that Cole's nomination of Butler for a brevet medal be upgraded to the Medal of Honor.

It is interesting to note that Admiral Caperton "withheld" his recommendations for the awards, stating that: "In view of the great distinction attached to the wearing of medals of honor, the necessity of protecting wearers of such medals, and to preserve its extraordinary distinctive character, the squadron commander [Caperton] holds in abeyance his recommendation upon this matter until reports of all [underlined] cases of distinguished services during the recent operations in Haiti have been received and their merits established."

The endorsements of Butler, Cole and Waller were all submitted by mid–January 1916, when Caperton declined to render his opinion. Fifteen months later, having received nothing from Caperton, Barnett wrote to the admiral to seek his opinion. On May 6, 1917, Caperton wrote back to state that, "while he appreciated the splendid work" referenced in the nominations, he "saw no reason to add anything" to his previous comment.

The likeliest explanation for Caperton's initial refusal to endorse the Medal of Honor for the six Marines is that no nominations had been made for members of the Navy who served in Haiti. His comment about waiting for "all" operations suggests he wanted to see some Navy nominations before commenting on those for the Marines. However, when none materialized between January 1916 and May 1917, or after, his refusal is harder to explain in neutral terms. It may be that Caperton allowed inter-service rivalry to prejudice his actions. There is also a darker possible explanation. As the top U.S. military officer in the Haiti operations in 1915–1916, Caperton may have expected to receive the medal himself, as Admiral Fletcher had after Vera Cruz. The fact that he didn't receive the medal probably says more about public reaction to the bevy of medals for Vera Cruz than about Caperton's leadership in Haiti.

Drawing on information from historian Hans Schmidt's biography of Smedley Butler, *Maverick Marine*, it seems likely that inter-service rivalry, combined with interpersonal animosity, was responsible for Caperton's unwillingness to endorse the medals for the Marines.

The Navy and Marines fought bitter bureaucratic battles for months over control of the various instruments of the occupation, wrote Schmidt. "The in-fighting featured a head-on clash between Colonel Waller and Admiral Caperton, both domineering personalities and jealous of their prerogatives. Each undermined the other in his 'unofficial' correspondence with Washington. Waller, commander of Marine Expeditionary Forces ashore, complained to [then-Assistant Commandant of the Marine Corps John] Lejeune that the admiral was 'insane' and that 'instead of backing up men working for him, he knifes them when they do well.' Butler referred to Caperton as 'old simpleton.' Meanwhile, Caperton, as senior U.S. officer in Haiti sitting in his battleship offshore, made a point of cultivating the local elite socially, and accused Waller of being 'very vindictive' and using 'intimidation' which made the occupation unpopular."[52]

Undeterred by Caperton's decision to abstain, the Marine commandant pressed ahead. Citing a "most careful review" and "a strictly impartial analysis" of the merits of each nominee, Barnett recommended all six Marines for the Medal of Honor. In Daly's case, he cited his "conspicuous gallantry during the engagements incident to the capture of Fort Dipitie and Fort Rivière." Daly received his medal on September 29, 1917, shortly before embarking for service in France. With the award of these medals, Daly and Butler became the first, and so far only, Marines ever to receive two Medals of Honor for separate actions.

Ten

Dominican Republic

Daly departed Haiti on January 6, 1916, but he had not seen the last of the island of Hispaniola. Just six months later he would return to confront a new and very different conflict.

When Daly left Haiti that January, his first stop was the Marine Barracks at the Brooklyn Navy Yard. There, he completed his fourth four-year enlistment on January 31 and reenlisted the same day with the rank of gunnery sergeant, back dated to April 5, 1915, the date of his temporary appointment to that rank before his deployment to Haiti.

He then began a well-earned two-month furlough, spending time with family members. His older brother, David, was living in Manhattan while his widowed mother, Ellen, was living in Brooklyn with his younger sister, Mary, her husband William Loeb, and their children.

Returning from furlough at the end of March, he was appointed acting first sergeant of the Marine Barracks detachment at the Brooklyn Navy Yard. On June 5, he was transferred to the 8th Marine Company stationed in New Orleans as a gunnery sergeant. When he arrived there, he was assigned to the U.S.S. *Machias*, a schooner-rigged gunboat commissioned in 1893 that conducted operations in the Caribbean, patrolling off Cuba, the Dominican Republic, and the Danish West Indies. It looked like a pleasant assignment, but it proved all too brief.[1]

Within days of his arrival in New Orleans, he and the 8th Marine Company sailed for the Dominican Republic, which shared the island of Hispaniola with Haiti.

A former Spanish colony, the Dominican Republic had gained its independence from Spain in 1821, only to lose it again the following year when Haiti invaded it. A popular uprising in 1844 drove the Haitians out, but the remainder of the 19th century witnessed one corrupt, cruel Dominican regime after another serve its own ends at the expense of the people.

"Devil Dog" Dan Daly

In a parallel to what had happened in Haiti, each of these new Dominican rulers borrowed heavily from foreign sources to enrich themselves and sustain their power, setting the stage for threats of military intervention from abroad to force repayment of debts. The most egregious of these strongmen was General Ulises Heureux, who came to power in 1882. He ruled the country with a heavy hand until 1899 when one of the leaders of a rival faction, General Ramon Caceras, shot him at point-blank range with a pistol on the main street of the town of Moca. Onlookers and Heureux's guards were too stunned to collar Caceres and he escaped unharmed.[2]

Caceres was part of a military cabal led by General Horacio Vasquez, who appointed the nation's wealthiest planter, Juan Isidro Jimenez, as the figurehead of the movement. The two men declared a new revolutionary government for the country with Jimenez as president and Vasquez as vice president. However, the regime soon degenerated into competing factions around Vasquez and Jimenez. Vasquez's followers, known as *horacios*, formed the southern-based Red Party, while Jimenez's supporters, known as *jimenistas*, became the northern-based Blue Party. "This feud led to a succession of weak compromise presidents, coups and countercoups during which each regime continued to borrow money abroad with which to buy arms to suppress revolution."[3] As the loans piled up, the foreign creditors pressed their respective governments to intervene.

The United States had had a strong interest in the commercial possibilities of the Dominican Republic since President Ulysses S. Grant had tried and failed to annex it in 1870. The United States also tried and failed to acquire land in the republic for a naval base. U.S. interest in the country peaked again in 1903–1904 when British, French and German warships bombarded coastal cities in Venezuela as part of an effort to force that country to pay its debts. In response, President Theodore Roosevelt had announced his corollary to the Monroe Doctrine, essentially declaring that the United States would act as the policeman of the Western Hemisphere to maintain order and ensure nations met their obligations to foreign creditors. This was intended to keep European nations from trying to establish new colonies in the Americas, but it also gave the United States license to intervene whenever and wherever it wanted.

In 1907, the United States pressured the Dominican Republic into a treaty that empowered U.S. officials to collect customs duties in the

Ten—Dominican Republic

republic and decide how to divide the revenue between government expenses and payments to foreign creditors. This arrangement worked well for a time and the nation's debt was gradually reduced.

During this period, Ramon Caceres, the same man who had assassinated Heureux seven years earlier, was elected president in 1906. While his presidency provided some stability, it did not end the power struggle between the *horacistas* and the *jimenistas*. What stability that existed ended in the November 1911 with the assassination of Caceras as he rode in his car through the capital city, Santo Domingo. The nation returned to revolving regimes, renewed borrowing and increased volatility.[4] Competition for political dominance led to repeated armed rebellions against whichever faction was in office at the moment as well as internal power struggles within each faction. As the two feuding factions splintered, two additional factions formed, further complicating efforts to bring order out of the chaotic situation.

By 1914, the country had gone through 43 presidents and 19 constitutions in the 70 years since the Dominicans had gained their independence from Haiti.

That year, the country was on the verge of civil war when U.S. President Woodrow Wilson dispatched a naval squadron to Santo Domingo harbor with the 5th Marine Regiment aboard. This show of force caused the rival factions to negotiate a truce and hold a presidential election in which Jimenez was elected. In hopes of maintaining order, the United States offered to support Jimenez against any new revolt, provided he abided by the terms of the 1907 treaty.

Before long, the United States added new demands. It insisted that a U.S. official be made a permanent overseer of all the government's revenues and expenditures, and that the army be replaced by a new national guard led by U.S. Marines.[5]

These demands finally united the rival Dominican factions to oppose U.S. meddling. However, this union was short-lived, owing to tensions between President Jimenez and his minister for war, General Desiderio Arias. On April 15, 1916, Jimenez sought to destroy Arias' power by secretly arresting two of Arias' top lieutenants who were the commanders of the national guard and the army garrison in the capital city. Jimenez then ordered Arias to come to the president's country villa, where he planned to arrest him too. Instead, Arias, who had learned of the arrests, used troops loyal to him to take control of the principal fortress in the capital city. He quickly drew public support and on May 2

"Devil Dog" Dan Daly

Arias pressured the Dominican Congress into impeaching Jimenez from office. Jimenez fled the city. He then quickly assembled his own loyal forces and returned. The rival forces were battling each other in Santo Domingo on May 5 when the first detachment of U.S. Marines landed in the capital city.[6] The First World War was well into its second year in Europe and President Wilson was worried about Germany stirring up trouble in America's backyard.

On May 5, the transport *Prairie* put 150 Marines ashore at Santo Domingo. The Marines were the 6th Company under Captain Frederic M. Wise, and the 9th under Captain Eugene Fortson. The 9th also had four 3-inch artillery pieces. They immediately moved to protect the U.S. legation and consulate, and to seize strategically located Fort San Jeronimo, a high-walled, stone fortress built by the Spanish. The gunboat *Castine* also landed a Marine detachment and a contingent of 130 bluejackets to augment the Marines.

The Marines soon found themselves facing about 250 Dominican army troops loyal to Arias who were squaring off against an estimated 800 army troops answering to Jimenez. Captain Wise, as the senior Marine commander ashore, boldly sought out Arias and negotiated safe passage for the foreign nationals in the city to be evacuated to the *Prairie*.[7]

Having been instructed by his superiors to help the government combat the rebels, Wise deployed his troops and field pieces to support an advance by Jimenez's forces. Despite this support, Jimenez abruptly resigned the presidency on May 7 and left the country. He gave as his reason that he did not want to be the cause of American guns being fired on his countrymen.[8]

Wise then negotiated a truce with the two warring sides, and the city settled into an uneasy quiet. Admiral Caperton arrived on May 12 and two days later met with Arias. Like Wise, the admiral had orders to support Jimenez's government. So, Caperton demanded Arias disband his army or the U.S. warships would bombard the city. Arias refused to disband but he did agree to remove his forces from the city. U.S. forces—375 Marines and 225 bluejackets—then moved to take control of the central city. They met no opposition.[9]

When Arias withdrew from Santo Domingo, he moved northwest about 100 miles over unpaved jungle and mountain roads to Santiago. The city sits in the hilly center of the Cibao Valley, a wide, fertile plain between two east-west mountain ranges in the north-central part of the

TEN—Dominican Republic

republic. At Santiago, Jimenez could gather additional forces and plan his next move.

No rail line linked Santo Domingo with Santiago at the time to move men and supplies from the capital to confront the rebels. The only rail link into Santiago ran in the opposite direction to the port of Puerto Plata on the north coast.[10] The republic's limited road system further isolated the north from the south.

Over the next seven weeks, the United States built up its troop strength in the Dominican Republic as two things became clear. The first was that government troops were either incapable or unwilling to forcibly disband the rebels. The second was that the U.S. military would need to occupy the entire country because the government had ceased to function.

This was a sizeable undertaking. The Dominican Republic occupies about 60 percent of the island of Hispaniola, compared to Haiti's 40 percent. The country is 240 miles long and 160 miles wide, or about half the size of Ohio. However, at the time of the landings in 1916, the republic had about 800,000 people, half as many as Haiti. Roughly two-thirds of the population lived in the north and one-third in the south.

On May 23, the 2nd Regiment led by Colonel Theodore P. Kane, plus three additional infantry companies, landed at Santo Domingo on the south coast. Naval vessels with four more Marine companies aboard patrolled the north coast. By May 28, the United States had 11 Marine companies in and around the republic. Most of these were from the 1st and 2nd regiments, which had been stationed in neighboring Haiti. About 750 of these Marines occupied the capital city.

On June 1, the Marines landed two companies each at Monte Cristi and Puerto Plata to secure these north coast ports west and north of Santiago, respectively. The Marines occupied Monte Cristi without firing a shot but they ran into 500 rebel riflemen in Puerto Plata and had to fight their way into the city.[11] Despite coming under rebel fire, the Marines at Puerto Plata did not return fire while heading to shore to avoid hitting noncombatants. One officer was shot in the head and killed and several men were wounded. Once ashore, however, the Marines swiftly captured Fort San Felipe and took control of the town.[12]

Admiral Caperton believed more troops were needed, and so, on June 4, the 4th Marine Regiment set out by train from San Diego, California, for New Orleans. Once there, it added the 8th Marine Company and Gunnery Sergeant Daly. Together, they sailed aboard the transport U.S.S. *Hancock*, and landed at Monte Cristi on June 21.[13]

Daly and the 8th company came ashore in small boats and landed at a jetty outside of town. The company commander was Captain Holland M. Smith.[14] Nicknamed "Howlin' Mad" by his men for his short temper, Smith later attributed the nickname to his "emphatic" way of speaking.[15] In any event, the name stuck and became part of Marine Corps lore. Prior to the Dominican Republic, Smith had served in the Philippines and Panama. He later served in World War I, and as a lieutenant general in World War II he commanded the V Amphibious Corps in the assaults on the islands of Tarawa, Kwajalein, Eniwetok, Saipan and Tinian.

Colonel Joseph H. Pendleton, commander of the 4th Regiment, was placed in overall command of the land forces and began preparing his advance on Santiago. Pendleton was a quiet, scholarly man and one of the best liked officers in the Marine Corps. An 1884 naval academy graduate, he had led Marine campaigns in Cuba, the Philippines and Nicaragua.

Pendleton had very little intelligence about the rebels. Arias reportedly had 1,000 men in Santiago and 100 men at a roadblock about 18 miles inland. Beyond that, nothing was known. The Marines also had little in the way of transport for their supplies. They had to purchase whatever they could find from the populace around Monte Cristi.[16]

Pendleton planned to deploy two columns. One column, his 4th Regiment, would march by road from Monte Cristi, about 70 miles from Santiago, down the Cibao Valley. The other column comprised of the 4th and 9th companies plus Marine detachments from the battleships *Rhode Island* and *New Jersey* would follow a rail line from Puerto Plata, about 40 miles from Santiago. The two columns would link up at the town of Navarette, 15 miles west of Santiago. Along the way, the second column would reopen the railroad for resupply of the combined force as it advanced on Santiago.[17]

On June 24, Pendleton issued a remarkable set of instructions to his troops. He said their mission in the republic was to "restore peace and order, protect life and property, and support the constituted government." In doing this, they were to be guided by the following principles[18]:

> Members of the command will therefore realize that we are not in an enemy's country, though many of the inhabitants may be inimical to us, and they will be careful to conduct themselves so as to inspire confidence among the people in the honesty of our intentions and the sincerity of our purpose.

Ten—*Dominican Republic*

Officers will act toward the people with courtesy, dignity and firmness, and will see that their men do nothing to arouse or foster the antagonism toward us that can be naturally expected towards an armed force that many interested malcontents will endeavor to persuade the citizens to look upon as invaders.

All commanding officers of posts, companies and detachments will carefully instruct their men in these matters, and will be diligent to enforce the principles herein laid down. While at all times being vigilant to guard against surprise and treachery they will be careful to avoid the appearance of constant suspicion, which attitude of mind, however, in private it is wise to maintain while any particle of the present trouble and unrest remains in the country.

Orders will be carried out with as little use of force as may be needed to attain the desired end, but armed opposition or attack will be sharply met and suppressed with forces of arms; this use of force to cease the moment the opposition has been overcome, the end attained and the safety of the troops assured. The same care and attention will be given to the wounded as would be given to our own, and prisoners, while carefully guarded, will be treated kindly, and as liberally as the ensuring of their safety will permit.

Under no circumstances will any subordinate commander carry out any punitive measure, or act of reprisal, without a direct order from the Commander of Forces.

The right of property will be carefully observed, men will be instructed and officers will watchful to enforce the instructions that nothing, no matter how apparently valueless, will be taken from any inhabitant of the country, or in any way appropriated, without remuneration, and the free consent of the owner. No force, threat or intimidation will, in any way, be allowed.

No shot will be fired by any enlisted member of these Forces, unless by command of an officer, or in pursuance of orders given by an officer, except that at any time it is proper to fire in case of actual defense of one's life or the life of another.

Two days later, June 26, Pendleton's column of 34 officers and 803 enlisted men began its march in the tropical summer heat and humidity on a road that was "little more than a muddy trail through the jungle of cactus and thorny brush."[19] A 15-man point team mounted on ponies led the column. Next came the advance guard, made up of the 2nd Battalion, which included Daly and the 8th company. The main body followed at about half a mile. The supply train, comprised of 24 mule carts, seven motor trucks and trailers, two motorized water carts, a tractor pulling four trailers, and 11 Ford touring cars, brought up the rear, guarded by the 6th Marine Company.[20]

The column set out just before dawn and ran into snipers about 12 miles out. The snipers fired from 600–700 yards and were put to flight by machine gun fire. The column halted for the night at 3:30 p.m. after covering about 17 miles. The relatively slow pace was due to the condition of the road, the obstacles encountered and how fast the mule-drawn carts could travel.

Captain Smith later recalled, "The rebels had dug deep trenches in the road to impede our progress and when we passed these obstacles we had to remove trees cut down to block our march."[21]

Combining animals and engines in the supply train presented other challenges. The motorized vehicles could not move as slowly as the mules without overheating, so they would drive ahead a ways and then stop to wait for the mule train to catch up. They repeated this herky-jerky gait several times a day.

About two miles ahead of their first day's stopping point, the Marines could see two hills that dominated the surrounding area. The first hill was about 75 feet high above the road. The second and taller hill stood behind the first. Trenches had been dug into the hills, and rebels could be seen moving about. The site was called Las Trencheras, and it held special significance for the rebels. In 1864, Dominicans dug in on these hills had defeated the Spanish. Given its history, the rebels considered the position impregnable.

Rather than launch an immediate assault, Pendleton set up camp to rest his troops and wait for the supply train to catch up. A heavy downpour had started and the dirt road had turned to mud. It would be 8 p.m. before the last of the supply train arrived.

Meanwhile, the 8th Company with the two motorized water carts was dispatched to fetch water from the Yaque del Norte River, four miles south of the camp.[22] Instead of water, Smith and Daly stumbled into a rebel buzz saw.

As Smith later recalled in his autobiography, "The rebels kept up a sharp fire from the woods. At one point, fire was so heavy that I took a small party of Marines and headed for the source. What followed was the most dangerous incident in my life up to that moment, almost as dangerous as some experiences in the Pacific when the Japanese were throwing everything around. Our party was cut off and we found ourselves surrounded by about a hundred Dominicans, who outnumbered us at least ten to one. We had to fight our way out and only sound Marine training saved our lives."[23]

It would be mid-day the next day, June 27, before Smith, Daly and

Ten—*Dominican Republic*

the rest of the company were able to rejoin the column at Las Trencheras. They had been under sniper fire the entire time.[24]

On, the morning of June 27, the Marines at Las Trencheras formed a firing line of four companies of about 80 men each, a total of about 325 men. They began their attack by firing two 3-inch field pieces and a platoon of machine guns at the rebel trenches from a nearby hill. When the advancing Marines were about a thousand yards from the first hill, the rebels opened fire with rifles. Most of the rebel bullets passed harmlessly over the heads of the Marines. As Marine machine gun fire moved along the trenches, the rebels' aim became even more erratic.

The pace of the Marine advance was slowed by thick underbrush, and one company found itself blocked by a swamp. The Marines continued to advance, with brief stops to fire starting at 750 yards, until they received the order to charge. At the foot of the hill, the sharp blast of a whistle sounded and the Marines ceased firing. Then, with the bright morning sun glinting off their 16-inch fixed bayonets, they launched themselves up the steep slope with a throaty roar. The assault swept up and over the trenches, but by then the rebels had, at the sound of a rebel bugle, retreated to the second line of trenches. When the Marines attacked those trenches, the rebels fled again. No dead or wounded rebels were found in either set of trenches, but five bodies were later found nearby. The action lasted about 45 minutes. Marine casualties were one dead and four wounded.[25]

This scenario at Las Trencheras repeated itself in the succeeding days. The rebels would fire on the column from ambush or in a night attack, then escape before the Marines could close with them. Progress was slowed by the condition of the road and by the need to stop to rebuild destroyed bridges. The column was fired on several times on June 28, and again on the 29th. On the 30th, the Marines drew "brisk fire" at Dona Antonia Alta, which was captured at the cost of one dead Marine. Another skirmish later that day occurred at Hautillo Palmas.[26]

The decisive engagement came on the eighth day of the march, July 3, at Guayacanas, 50 miles from Monte Cristi and 27 miles from Santiago. From a rebel captured by a patrol, the Marines learned that a large force of rebels was entrenched on a low ridge just beyond the town. A deep railroad cut sliced through the middle of the ridge. Approaching Guayacanas, the column came under fire. Marine skirmishes drove these outposts back, clearing the way for the advance.

"Devil Dog" Dan Daly

A Marine reconnaissance patrol confirmed the prisoner's information. They also reported that dense brush covered the approaches to the hill, trenches were dug into the ridge, the ground 200 yards in front of the trenches had been cleared to create a field of fire, and there was a felled palm log blocking the road 150 yards in front of the trenches. Unfortunately, there was no suitable location for the artillery to support this attack.

At 9 a.m., three Marine companies set out through the thick brush toward the ridge. The 27th and 29th companies headed toward the left flank of the ridge while the 26th company moved toward the right flank. Meanwhile, Major Robert H. Dunlap advanced up the road in the center with a Benét-Mercié machine gun crew. He and the crew soon found themselves well ahead of the rifle companies. Emerging into the cleared space 200 yards in front of the ridge, they came under rebel fire. Rushing forward, they took cover behind the felled log.

Corporal Joseph Glowin placed his gun behind the log and fired at the trenches. Before long he caught a bullet but continued to fire. Wounded a second time, he refused to leave his gun. Fellow Marines had to drag him under cover. Dunlap took over Glowin's gun and fired until it jammed. A second Benét-Mercié gun and crew arrived and began firing but their gun soon jammed too.

First Sergeant Roswell Winans of the 28th company then arrived with a Colt machine gun. He placed it behind the log, seated himself on the tripod in an exposed position, and began firing. When the last round of a 250-cartridge belt jammed, he coolly stood up in full view of the rebels and cleared the blockage while bullets snapped around him. He resumed firing and continued until the rebels retreated.[27]

Supported by these machine guns, the rifle companies advanced toward the ridge. The companies on the left hacked their way through a dense cactus hedge and reached the ridge. "With a loud cheer the Marines of these two companies charged the northern enemy trench." When the rebel commander, General Maximo Gabral, was shot and killed, the Dominicans fled the entire ridge even though Marines on the right flank had yet to reach the trenches there.[28]

Both Glowin and Winans received the Medal of Honor for exposing themselves to enemy fire at the hottest spot on the firing line. Seven out of the 10 Marines wounded in this action were hit within 20 feet of their positions, as was the one man killed.[29] Rebel losses at Guayacanas were at least 27 dead and five captured. Winans

Ten—Dominican Republic

subsequently served as a captain in France in World War I and as a colonel in World War II. Glowin also served in World War I and later as a Detroit police officer.

While the main fight occurred at the trenches, the 6th Marine Company, led by Captain Julian C. Smith, a future lieutenant general, came under fire while escorting the supply train. A rebel force had worked around to the rear of the column and attacked, but they were driven off.

The next day, July 4, the column reached Navarette for its link up with the column from Puerto Plata. That column, commanded by Major Hiram Bearss, had encountered a force of 200 rebels at Alta Mira on June 29. While his main force pressed forward along the rail line, Bearss had sent the 4th Company over a mountain trail to turn the rebels' flank. The rebels pulled back to the entrance to a tunnel. There, Bearss once again used frontal and flank attacks to drive the rebels back. Then he and 60 men dashed the length of the 300-foot tunnel to secure the other end and prevent the rebels from destroying the rail line. Two Marines were wounded in the fight, which cost the rebels an estimated 50 casualties and sent them running. After building a bridge, Bearss' column arrived at Navarette on July 4, the same day as Pendleton's column.[30]

As the combined forces made ready to push on to Santiago, a delegation from Arias arrived at Navarette. He had agreed with Admiral Caperton to disband his forces. He asked that Pendleton delay his entry into Santiago to allow this to happen. Pendleton agreed but, as a precaution, he moved his troops forward to secure key points ahead. On July 6, the combined U.S. force entered Santiago and the rebellion ended. The Marines spent the next few months rounding up individual rebel leaders who engaged in banditry. They also disarmed the populace.

However, a rebellion sprang up in the eastern provinces of the republic in 1917 and hit-and-run attacks continued until 1921, when a negotiated agreement was reached. It provided for a provisional presidency in 1922 followed by elections and return to Dominican control in 1924. The occupation officially ended that year, and the last Marine contingents withdrew.

Daly returned to New Orleans on the *Machias*. There, on August 3, 1916, he was appointed first sergeant with a date of rank of April 5, 1915. He spent much of the remainder of 1916 in hospital with another bout of gastritis, first in New Orleans and then at the naval hospital in Washington, D.C.

"Devil Dog" Dan Daly

In January 1917, he reported aboard the U.S.S. *Montana*, an armored cruiser commissioned in 1908. In May he was assigned to detached duty at the Savage Arms Co. in Utica, New York, where he filled the post of acting first sergeant. Once again, this quiet period proved very short. World events were about to present Daly with the biggest fight of his life.

Eleven

Over There

The third and by far the most cataclysmic of the three armed conflicts that erupted in 1914 that would directly affect Daly and make him a living legend began half a world away. On June 28, 1914, a Serbian nationalist assassinated the heir to the Austro-Hungarian throne in the Bosnian capital, Sarajevo.

Within a month, all of Europe would be at war and in less than three years the United States would be drawn into a global conflict. Dubbed "The Great War," it changed the lives of millions, the fate of nations, and the future of mankind.

In January 1917, when Germany resumed its campaign of unrestricted submarine warfare in hopes of breaking the stalemate on the war's Western Front, Daly had just reported aboard the U.S.S. *Montana* at the Philadelphia Navy Yard. After German U-boats sunk seven American merchant ships, Congress declared war on April 6, and Daly prepared once again for combat.

On July 18, Daly joined the 73rd Machine Gun Company at the newly established Marine base at Quantico, Virginia. It was located on 6,000 acres of woodland, 35 miles south of Washington, D.C., on the west bank of the Potomac River. He was immediately made the company's acting first sergeant, with the rank made permanent on August 21.

Daly's mission, like that of the other seasoned professionals of the Marine Corps, was to turn the sudden influx of raw recruits into combat-ready fighting men. In the run-up to America's entry into the war, Congress had vastly expanded the authorized strength of the Marine Corps in 1916 from 10,265 officers and men to 18,093, with 7,000 more authorized in March 1917. Actually filling these slots, however, didn't happen overnight. Recruitment before war was declared in April 1917 was slow. The Marine Corps entered the war with 419 officers and 13,214 enlisted personnel in uniform.[1] After war was declared,

"Devil Dog" Dan Daly

the stream of volunteers became a flood. By the war's end just 19 months later, there were 2,400 officers and 70,000 enlisted Marines, a five-fold increase over the old corps.

Spurred by the recruiting slogan "First to Fight," Major General Commandant George Barnett pressed Secretary of War Newton Baker to include a Marine regiment in the first convoy of troops sent to France. Later, he would try and fail to get permission for an entire and independent Marine Division. Barnett was supported in these efforts by Secretary of the Navy Josephus Daniels and Assistant Secretary of the Navy Franklin D. Roosevelt. Once war was declared, Baker secured President Wilson's approval of Barnett's initial request. To achieve this, Marine companies with expeditionary experience in Cuba, Haiti and the Dominican Republic, plus shipboard detachments, were pulled together to form the 5th Marine Regiment. Led by Colonel Charles Doyen, a veteran of Cuba, the Philippines and the Dominican Republic, the regiment quickly assembled at Quantico and sailed for France on June 14 with the Army's 1st Infantry Division. Among the regiment's senior officers were Colonel Wendell Neville, Daly's battalion commander at Vera Cruz, and Lieutenant Colonel Hiram Bearss, who led the Puerto Plata column in the march on Santiago. Both men were Medal of Honor recipients.

Neville graduated from the Naval Academy in 1890 and was commissioned in the Marine Corps two years later. During the Spanish-American War, he participated in a daring battalion attack at Guantanamo Bay that earned him a brevet promotion to captain. During the Boxer Rebellion in 1900, he fought in four battles as part of the international force that relieved the siege of the legations in Peking. In 1914, he commanded the 2nd Base Force Regiment at Vera Cruz and was awarded the Medal of Honor. He was promoted to colonel in 1916.

Bearss attended several universities in his youth where he majored in sports and minored in pranks but never graduated. He joined the Marine Corps during the Spanish-American War and earned a commission. He served in the Philippines as part of Major Littleton Waller's battalion on Samar and earned the Medal of Honor in 1901 for leading an attack on a cliff-top fort. He also saw action at Vera Cruz in 1914 and in the Dominican Republic in 1916.

As soon as the 5th Marines departed, training at Quantico focused on getting the 6th Marine Regiment filled out and ready. Daly and the 73rd Machine Gun Company were assigned to this new regiment, which was comprised mostly of inexperienced volunteers. Formed on July 11, the 6th Marine Regiment was unusual in that 60 percent of its volunteers were college men. In fact, two-thirds of one company came from a single school—300 students at the University of Minnesota had enlisted as a group.[2] The high percentage of college men in the ranks is all the more remarkable because during this period the majority of Americans never even completed high school, let alone went on to college.[3]

The 5th and 6th Marines were larger than previous Marine regiments. They had three infantry battalions of four rifle companies each, a machine gun company, a supply company and a headquarters company. This made them equivalent in size to an entire British or French division.

Each machine gun company was issued 16 Lewis guns and 33 hand carts to transport their equipment and supplies. In addition to learning how to fire and maintain their weapons, the recruits also received training in trench construction, concrete pillbox construction, trench warfare tactics, open warfare tactics and chemical warfare. After the Marines arrived in France, their prized Lewis guns would be replaced with the Hotchkiss M1914 machine guns used by the French Army. Although the Marines were unhappy at having to give up their Lewis guns after using them to good effect in Haiti and the Dominican Republic, the Hotchkiss proved sturdy and reliable.

The Hotchkiss was a gas-operated, air-cooled gun with a maximum rate of fire of 450 to 600 rounds per minute, and a sustained rate of 120 per minute. It was usually fired in 8–10 round bursts for greater accuracy. It used 8-millimeter (.323 caliber) Lebel ammunition, which was fed into the side of the gun on a strip of 24 cartridges. This short strip meant the gun had to be reloaded many times a minute during firing. It also meant a single gunner could not easily operate the gun. Each gun had a three-man crew. The gun's maximum effective range was a little over 4,000 yards. It weighed about 52 pounds, and was fired from a 53-pound tripod.[4]

Although filled with rookies, the 6th Marines was led by seasoned veterans, many with storied careers like Daly. They included the sergeant major, John H. Quick, a Medal of Honor winner in Cuba during the Spanish-American War; the regimental commander, Colonel Albertus E. Catlin, who commanded the Marine detachment aboard the *Maine* when she blew up and won the Medal of Honor at Vera Cruz; the 1st Battalion commander, Major John "Johnny the Hard" Hughes, who won the Medal of Honor at Vera Cruz while serving as Daly's company

"Devil Dog" Dan Daly

commander; the 2nd Battalion commander, Major Thomas Holcomb, a future Marine Corps commandant; 2nd Lieutenant Clifton B. Cates, also a future Marine Corps commandant, and several other future flag officers.

Daly's company commander was Captain Maurice Edwin Shearer. Born in 1879, he began his military career by dropping out of high school to fight in the Spanish-American War. He joined the 27th Battery, Indiana Volunteer Artillery and served in Puerto Rico. After the war, he returned briefly to civilian life before joining the Marine Corps in 1901. He rose to sergeant before being commissioned in 1905. He was promoted to captain in 1916 and took command of the 73rd Machine Gun Company when it was formed in July 1917.

The training schedule was pretty intense, but the surroundings would have gotten a smile out of Daly. The newly built wooden barracks had a clean pine smell, which was a vast improvement over the pungent odors of Peking, the stinking jungles of the Caribbean, or even some of the decaying Marine quarters of years past. The barracks at Quantico had new steel cots with real mattresses, separate washrooms and showers. Each barracks housed one platoon.[5]

People who knew Daly at this time described him as a tough task master and a strict but fair disciplinarian. He demanded exemplary attention to detail, and accepted nothing less than excellence.[6] One recruit recalled an inspection by him. "Daly made a sharp left turn and walked right up to me within inches. His steel grey eyes met mine like a laser beam. I can still see him. He said, 'What is your name?' I replied name and PFC. He then said, 'Your uniform freshly pressed?' I answered. 'No Sir, I wore it on liberty last evening for only two hours.' He replied immediately, 'Sergeant, put this man on the restriction list. No shore liberty for two weeks.'"[7]

He required a lot from his men but like any good NCO, he went out of his way to look out for them. "That such a man should be popular as well as respected owes to a tough-grained fair mindedness at all times and a never slackened vigilance to protect the rights and welfare of those under him," concluded historian Frank Hough.[8] In fact, he was an inspiration to his fellow Marines, including the officers, many of whom would later recall gathering around Daly to hear him talk about "the old days."

The training continued into September when the 6th Marines took trains to Philadelphia and sailed to France. Daly and the 73rd Machine

ELEVEN—Over There

Gun Company sailed aboard the U.S.S. *DeKalb*, a former German ocean liner/auxiliary cruiser seized at the outset of the war and used by the U.S. Navy as a transport. The *DeKalb* sailed to New York harbor, where it joined a convoy before heading for France. Colonel Catlin and the regimental headquarters and supply companies sailed on the same ship. During the trip across the Atlantic, the Marines engaged in calisthenics and abandon ship drills. No submarines were sighted and the crossing was uneventful.

Daly landed at St. Nazaire, on France's southwest coast on November 1.⁹ He and his men expected to be sent immediately to the front, so they were sorely disappointed when they were instead put to work unloading ships. The same fate had befallen the 5th Marines when they landed four months earlier.

It seems that while the Wilson administration supported sending Marines to France, General John J. Pershing had other ideas. As the commander of the American Expeditionary Force, he had actively opposed having Marines in the AEF. He wanted an all-Army show. When he was overruled by Baker, he initially sought to use the Marines as stevedores and guards.

In early 1918, the 5th and 6th Marines were finally brought together with the 6th Machine Gun Battalion to form the 4th Marine

Daly as a first sergeant, probably in France, in 1918 during the time he fought in World War I (Marine Corps History Division Archive).

"Devil Dog" Dan Daly

Brigade. As a result, there were simply too many Marines in France to sideline them any longer, especially with steady pressure from the French for more front-line troops.

4th Marine Brigade

5th Marine Regiment

1st Battalion	*2nd Battalion*	*3rd Battalion*
17th Company	18th Company	16th Company
49th Company	43rd Company	20th Company
66th Company	51st Company	45th Company
67th Company	55th Company	47th Company
8th Machine Gun Company		

6th Marine Regiment

1st Battalion	*2nd Battalion*	*3rd Battalion*
74th Company	78th Company	82nd Company
75th Company	79th Company	83nd Company
76th Company	80th Company	84th Company
95th Company	96th Company	97th Company
73rd Machine Gun Company		

6th Machine Gun Battalion

15th Company	23rd Company	77th Company	81st Company

The 6th Marines were shipped by rail to a training area near Bourmont, about 150 miles east of Paris in northeast France. Instead of being seated in passenger cars, they were transported like freight in box cars. There was a foot-thick layer of straw on the floor for the men to sit or lay on. The cars were called "forty-and-eights" because they could hold either 40 men or eight horses. The cars measured eight feet wide by 20 feet long. With 40 men assigned to each car, there was only enough room for each man to sit with legs bent. The 500-mile trip took three days and nights. There were many stops, as the war time rail lines were heavily congested. The doors were kept shut except during stops to keep frigid blasts of air out of the unheated cars. As a result, the air in the cars became quite foul while the train was moving. It smelled like a barnyard, recalled some Marines. While some of the new Marines grumbled about the cold, damp, stink and cramped quarters of the boxcars, Daly had experienced much worse and had no illusions about the truly grim conditions that awaited the Marines on the battle front.

Eleven—Over There

The new brigade had 280 officers and 9,164 enlisted men under the command of Colonel Doyen, newly promoted to brigadier general. While it was a big brigade, it was, in the words of historian S.L.A. Marshall, "a little raft of sea soldiers in an ocean of Army."[10] The brigade was made a part of the Army's 2nd Infantry Division, which numbered 28,000 men, making it more than twice the size of the French and British divisions. There were two brigades in the division. The other brigade, the 3rd, was comprised of two Army infantry regiments, the 9th and 23rd.

The division commander was Army Major General Omar Bundy. An 1883 graduate of West Point, he was a veteran of the Indian wars, the Spanish-American War, Philippine Insurrection and the Moro Expedition. Historian Edward Lengel described Bundy as a "thoughtful soldier" but one who "lacked a forceful personality."[11]

In addition to being a part of an Army division, the Marines were required to dress the part. They had to turn in their khakis and greens, and put on Army olive drab uniforms. The stated reasons were the need to simplify supply and to make unit identification by the enemy more difficult. Likewise, the Marines had to surrender their campaign field hats for Army overseas caps and British-style steel helmets. While practical, the changes also had the effect of making the Marines invisible within Pershing's AEF.

The training at Bourmont included rifle marksmanship, bayonet fighting, gas attack drills and practice throwing hand grenades, storming an enemy trench, attacking pillboxes and eliminating strong-points.[12] The Marines were billeted in 11 French villages in the area. As part of their training, the Marines dug a series of trenches to simulate those on the front lines. For two months, they spent an average of four to six hours a day in training at these trenches. Depending on each town's location, the trenches were located eight to 13 miles from where the Marines were billeted. This meant they had to march 16 to 26 miles a day to reach the trenches and return to their billets, and they did so carrying their 8.7-pound rifle and 60-pound pack. This was during wintertime and it frequently rained and snowed. As a result, when the Marines finally went into action they proved to be better prepared for the rigors of combat than their Army counterparts.[13]

On March 17, the brigade entered the trenches southeast of Verdun, the French stronghold that had witnessed titanic artillery duels and infantry assaults in 1916 that produced nearly a million French and

German casualties but no break in the stalemate of the trenches. Daly's company was billeted at a place dubbed Camp Massa, hidden in a wood. Here the Marines received instruction from the French about life and war in the trenches. This included "cooties" (lice) in the bedrolls and clothing, rats the size of house cats, enemy raiding parties, night patrols into no-man's-land, and "wire parties" (stringing barbed wire at night).

The Marine battalions rotated in and out of the trenches during this period. On average, a battalion spent 20 days in the trenches and 20 days in the rear, where the men could get some rest, eat regular meals, take a shower and get rid of the cooties infesting them. While they were in the front-line trenches, they lived in dugouts built into the rear side of the trench. These reinforced caves varied in size. Some only had room for three or four men, while others could accommodate up to 40 men. The circuitous entranceway was intended to shield the men inside from bursting shells, and burlap curtains doused with chemicals to neutralize poison gas hung at the entrance.

During this period, Daly's machine gun company had a dog that someone had somehow managed to bring along from Haiti.[14] There were no dogs assigned to the Marine brigade, but other units also had dogs within their ranks. They proved useful in detecting an approaching enemy raiding party and killing the rats that raided food stored in the dugouts when the rats weren't feasting on corpses in no man's land.

Although the Marines' sector at Verdun was relatively quiet, as it was intended to be a training opportunity, artillery barrages and poison gas still took a toll. The brigade had 128 killed and 744 wounded in less than eight weeks there.[15] Daly and his fellow Marines also had to contend with mud so thick that just walking was a chore, water-filled trenches that caused trench foot, and lack of hot food and clean water that led to diarrhea and dysentery. They also had to crawl out into no man's land at night to string wire, establish listening posts and conduct raids. No man's land in this sector tended to be about three-quarters of a mile wide. If a Marine patrol was discovered, the Germans would lay down a barrage to cut them off from their own trenches and walk the shelling back toward the German lines hoping to kill the intruders. Sometimes the Marine patrols ran into German patrols and sudden, fierce, confused firefights broke out. If a man was killed in one of these skirmishes, his fellow Marines sometimes had to leave him where he fell in order to escape from no man's land. This only intensified their fury at the enemy.

Eleven—Over There

On May 1, Shearer, who was now a major, was put in command of the 1st Battalion, 6th Regiment while Major Hughes was away attending the School of the Line at Langres. Each of the officers spent time in one of the specialized schools intended to supplement their training.

Shearer was succeeded as Daly's company commander by Captain Roy Cleveland Swink. Born in Stroudsburg, Pennsylvania, in 1893, Swink was a 1916 graduate of the U.S. Naval Academy. He had been with the 73rd Machine Gun Company since its formation and had advanced from second lieutenant to first lieutenant to captain by October 1917 under Shearer's command. He would lead the company through the coming engagements at Chateau Thierry and Belleau Wood.

While these changes were taking place in Daly's company, a much more significant and unsettling change occurred on May 7, two days before the brigade completed its training at Verdun. On that date, Brigadier General Doyen was forced to relinquish command of the 4th Marine Brigade. He had failed an Army physical and was being sent home to a training command as part of Pershing's purge of AEF officers he deemed too old or infirm for a field command. (Doyen died of influenza on October 6, 1918.) His departure was a shock to the Marines, made even greater by Pershing's choice to replace him. Instead of elevating a Marine to the post, Pershing appointed an Army officer, his chief of staff and good friend from their days chasing Pancho Villa in Mexico, Brigadier General James G. Harbord.

Born in 1866, Harbord had graduated from Kansas State Agricultural College in 1886. He spent two years there as an instructor before enlisting in the Army. In 1891, he was commissioned in the 5th Cavalry Regiment. He had not seen action in the Spanish-American War but had served in the occupation of Cuba. Later, after serving on the staff of the Secretary of War, he secured a transfer to the Philippines where he served with the 11th Cavalry and then as assistant chief of the Philippine Constabulary. He took command of a National Guard unit guarding the U.S.-Mexico border at Calexico in 1914, and then joined Pershing's fruitless pursuit of Villa in 1916 before attending the Army War College in Washington, D.C. When Pershing shipped out for France, Harbord went with him as AEF chief of staff.

Compared to Bundy, the mild-mannered division commander, Harbord was "nothing if not forceful," wrote historian Edward Lengel. "He had to be, commanding two Marine regiments, the 5th and 6th, led by colonels who were Medal of Honor recipients. Harbord also was an outgoing, almost irrationally optimistic man." This would incite criticism of his leadership later.[16]

Several officers in the 4th Brigade spoke out immediately against what they perceived as unfairness to Doyen and an insult to the corps of putting an Army officer in charge of a Marine unit. Higher ups had to step in to quash the dissent. The *Washington Post* reported: "Junior officers were admonished to remain silent, and several brigade staff members were placed under arrest for continuing to question the relief after being told to shut up. Major Holland M. Smith listed staff majors Bennet Puryear Jr., Maurice E. Shearer, and Henry E. Manney Jr. as members of the Marine cabal opposed to Doyen's ouster."[17] Smith was the brigade adjutant at the time. None of those arrested was apparently ever formally disciplined.

Colonel Wendell Neville, commanding the 5th Marines, was the brigade's senior officer and had been expected to succeed Doyen when he was removed. When Harbord arrived to take command instead, Neville handed him a pair of Marine Corps emblems for his collar. "It was half a greeting and half a challenge," wrote historian and Brigadier General Edwin H. Simmons. Harbord put the emblems on without indicating which half of Neville's gesture he accepted.

Colonel Albertus Catlin, commanding the 6th Marines, knew Harbord from their time together as at the War College and had a favorable view of him. In his post-war memoir, Catlin stated that Harbord proved "popular with the men, talked with them often, and obviously had their interests at heart."[18]

When Harbord assumed command, he said Pershing had told him, "You are to have charge of the finest body of troops in France, and if they fail to live up to that reputation I shall know whom to blame."[19] If true, Pershing had apparently changed his mind about having Marines in his command. Of course, it's also possible the notoriously flinty general was simply letting Harbord know he could expect no favors from his friend and mentor.

In any event, Harbord had precious little time to familiarize himself with his new command before the brigade was plunged into a desperate battle.

Twelve

Chateau Thierry

By the spring of 1918, the Germans were frantic to win the war before the arrival of America's fresh troops could tip the balance in favor of the Allies. They launched three offensives in quick succession. The first, in March, targeted the Somme sector in Flanders. The second, in April, struck in the Amiens area, south of Flanders. The third blow came on May 27 through the Chemin des Dames sector in the Aisne front, farther south of the first two offensives. General Erich Ludendorff's goal was to divert French forces in preparation for an all-out German offensive against the British in Flanders that he hoped would finally lead to victory.

Ludendorff struck with 17 divisions, followed by 25 more, and 6,000 artillery pieces. The attack on the Chemin des Dames, a 20-mile-long ridge northeast of Paris between Soissons and Rheims, took the French by surprise. They were driven back so fast that the advancing Germans captured river bridges intact and a large cache of supplies at Soissons. The Germans penetrated 12 miles the first day, the deepest drive since the early days of the war, and crushed four French divisions. By the end of the second day, the offensive had smashed eight more Allied divisions and driven a forty-mile-wide gap in the Allied line 15 miles deep. The Germans had not expected such success and had outrun their ability to resupply their spearhead.[1]

The one bright spot for the Allies on that dark day came in the first American action of the war. The 1st Infantry Division attacked and captured a German salient at Cantigny on the Somme River. Seven German counterattacks over the next 24 hours failed to dislodge the Americans.

As the German juggernaut in the Chemin des Dames sector rolled south, the U.S. 2nd and 3rd infantry divisions were rushed by truck into the gap that had been torn in the Allied line. Secretary of the Navy

"Devil Dog" Dan Daly

Josephus Daniels later described the scene: "On this trip the camions [trucks] containing the Americans were the only traffic traveling in the direction of the Germans; everything else was going the other way—refugees, old men and women, small children, riding on every conceivable conveyance, many trudging along the side of the road driving a cow or a calf before them, all of them covered with the white dust which the camion caravan was whirling up as it rolled along; along that road only one organization was advancing, the United States Marines."[2]

Years later, a private in the 2nd Battalion, 6th Regiment wrote movingly of the war's toll on civilians that he saw on this ride. "As we moved deeper into this stream of human misery, our men for the first time were brought face to face with the fact that war was a sad business, a costly one whose product was mostly misery and despair, pain and death, a kind of reward only the devil and his kind could want or enjoy.... One old man was seen pushing a wheelbarrow before him on which was sitting a feeble old lady. There were children, and some young mothers with babies in their arms, and others in a family way. Some of the children and babies were sick. One baby had died and the mother was beside the road weeping over the body of her lost child."[3]

The troop trucks were canvas covered with hard wooden benches affixed to either side of the truck bed and a bench down the middle. Each truck carried 25 Marines sitting shoulder to shoulder. The solid rubber tires and primitive suspension systems transmitted every bump in the road into the backsides of the tightly packed Marines like the slap of a thick, wooden paddle.

Daly would forever remember the 30-hour, bone-jarring truck ride through 72 miles of French countryside; the clusters of villagers tossing flowers and encouragement at the passing Americans early in the journey; later, the steady stream of forlorn, frightened women, children and old men hurrying south with whatever they could push or carry as he headed north into battle; and finally the hollow-eyed French soldiers stumbling away from the front. Daly had witnessed a great deal in his career, but these scenes were unlike any he had seen before.

By June 1, the Germans had advanced to the Marne River, 50 miles from Paris, and the French government was preparing to flee the capital. Arriving on the south bank of the Marne River, the U.S. 3rd Infantry Division dug in at the main bridge at Chateau Thierry. They held back the German tide until the bridge could be blown up, putting the wide, swift Marne River between the frenzied forces. Colonel Catlin

Twelve—Chateau Thierry

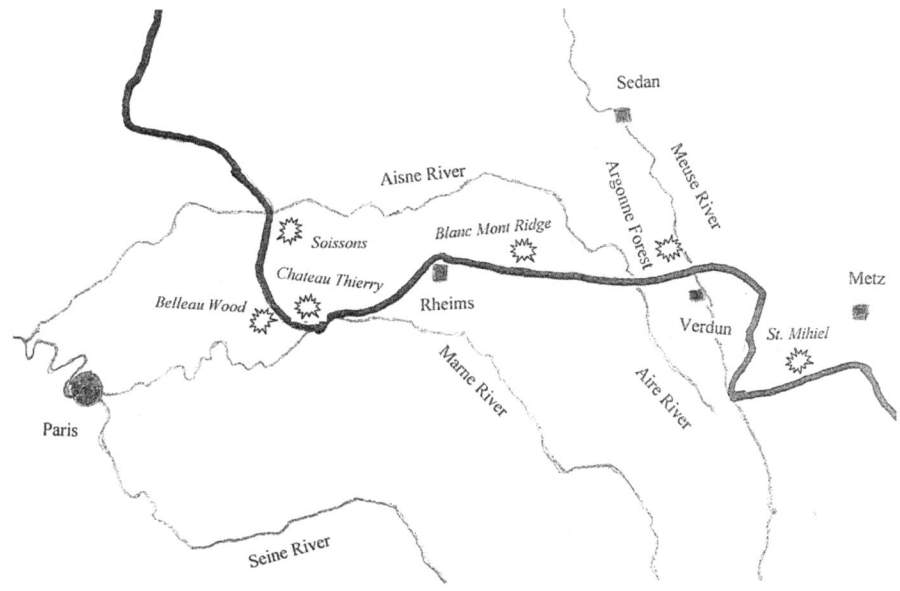

Map of the 2nd Division's World War I battles sites. The solid black line is the battle line after the German offensive of May 1918. Chateau Thierry (May 31–June 3), Belleau Wood (June 6–26) and Soissons (July 18–19) are on left, northeast of Paris. St. Mihiel (September 12–15) is on the right, east of Verdun. Blanc Mont Ridge (October 3–10) is in the center, near Rheims. The Meuse-Argonne Offensive (November 1–11) was fought between the Aire and Meuse rivers, north of Verdun (author's map).

later described the fighting in the streets and at the bridge as "a wild demoniacal tempest of machine gun and rifle fire."[4] The 3rd Division's ferocious defense at Chateau Thierry earned it the nickname "The Rock of the Marne."

Meanwhile, the Germans widened their wedge westward from Chateau Thierry seeking a weak spot through which to continue their push toward Paris. They seized Hill 204, due west of Chateau Thierry. This gave them a commanding view of the Rheims-Paris highway about a mile northwest. Continuing northwest, the Germans occupied the village of Bouresches and the Bois de Belleau.

Belleau Wood was a dense tangle of tall trees averaging about five inches in diameter, with thick underbrush, huge boulders, narrow ravines and steep ridges. The trees grew so close together, Catlin later recalled, "that when our men got in they found they could see not more than fifteen to twenty feet through the wood, except where ax or shell fire had made small clearings."[5]

Supplementing these natural defensive features, the Germans had quickly established three lines of trenches within the wood. One line faced Lucy-le-Bocage and Bouresches. A second line ran east-to-west across the narrow midsection of the wood with barbed wire entanglements along its front. A third line ran across the northern edge of the wood.[6]

Altogether, the kidney-shaped wood measured roughly 1,000 yards east-to-west by 2,000 yards north-to-south. Flat open fields surrounded the wood, which stood on slightly higher ground than the adjacent fields. It had been used as a private hunting preserve before the war. Now, instead of sportsmen hunting gaily-colored game birds, men in field gray and olive drab would hunt each other in this pristine killing ground.

As the Germans shifted the angle of their attack westward, the U.S. 2nd Infantry Division, with the 4th Brigade Marines, took up a position west of the 3rd Division, north of Montreuil-aux-Lionsat, straddling the Rheims-Paris highway and barring the doorway to the blacked-out City of Light. The division's 3rd Brigade, comprised of two Army regiments, was assigned the east side of the highway; the 4th Brigade the west side. This put the Germans' expanded salient squarely in front of the 2nd Division's assigned position.

The 4th Brigade was told to establish a line starting about 15 miles northwest of Chateau Thierry at Les Mares Farm, then east toward Hill 142, which stood west of the Bois de Belleau, then south through Champillon, east through Lucy-le-Bocage and the Bois de la Clerembauts to the Triangle Farm on the Rheims-Paris highway. The division's Army brigade was told to form a line south from the Triangle Farm southeast through le Thiolet, the southern edge of the Bois de le Marlette and la Nouette, facing Hill 204.[7]

Climbing down from the trucks in the pre-dawn darkness after the epic ride, Daly and his fellow Marines were stiff, tired and hungry.[8] Their only food or water during the ride came from what they carried in their packs. "When they arrived they were grey with dust and bleary-eyed with fatigue," Colonel Catlin later recalled. "They looked more like miners emerging from an all-night shift than like fresh troops ready to plunge into battle."[9]

After a brief rest, the Marine Brigade moved up to the defensive

TWELVE—Chateau Thierry

line. The 2nd Battalion, 5th Regiment, commanded by Lieutenant Colonel Frederic Wise, dug in between Les Mares Farm and Hill 142. The stocky, hard-nosed, hot-tempered Wise was an 1899 graduate of the Naval Academy and had seen action in the Boxer Rebellion, the Vera Cruz landing, Haiti and the Dominican Republic.

The 1st Battalion, 6th Regiment, led by Major Shearer, formed a line northeast of Lucy-le Bocage, with Bouresches to its right and Belleau Wood to its front. Lucy-le-Bocage, or "Lucy Birdcage" as it was called by the Marines, was a small village with a stone church tower and about 150 residents at the junction of five local roads.

The 2nd Battalion, 6th Regiment, Major Thomas Holcomb commanding, established a line eastward from Lucy-le Bocage on the left to Triangle Farm on the right. The modest, yet efficient Holcomb was appointed a Marine Corps second lieutenant from civilian life in 1900 and served in China and the Philippines prior to World War I.

The 3rd Battalion, 6th Regiment, with Major Berton W. Sibley at the helm, took up a reserve position southwest of Lucy-le-Bocage. Sibley was a short, wiry man noted for his physical endurance. After graduating with honors from Norwich University, a private military college, he was commissioned in the Marine Corps in 1900. He served in the Philippine-American War and later in Cuba.

The 2nd and 3rd Battalions of the 5th Regiment were also in reserve. The 6th Machine Gun Battalion, led by Major Edward B. Cole and later by Major Littleton Waller, namesake son of Daly's commander in Haiti, was distributed along the line. The younger Waller was commissioned in 1907 and saw action at Vera Cruz in 1914.

Harbord set up his headquarters at La Voie du Chatel, southwest of Lucy-le-Bocage, hoping to facilitate contact with the French on his left flank.[10]

Looking out across the flat, open fields with the waving grain and distant woods, Daly could see thatched-roof stone houses and large barns surrounded by stone walls that turned each farm into a fortified strong point for whichever side in the fighting held them.

There were no prepared fighting positions. The weary Marines had only enough time to dig a shallow trench and prepare to repel an expected German attack. It would be two more days before the supply train caught up to the troops. To dig in, the Marines used the lids of their mess kits and bayonets in lieu of shovels, which were with the supply train many miles away. Not knowing how soon the Germans would

117

be upon them, the Marines went right to work. "You'd be surprised to know just how much digging you can do under those circumstances,"[11] Marine Private John C. Geiger later wrote of that moment. The machine gun crews, like Daly's men, had the harder task. Their weapons and equipment were heavier than that of the riflemen and required much greater exertion to unload and manhandle into position.

The German's pell-mell advance and the resulting mad dash of the Americans to plug the yawning gap in the Allied line had produced something rarely seen on the Western Front since 1914. The war of position, with layers of trench lines, had suddenly given way to a war of movement, with hastily erected defenses and rapidly devised assaults. This was a Marine's kind of a fight.

In the words of Lieutenant Colonel Edwin N. McClellan, director of the Marine Corps Historical Section, what followed was a "magnificently stubborn defensive lasting a week."[12]

"On the night of June 2 the French retreat became general," Colonel Catlin later wrote. "They passed through to the rear in large numbers, both stragglers and organized units, and we suddenly realized that our line, which had been placed here for support, had become, through the fortunes of battle, the front. The United States Marines stood face to face with the oncoming hordes of Attila." To close a gap created by the French withdrawal, Harbord put three reserve companies into the line next to Wise's battalion of the 5th Regiment.[13] A platoon of Daly's 73rd Machine Gun Company was attached to these three companies to bolster their fire power.[14]

This meant the 6th Regiment, which Daly was a part, held a front nearly five miles long, with one company in reserve. Catlin issued an order to the men of the 6th Regiment: "The Germans are advancing and as far as I know we are the only troops between them and an open gate. We will occupy this line and hold at all costs." Hold at all costs. Every Marine in the front line that day knew what that meant: Victory or death. Not for the last time would they face such an uncompromising situation.

In a published tribute to the Marine Brigade, Secretary of the Navy Daniels described the key action:

> [A]t 3 o'clock ... began the battle of Chateau Thierry, with the Americans holding the line against the most vicious wedge of the German advance. The advance of the Germans was across the wheat field, driving at Hill 166 and advancing in smooth columns. The United States Marines, trained to

Twelve—Chateau Thierry

keen observation upon the rifle range, nearly every one of them wearing a marksman's medal or better, that of the sharpshooter or expert rifleman, did not wait for those gray clad hordes to advance nearer. Calmly they set their sights and aimed with the same precision that they had shown upon the rifle ranges at Paris Island [correct spelling at the time], Mare Island and Quantico. Incessantly their rifles cracked, and with their fire came the support of the artillery. The machine gun fire, incessant also, began to make its inroads upon the advancing forces. Closer and closer the shrapnel burst to its targets.

Caught in a seething wave of machine gun fire, of scattering shrapnel, of accurate rifle fire, the Germans found themselves in a position in which further advance could only mean absolute suicide. The lines hesitated. They stopped. They broke for cover, while Marines raked the woods and ravines in which they had taken refuge with machine gun and rifle to prevent them from making another attempt to advance by infiltrating through. Above, a French airplane was checking up on the artillery fire. Surprised by the fact that men should deliberately set their sights, adjust their range and then fire deliberately at an advancing foe, each man picking his target, instead of firing merely in the direction of the enemy, the aviator signaled below "Bravo." In the rear that word was echoed again and again. The German drive on Paris had been stopped.[15]

By sheer tenacity and massed machine guns, the two divisions broke the tip of the German spear.[16] The Germans attacked in waves, but Marine machine gun and rifle fire decimated their ranks. The Germans tried flanking the Marines but were stopped cold. They pounded the Marine positions with artillery but the defenders refused to budge.[17]

"It was a terrible slaughter; the mere thought of such wholesale killing is enough to curdle Christian blood," recalled Colonel Catlin. "But we had whipped the Hun. We had turned that part of his advance into a rout. We had tasted his blood and we had not forgotten the blood of our own who had been slain. We had had our first fight where fighting meant so much, and it would not have been human to refrain from cheering when it was over."[18]

Although the German advance had been halted, the ultimate outcome of the battle was still in doubt. The following day, the 2nd Infantry Division was deployed along a 12-mile front west of Chateau Thierry. The Germans still might break through and drive all the way to Paris to win the war.

When Daly wasn't listening to the scream and crash of German shells, he would have been able to hear his stomach rumbling. It would be two more days after the Marines arrived on the Marne before actual meals arrived at the front. He and his fellow Marines had to exist on the reserve rations they carried: a pound of bread and three-quarters of a pound of cold bacon a day. Colonel Catlin later remarked, "It came pretty close to hardship, but I heard no one complain."[19] Daly could reflect back to Peking when the defenders lived on horsemeat and rice for weeks.

For the next two days, the 2nd Division consolidated its position, brought up its artillery, endured bombardment and prepared to resist the highly anticipated major German assault. However, the Germans were tired from their surprisingly rapid advance, the fighting in and around Chateau Thierry and in need of supplies. So, while they made a number of small-scale attacks on the Allied lines that were beaten back, they made no major push during this time.

In Catlin's view, the German delay proved fateful. "They waited a day or two too long," allowing time for the American artillery to arrive, he later wrote. "Infantry action has accomplished wonders in this war on both sides, but however brilliant their performance, foot soldiers are not enough to check a big drive or carry through a big offensive.... [T]he Boche made his fatal mistake when he gave us time to bring up our guns."[20]

A French division on the left of the Marines attempted an attack on the German positions on June 3 but it only succeeded in demonstrating how exhausted the French troops were after the running battle of the past seven days. It was now clear that any attempt to dislodge the Germans would have to be made primarily by the Americans.

The Marines spent June 4 further concentrating their forces. Wise's 2nd of the 5th was relieved by a French unit and went into reserve, as did Hughes' 1st of the 6th (with Shearer still in command), which was replaced by Major Benjamin Berry's 3rd of the 5th. The platoon of Daly's 73rd Machine Gun Company remained in place with the 5th Regiment during this changeover.[21] The French now held the line north of Hill 142 and Berry held the line from there to Lucy-le-Bocage. Holcomb's 2nd of the 6th moved up to link up with Berry at Lucy. The Army's 23rd Infantry Regiment took up a position on Holcomb's right flank, running from the Triangle Farm to the Paris highway, making contact with the Army's 9th Infantry Regiment there. These moves meant the Marines had two battalions on a shorter front line with four battalions in reserve, ready to support any advance.

Twelve—Chateau Thierry

Late on June 4 the rolling kitchens finally arrived two miles behind the lines. At last there was the prospect of a hot meal for the half-starved Marines. But war is hell in many ways, and German shot and shell weren't the only things the Marines had to contend with. There was also "monkey meat." In his operations report, Major General Bundy wrote: "Only one hot meal was served during the twenty-four-hour day, and it was frequently cold by the time it reached the men in the front line. This continued during the entire forty days in which the division held the front line. We received the French ration, a part of which was canned beef shipped from Madagascar. It had a peculiar taste which our men did not like. They called it 'monkey meat,' and it soon became known by that name throughout our army."[22] Some accounts say "monkey meat" was actually Argentine beef mixed with carrots, a standard French ration. Wherever it came from, American Marines came to despise it.

In preparation for an assault of Belleau Wood, a pre-dawn attack on June 5 by a French unit and Berry's battalion took the German defenders of Hill 165 by surprise. The German guns on the hill were put out of action and the German line was driven north more than a mile.[23] Berry's battalion was now in position facing the west side of the wood while Holcomb's battalion was dug in near the south side.

A total of 74 Marines died in the five days of fighting that stopped the German offensive, including one from Daly's 73rd Machine Gun Company.[24] Daly was active throughout the fighting, and on June 5 he distinguished himself when he risked being blown to bits to extinguish a fire in the brigade's ammunition dump. Daly and his men were dug in near Lucy-le-Bocage to repel any attack by the Germans aimed at retaking the vital junction of five roads. When a German artillery barrage fell on him and his men, it ignited a blaze in the ammo dump. "Flames, exploding shells and tracer bullets made the place look like a Fourth of July celebration," wrote historian Raymond Tassin. Daly pulled together a group of his men and led them into the inferno. Despite the enemy shelling, they soon put out the fire, preventing a potentially huge conflagration.[25] This was the first of four acts in the coming days that would lead Daly's superiors to recommend him for a third Medal of Honor.

While the fate of the Allied cause on the Marne was still very much in doubt, a French colonel loudly advised the arriving Marines to retreat while they still had the chance. This led to a celebrated moment in the

"Devil Dog" Dan Daly

Marines' involvement in this war. Hearing the Frenchman's advice, Captain Lloyd C. Williams of the 5th Marines, shouted back: "Retreat, hell! We just got here!"

For Daly and the rest of the 4th Brigade, their war was just beginning.

Thirteen

Belleau Wood

June 6, 1918, would become the single bloodiest day in Marine Corps history up to that time. In fact, more Marines would become casualties that day than in all of the days *combined* since the founding of the corps in 1775.[1] June 6 would also prove to be a turning point in World War I, in the history of the Marine Corps, and in the legend of Dan Daly.

The fighting that grimly historic day began in the wee hours.

While the 3rd Infantry Division was assigned to attack Hill 204 west of Chateau Thierry, the 2nd Infantry Division was ordered to assault key points in the German line farther west. On the left wing of the 2nd Division, the 4th Brigade Marines were tasked with seizing Belleau Wood and the village of Bouresches. General Harbord, commanding the brigade, expected both objectives to be secured by nightfall. His timetable would prove as woefully wrong as his preparation.

Although Colonel Catlin was uneasy about attacking the Bois de Belleau, likening it to "entering a dark room filled with assassins," he also saw the necessity for capturing the wood. He outlined his reasons for this belief in his memoir:

"There were sound strategic reasons for this remarkable order. In the first place, pressure had to be relieved northwest of Chateau Thierry before that position could be made secure. Belleau Wood now formed a dangerous salient in our curving line, and to straighten that line ... it was necessary to take Bouresches and at least a part of the wood. In the second place, Belleau Wood was too strong a natural fortress to be allowed to remain in the hands of a powerful enemy on our immediate front. It was strongly garrisoned with infantry and machine gunners, and the big guns were coming up. For the Germans it formed a base of attack that threatened our whole line to the south. So long as they held it a sudden thrust was possible at any time, and such a thrust might mean untold disaster, probably the quick advance on Paris. For us it was an effective barricade. The Allies could not advance with that thorn in our side.... It would have been suicidal to wait for the German attack. An assumption of the offensive was the only solution."[2]

Harbord didn't issue his orders until just hours before he expected his unit commanders to begin the attack. Major Julius Turrill, whose 1st Battalion, 5th Regiment (1/5) was expected to kick off the attack at 3:45 a.m., didn't receive his orders until 10:00 p.m. on the 5th. (The short, stocky Turrill had been commissioned in 1899 and had served in the Philippines, Cuba, Guam and at sea.) His assignment was to drive German gunners off Hill 142 northwest of Belleau Wood so the Marine regiments tasked with attacking the wood itself could do so without flanking fire from 142.

Despite the last-minute orders and the need to move into position in total darkness, Turrill and the two companies of the 1/5 that he could muster in time launched their pre-dawn assault on Hill 142 at the appointed hour, 3:45 a.m. The missing companies and a promised machine gun company did not arrive until much later, after the initial assault. Turrill's attack force moved out from Hill 176 toward their objective in waves with fixed bayonets. The German artillery and machine gun fire tore gaping holes in the ranks of the approaching Marines, but they kept advancing, often crawling to avoid being slaughtered by the massed machine guns. Three fresh companies of Prussian infantry awaited them with 18 light machine guns and six heavy machine guns. The determined Marine assault crept up the rise of Hill 142. When they were close enough, the Marines advanced in rushes, bayoneting the Germans behind the guns in a savage melee. As the front-line Germans fell, those defenders farther back along the mile-long, rocky, wooded ridge, with a ravine on either side, fell back until they were driven off, killed or captured.

In the excitement of the moment, Captain George W. Hamilton, leading the 49th Company along the right side of the ridge, pursued the fleeing Germans down off the ridge with the remnants of his company. "They went down the brushy slope," recalled Lieutenant John Thomason, "across a little run, across a road where two heavy Maxim were caught sitting, and mopped up [enemy troops on] the next long smooth slope." It was only then that Hamilton concluded they had overshot the objective. Realizing he couldn't continue advancing with only a handful of men, nor could he hold where he was, he and his men crawled

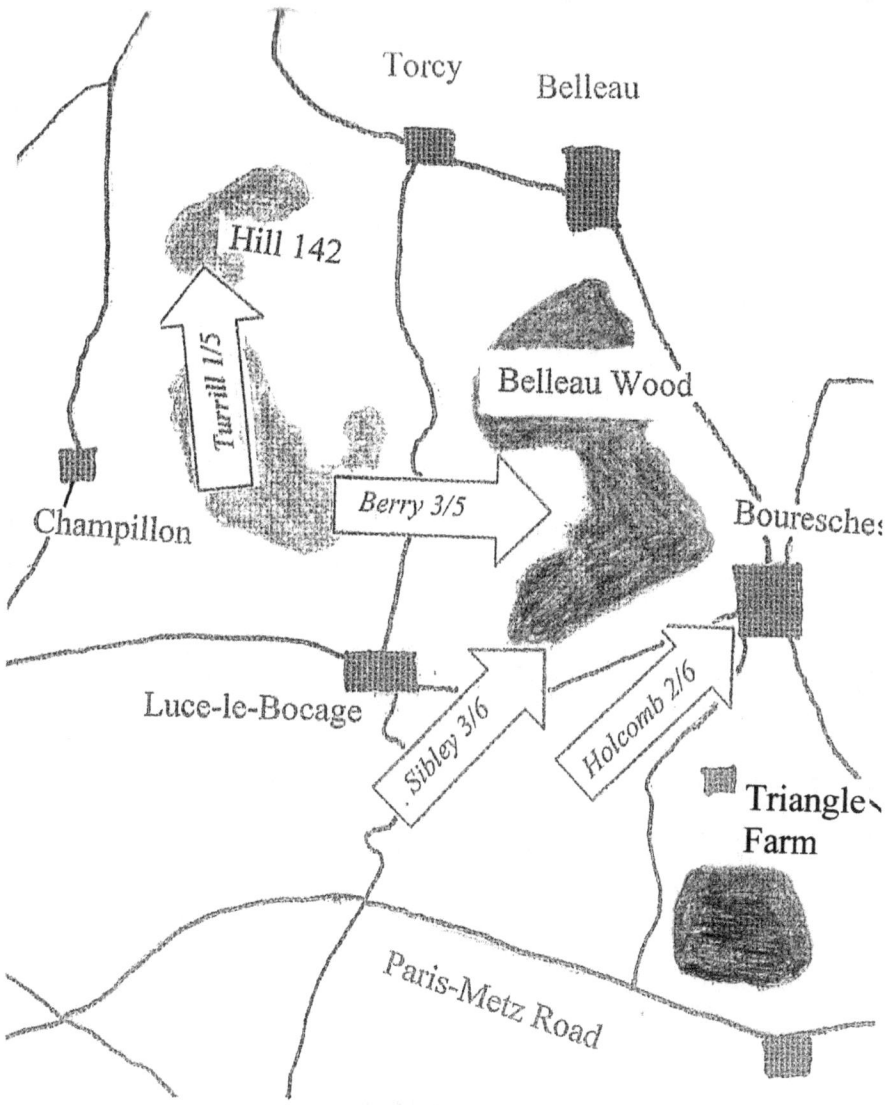

Map of Belleau Wood showing the Marine assaults on the first day of the battle. Turrill's battalion attacked Hill 142 beginning at 3:45 in the morning. Beginning at 5:00 in the afternoon, Berry's battalion charged the west side of Belleau Wood while Sibley's battalion assaulted the southern edge of the wood and Holcomb's battalion attacked the village of Bouresches (author's map).

through a drainage ditch back to the ridge and dug in. Hamilton had lost more than half his company but they had taken Hill 142.

However, the fight for the hill did not end there. The Germans swiftly mounted a series of counterattacks. Most of the officers and roughly half the enlisted Marines from Turrill's two companies were killed or wounded taking the hill. Turrill sent urgent messages back to Colonel Neville seeking ammunition, water and, above all, more men. Neville rushed supplies forward but they arrived more than a mile from the fighting, and a frustrated Turrill could spare no men to lug them forward.

As the surviving Marines prepared to meet the fourth counterattack, Gunnery Sergeant Ernest August Janson spotted 12 German soldiers crawling toward his position dragging five light machine guns. Shouting a warning to his men, Janson charged alone down the slope directly into the enemy force. He bayoneted the two leaders of the German detachment and drove the remainder away, forcing them to abandon their machine guns. Despite a serious chest wound, he then returned to his men, and continued the fight for the hill until finally dispatched to a field hospital. His daring charge was the first action by a Marine in World War I to result in an award of the Medal of Honor.[3]

By afternoon, Hill 142 had been secured, but at a very high cost. Casualties among Turrill's two companies totaled eight officers and 325 men.[4] In addition, three companies that came up in support of Turrill's force lost three officers and 126 men.

The capture of Hill 142, of course, was just the prelude to the attack on Belleau Wood. Colonel Catlin later recalled "the dark threat of Belleau Wood as full of menace as a tiger's foot, dangerous as a live wire, poisonous with gas, bristling with machine guns, alive with snipers, scornfully beckoning us to come on and be slain, waiting for us like a dragon in its den."[5]

At 2:05 p.m., General Harbord issued orders for the next phase of his plan to begin in just three hours. Major Benjamin S. Berry's 3/5 would assault the west side of Belleau Wood while Sibley's 3/6 would attack the south side, and Holcomb's 2/6 would seize Bouresches, a village of some 60 stone masonry buildings just east of the wood.

(Berry had graduated from Pennsylvania Military College and joined the Marine Corps in 1904. He had seen action in Santo Domingo in 1916. While a captain commanding the 45th Company, 3/5, at Verdun, he and 11 of his men earned the French Croix de Guerre for repelling an enemy raid. He took command of the 3/5 in May 1918.)

THIRTEEN—*Belleau Wood*

No reconnaissance had been made of these objectives, so the attacking Marines had no clear idea what they were walking into. Harbord had taken the word of the French that the Germans had not yet established themselves there in any numbers. However, the 461st Infantry Regiment had in fact over a thousand men dug in and waiting in the wood. The two Marine battalions assigned to assault the wood each numbered about 1,000 men.[6] However, only half of each battalion could be used in the first rush. Thus, the Marines faced an almost insurmountable task. They had to attack and capture a strongly fortified position held by an enemy force equal in size to their own. As Colonel Catlin later observed, "Even to a Marine it seemed hardly enough men."[7]

Harbord's attack order put Catlin, commanding the 6th Marine Regiment, in overall command of the attack by the three battalions. However, Catlin didn't receive Harbord's order until 3:45 p.m., a little more than an hour before the attack he was to command was to begin. Catlin met with Sibley and Holcomb to go over the plan. He also tried to telephone Berry before the attack but Berry was already moving into position and was beyond Catlin's reach. The lack of preparation caused Catlin "considerable anxiety," he later wrote. "It looked as though we would have to attack without proper coordination, and as a matter of fact, that is what we did. I was fully aware of the difficulties of the situation, especially for Berry. He had 400 yards of open wheat field to cross in the face of galling fire, and I did not believe he could ever reach the woods. It looked as though Sibley's battalion would have to bear the brunt of the action."[8]

Despite Catlin's concerns, at precisely 5 p.m., Berry's battalion stepped off at a rapid walking pace toward the west side of Belleau Wood and Sibley's 3/6 moved out smartly along the Lucy-Bouresches road toward the south end of the wood. There were no blaring bugles, no flashing sabers, no melodramatic poses, just the shrill tweets of NCO's whistles and Marine officers calling out to their men: "Follow me."

Berry's Marines left the shelter of a wood and entered the poppy-studded wheat fields in four long, neatly spaced waves. The men in each line were about five yards apart, and each line was about 20 yards behind the line ahead of it. The lines each stretched about a third of a mile from end to end. The blood-red poppies likely reminded Daly of the blood splatters that stained the stone surface atop the Tartar Wall.

The 3/5 had to cross at least 400 yards of open ground to reach the

"Devil Dog" Dan Daly

wood. Walking at a brisk pace, a man could cover 400 yards in three to four minutes. But striding briskly while enduring a murderous storm of enemy shot and shell for four minutes is no walk in the park. However, running across the field was out of the question. A man would be momentarily out of breath after running hard for nearly a quarter of a mile with a rifle and pack, to say nothing of trying to keep his emotions in check under heavy fire. If he arrived at the wood at all, the attacker would face a well-armed defender who was rested and ready.

While Berry's and Sibley's battalions attacked toward the wood, Major Thomas Holcomb's 2/6 skirted the south end of the wood and moved toward Bouresches, on the far side.

Berry's Marines had advanced only a short distance before German machine guns hidden in the darkness of the wood unleashed a torrent of lead. It quickly became apparent that the enemy was more than ready to meet any assault. Every inch of the vast fields of swaying wheat was covered by interlocking arcs of German machine gun fire. The German fusillade quickly mowed down the first rank of advancing Marines like a giant scythe.

The following ranks of Berry's Marines began diving to the ground, seeking whatever cover they could beneath the knee-high wheat. Their advance continued at a crawl, quite literally. The Marines crawled toward the wood, occasionally rising up, taking aim and firing at whatever target presented itself before dropping back down to the illusory protection of the wheat. Their progress toward the wood was agonizingly slow, and the steady stream of bullets from the German machine guns gradually reduced the slender stalks of wheat to chaff and the bodies of many Marines to mangled corpses and writhing wounded. The closer the Marines crawled toward the deadly wood, the closer the attack came to stalling out. As the casualties mounted so did the fear, and panic gradually turned into paralysis.

Most of Berry's Marines got no closer to the wood than 100 yards before the sheer volume of the enemy fire ground them to a halt. Here and there, small clusters of Marines, including Berry, managed to actually penetrate the wood, but here they were essentially cut off from further support. About an hour after the attack began, Berry sent a runner back to Harbord with a report that "What is left of the battalion is in the woods close by. Do not know whether we will be able to stand or not. Increase artillery." As darkness descended, those Marines still alive in the wheat field and able to move began crawling away from the wood,

Thirteen—Belleau Wood

back the way they came, trying to escape death among the shattered wheat stalks.

Berry's battalion had lost four officers and 268 men killed or wounded in about an hour.[9]

Floyd Gibbons, a war correspondent for the *Chicago Tribune*, accompanied Berry's 3/5 into the wheat field and later recounted what he saw. Before joining the advance, Gibbons handed a dispatch about the coming battle to his driver with instructions to deliver it to Paris for transmission to his newspaper.[10] This dispatch would have serious, unforeseen consequences that will be discussed later.

Once in the wheat field, Gibbons was about 10 yards behind Berry when he saw the major turn toward him and shout, "Get down everybody."

"We all fell on our faces," Gibbons continued. "And then it began to come hot and fast. Perfectly withering volleys of lead swept the tops of the oats just over us.... Then I heard a shout in front of me. It came from Major Berry.... The major was making an effort to get to his feet. With his right hand he was savagely grasping his left wrist. 'My hand's gone,' he shouted.... A ball had entered his left arm at the elbow, had traveled down the side of the bone, tearing away muscles and nerves of the forearm and lodging itself in the palm of his hand. His pain was excruciating."[11]

Gibbons shouted at the major to get down, to take whatever cover he could find in the wheat. But Berry would have none of it. "We've got to get out of here," the major yelled back. "We've got to get forward. They'll start shelling this open field in a few minutes." Berry was about 20 yards from the edge of Belleau Wood. Gibbons was about 10 yards behind Berry. Gibbons urged Berry to get down and wait until he could crawl to where the major was. Using his toes and elbows, Gibbons began crawling toward Berry. As he did, Gibbons felt a pain like the "lighted end of a cigarette" on his upper left arm. A bullet tore through his bicep muscle. Moments later, a second bullet "nicked" the top of his left shoulder. Again there was the momentary burning sensation, nothing more. So Gibbons resumed crawling toward Berry. As he did so, he was struck by a third bullet. This one ricocheted off the ground, went through his left eye and exited out his forehead.

Gibbons later described the moment as follows: "Then there was a crash. It sounded to me like someone had dropped a glass bottle into a porcelain bathtub. A barrel of whitewash tipped over and it seemed that everything in the world turned white. That was the sensation. I did not recognize it because I have often been led to believe and often heard it said that when one receives a blow on the head everything turns black."[12]

Gibbons was still conscious but dazed. Blood poured from his hideous wound. "I got as close to the ground as a piece of paper on top of a table," he said. "I remember regretting sincerely that the war had reached the stage of open movement and one consequence of which was that there wasn't a shell hole anywhere to crawl into."[13]

Gibbons miraculously survived and after 10 days in the hospital, he returned to the front, missing his left eye with a large bandage over his empty eye socket and fractured forehead. Major Berry was not quite so lucky. He remained in the wood, in command of the remnants of his battalion, until he was finally convinced to seek medical attention in the rear. Berry was out of the war.

While Berry's 3/5 was being torn apart on the west side of Belleau Wood, Sibley's 3/6 launched itself down the road from Lucy-le-Bocage along the southern edge of the wood. The battalion split into two parts, with two companies on either side of the road. After moving past the southwest corner of the wood, the battalion turned and advanced into the wheat field where it ran into a wall of German artillery and machine gun fire.

Colonel Catlin watched Sibley's men advance. "It was one of the most beautiful sights I have ever witnessed," he recalled in his memoir. "The battalion pivoted on its right, the left sweeping across the open ground in four waves, as steadily and correctly as though on parade," he later wrote. "They walked at the regulation pace…. Oh, it took courage and steady nerves to do that in the face of the enemy's machine gun fire."[14]

Daly and the 73rd Machine Gun Company were attached to Sibley's battalion. They were at the edge of the wheat field near Lucy-le-Bocage. As Sibley's battalion went in, Daly's platoon poured suppressing fire on the Germans in the wood. The German gunners returned fire with a vengeance. When the order came to join Sibley's men trying to get into the wood, Daly's platoon momentarily wavered in the face of the punishing enemy fire. It was at this moment that Daly launched himself into action.[15]

Catlin later recalled the moment: "Into a veritable hell of hissing bullets, into that death-dealing torrent, with heads bent as though facing a March gale, the shattered lines of Marines pushed on. The headed

Thirteen—Belleau Wood

wheat bowed and waved in that metal cloud-burst like meadow grass in a summer breeze. The advancing lines wavered, and the voice of a Sergeant was heard above the roar, 'Come on — — – —! Do you want to live forever?'"[16]

Despite heavy casualties, Sibley's Marines entered the wood and went to work with bullets and bayonets on the Germans there. By 8:30 p.m., as darkness settled over the battlefield, the advance of the 3/6 was finally halted for the night by heavy enemy fire. Against great odds, Sibley's men had cleared nearly a mile across the southern quarter of the wood and reached its eastern edge, the first objective. They dug in and endured a night of shelling and poison gas.

Sibley's battalion had lost five officers and 194 men in less than four hours.

About the time Sibley's Marines reached the wood, a sniper's bullet struck Colonel Catlin in the chest, slamming him to the ground and putting him out of action, and ultimately out of the war. Catlin had been observing the attack through field glasses while standing on a small rise screened by bushes.[17] He was about 300 yards from Belleau Wood and near where Berry's right flank almost touched Sibley's left at the start of the attack.[18] When Lieutenant Colonel Harry Lee, the regiment's second-in-command, learned of Catlin's wounding, he rushed to the front and took charge of the 6th Regiment. (Lee's troops called him "Light Horse Harry," based on the mistaken belief that he was a direct descendant of the Revolutionary War hero of that name. He spent seven years in the District of Columbia National Guard before being commissioned in the Marine Corps in 1898. Powerfully built with a dominating manner, he had served in the Philippines, China, Nicaragua, Cuba, Haiti and the Dominican Republic as well as at sea aboard battleships.)

While Sibley's battalion fought its way into the wood, elements of Holcomb's 2/6 battalion, supported in part by four guns from Daly's 73rd Machine Gun Company, moved out toward Bouresches. The village, about three-quarters of a mile east of Belleau Wood, consisted of one- and two-story masonry homes, a church and a few shops. Its thousand or so residents had fled at the approach of the warring forces.

The Marines advanced in a skirmish line through 600 yards of wheat fields under heavy fire and suffered heavy losses. At one point, much of the remaining attack force was forced to hit the dirt or take cover in a ravine. What was left of one platoon, 24 men led by Second Lieutenant Clifton B. Cates, a future Marine Corps commandant, doggedly continued onward. Rushing the German machine guns, they overpowered the crews and turned the guns on the village's roughly 100 German defenders.

The village was about 500 yards across with three main avenues. Cates divided his tiny force into sections and began to systematically wipe out the machine gun nests and snipers that infested the village. "[T]he place bristled with machine guns," Cates later recalled. "There were guns at the street corners, behind barricades, and even on the housetops, but the Marines kept on. They attacked with rifle, bayonet, and grenade. They were outnumbered when they started, and one by one they were put out of the fighting. But they kept going, taking gun after gun, until the Germans, for all their numbers and advantage of position, began to fall back." By the time most of the town had been cleared, Cates was down to 21 men.[19]

To discourage the Germans from counterattacking, Cates had his men repeatedly change positions within the village and fire their weapons to make it appear he had many more men than he had. Within a few hours, more Marines from the 2/6 and the 3/6 reached the village, and by 11 p.m. at least 600 Marines were in the village, enabling them to hold on against the inevitable German counterattacks.[20]

The bloodiest day in Marine Corps history up to that time finally ended with the Marines in tenuous possession of toeholds inside Belleau Wood and Bouresches. But these gains had come at a tragically high price. Roughly half of the Marines engaged that day were either killed or wounded. The four assault battalions, the 1/5, 3/5, 2/6, 3/6, were shattered. Those veteran Marines who remained, like Daly, would continue the fight with the gaping holes in the ranks filled by untested replacements.

What had been intended as a coordinated attack by three battalions had devolved into a confused struggle by platoons, squads and even individual Marines to simply survive through the night in hopes that the dawn would bring some change of fortune. Few of those company and platoon leaders still in action had a clear idea where they were in the wood or where their nearest units might be. One company leader gave up trying to find units to form a line and drew his men into a British Square in which the four platoons each formed one side of a square so that an attack from any direction could be resisted. Then they waited for whatever came next.[21]

Upon returning to the front, Floyd Gibbons wrote a dispatch that

Thirteen—Belleau Wood

provided some of what he observed during the June 6 attack on Belleau Wood and some of what he learned later from Major Frank E. Evans, the 6th Regiment's adjutant, and others. The dispatch told of an unnamed gunnery sergeant who inspired his men to rise up and charge forward with a few choice words:

> "The enemy gun fire was terrific. The oats and the wheat in the open field were waving, and snapping off, not from the wind but from rifle and machine gun fire of German veterans in their well-concealed positions. A runner came scrambling through the brush, and handed the old Gunnery Sergeant a sheet of paper. He read it quickly, then glanced along the line of his dug-in platoon. He stood up and made a forward motion to his men. There was [a] slight hesitation. Who the hell could blame them? Machine gun and rifle bullets were kicking up dirt, closer and closer. The sergeant ran out to the center of his platoon—he swung his bayonet-rifle over his head with a forward sweep. He yelled to his men: 'Come on, you sons-of-bitches. Do you want to live forever?'"[22]

Gibbons reported that the Marines around the sergeant rose up from the ground with a roar and followed him into the mouth of hell.

Later, in his book about his war time experiences, Gibbons offered the following, more detailed, telling of that story:

> A small platoon line of marines lay on their faces and bellies under the trees at the edge of the wheat field. Two hundred yards across the flat field the enemy was located in trees. I peered into the trees but could see nothing, yet I knew that every leaf in the foliage screened scores of German machine guns that swept the field with lead. The bullets nipped the tops of the young trees three feet from the ground on which the marines lay. The minute for the marine advance was approaching. An old gunnery sergeant commanded the platoon in the absence of the lieutenant, who had been shot and was out of the fight. This old sergeant was a marine veteran. His cheeks were bronzed with the wind and sun of the seven seas. The service bar across his left breast showed that he had fought in the Philippines, in Santo Domingo, at the walls of Pekin, and in the streets of Vera Cruz.... As the minute for the advance arrived, he rose from the trees first and jumped out onto the exposed edge of the field that ran with lead, across which he and his men were to charge. Then he turned to give the charge order to the men of his platoon—his mates—the men he loved. He said: "COME ON, YOU SONS-O'-BITCHES! DO YOU WANT TO LIVE FOREVER?"[23]

Historians have debated how Gibbons could have witnessed and heard Daly's famed battle cry, given that Gibbons was with Berry on the west side of the wood and Daly was with Sibley's battalion on the south side. It seems likely that Gibbons did not personally witness this act but learned of it later from Marines who witnessed the attack. In his post-war memoir, Gibbons thanked Major Frank E. Evans, adjutant of the 6th Regiment, for providing him with much of what he wrote about the battle that occurred while in the hospital.[24]

In their history of the Marines in World War I, Edwin Simmons and Joseph Alexander concluded: "It is highly likely that Daly screamed those words, or words to that effect, at some time during the critical moment of the initial assaults on Belleau Wood."[25] Historian Alex Axelrod reached the same conclusion in his book about Belleau Wood: "A real marine in a real battle, Daly really did say something that ended with the rhetorical question, 'Do you want to live forever?' That the versions of the legend surrounding Daly and his battle cry vary in the details does not diminish the reality the legend is based on. Both Catlin and Gibbons seized on the phrase, changing its location a bit, and in Gibbon's case even claiming to have heard it personally, for much the same reason that the marines marched against Belleau Wood in the elaborately choreographed line of sections formation; to impose order on chaos, to make sense of it, to extract some greater meaning from it."[26]

Gibbons didn't name the sergeant but as the foregoing excerpts show, it has since been generally accepted that the sergeant was Daly. He was never one to seek out fame, so the fact that he never denied being the sergeant in question tends to support the accepted conclusion. In later years, Daly only quibbled over the words he reportedly spoke that day, offering instead: "For Christ sake, men, come on! Do you want to live forever?" Whatever the truth, Gibbons' version is the one everyone remembers[27] and the one carved into the wall of the National Museum of the Marine Corps at Quantico.

The battle for possession of Belleau Wood would go on for 20 more grueling days at a horrendous cost in casualties to both sides. It was a desperate struggle fought at extremely close quarters, often with bayonets, rifle butts or bare hands. The wood was honeycombed with machine guns, each positioned to leave no hiding spot. However, the Marines soon devised a successful means of attack. "The most effective method was to run to the rear of each gun in turn and overpower the crew," recalled Catlin. "But each flanking position was covered by another gun which had to be taken immediately. It was a furious dash from next to next, with no time for breath.... It was man to man, there in the dark recesses of the woods, with no gallery to cheer the gladiators, and it was the best man that won."[28]

THIRTEEN—*Belleau Wood*

Both sides spent June 7 licking their wounds, repositioning their forces for a continuation of the fighting and attempting to resupply the front-line forces. Sibley sent out two-man intelligence teams to scout enemy positions. The teams frequently came under fire from snipers. Corporal Joseph Rendinell later recalled being sent out on one of these missions. "The woods was [*sic*] trackless jungle and there was [*sic*] Germans in trees, behind woodpiles, in ravines, hid behind piles of stones. We had to advance from tree to tree, looking all around to see where those shots was [*sic*] coming from. It was like playing Hide & Seek, only if you lost you were out for keeps."[29]

The piles of dead in the wheat fields and the woods attested to the fierceness of the struggle. "The dead out in the wheat fields near Belleau Wood laid where they had fallen. We had no chance to bury them." Corporal Rendinell recalled. "One place a Marine corporal and three Germans laying together in a heap, a story untold. At another place, a Marine in a prone position with his rifle to his shoulder & finger on the trigger, just as he died. Another with his baynote [*sic*] still in a German and both dead."[30]

The Germans delivered a heavy artillery barrage on Sibley's battalion in the southern end of the wood on June 7. During the bombardment, Daly visited each of his company's machine gun crews to offer encouragement and steady their nerves. The crews were posted over a wide portion of the front, from one side of the southern wood to the other as well in Bouresches, which could only be reached by crossing an open wheat field. His action was deemed sufficiently worthy of note to be recounted in a later recommendation for the Medal of Honor.[31]

Sibley led the 3/6 battalion forward on June 8 in an attempt to take four strong points located in the south wood. However, his casualties in these efforts proved so great that General Harbord allowed him to withdraw to the edge of the wood so that artillery could soften up the enemy. The Germans responded with their own heavy barrage on the Marines. That dark night, Sibley's battalion, minus one company, was relieved by Hughes' 1/6, and Sibley's 3/6 Marines had their first hot meal in a week.

On the west side of the wood, Major Shearer took command of the 3/5, succeeding the wounded Berry. Shearer's first order from General Harbord was to take the badly mauled battalion to Bouresches, on the opposite side of the wood, to relieve Holcomb's 2/6. Apparently, Harbord still lacked a clear understanding of the battered condition of his front-line forces.

"Devil Dog" Dan Daly

At 4:30 a.m. on June 10, Hughes and the 1/6, supported by Daly's 73rd Machine Gun Company, attacked. Hughes' objective that day was a line running east-to-west across the narrow waist of the wood. As a sign of the continuing confusion, Hughes' attack occupied the area of the south wood that Sibley had seized before withdrawing the previous night. This was 800 yards south of the actual objective. Based on his misreading of the situation, Hughes' upbeat messages back to brigade headquarters led Harbord to believe that far more ground had been taken.[32]

During this advance, Daly attacked an enemy machine gun emplacement singlehanded. Working his way to a ditch near the gun, Daly armed three grenades and tossed them into the gun pit in quick succession. The explosions silenced the gun. He then drew his .45-caliber semi-automatic pistol and charged. He shot and killed the officer in charge of the gun crew and the remaining Germans threw up their hands in surrender. He reportedly took 14 prisoners.[33]

Later that day, Daly repeatedly braved enemy fire to retrieve wounded Marines trapped between the warring forces.[34] One account credits him with rescuing 12 Marines that day.[35]

These events were the third and fourth of four exploits cited by Daly's superiors in their recommendation for his third Medal of Honor.

Around noon on June 10, Shearer and the 3/5 completed the relief of Holcomb's 2/6 at Bouresches. Harbord now believed, mistakenly, that his forces controlled the entire southern portion of the wood and so he issued an order for the following day for Hughes' 1/6 and Wise's 2/5 to attack and capture the entire northern portion of the wood. Harbord's error was subsequently compounded by confusion among the unit commanders over their respective tasks, resulting in heavy casualties the next day.[36]

As June 11 began to dawn, Wise's 2/5 attacked the west side of the wood. However, owing to a dense morning mist, the attack angled south instead of north and proceeded through the same wheat field as Berry's 3/5 had done five days earlier. Sadly, Wise's Marines met much the same fate as Berry's. Despite heavy losses, they penetrated the wood and began the bloody business of knocking out the German machine guns there.

Shortly after noon, based on messages from Hughes and Wise that they had reached their objectives, Harbord concluded that the northern

Thirteen—*Belleau Wood*

portion of the wood was now in Marine hands. Not until later that day did the unit commanders discover their errors in location and realize most of the wood was still in enemy hands. Wise's battalion had actually attacked straight across the narrow midsection of the wood and reached its eastern edge. Wise later recalled the difficulties of trying to "orient themselves in the heavy underbrush. There were no landmarks, once you got into those woods. If you turned around twice you lost all sense of direction and only your compass could straighten you out."[37]

Remarking on this part of the battle, historian Alan Axelrod wrote: "The marines, having approached and then entered Belleau Wood from the wrong direction and at the wrong place, were being torn to shreds, there was no denying that. Yet, disorganized and disoriented in the woods, they were nevertheless giving better than they got."[38]

The following day, June 12, Harbord and Bundy, the 2nd Division commander, finally realized that any congratulations for driving the Germans out of Belleau Wood were premature.

Newspaper headlines back home had heralded a success that the Marines fighting in the wood now had to deliver on. Wise's 2/5 began advancing into the northern portion of the wood on the afternoon of June 12. German resistance was fierce and Marine losses were heavy. The 2/5 attacked high ground studded with enemy machine guns and covered on the flanks by riflemen. Despite the difficult terrain and volume of enemy fire, the Marines drove the Germans off the heights with bullets, bayonets and bare fists. From there, the Marines could see to the end of the wood, still some distance ahead. Hughes' 1/6 came up and helped secure the line. The depleted Marine units had secured the day's objective, now the question was could they hold it if the Germans counterattacked.

In the early morning hours of June 13, the Germans did in fact launch a counterattack to reclaim the high ground they had lost. The hard-pressed Marines, sorely in need of sleep, food and ammunition, succeeded in repelling the attackers. A German counterattack also targeted Bouresches, with the same result. The Germans pushed their way into the village but the Marines of Shearer's 3/5 pushed them back out.[39] These attacks, and heavy German shelling, took a further toll on the Marines. Late in the day, Holcomb's 2/6 was ordered to relieve Wise's severely battered 2/5 on the high ground in the northern portion of the wood. Two-thirds of Wise's men were dead or wounded. Wise informed Harbord, "[I] have one replacement officer per company left and about

"Devil Dog" Dan Daly

three hundred men, not including replacements." Three days earlier, he had had 30 officers and a thousand men.[40]

Despite the gains made, and heavy losses, Harbord was unhappy that Wise had not secured the entire wood and wasted no time letting him know it. That night, Harbord ordered the 5th and 6th Regiments to form a continuous east-west line across the northern portion of Belleau Wood, extending from Champillon Brook on the west, to Bouresches, on the east.

On June 14, several of the Marine battalions were subjected to a lengthy bombarded by 7,000 mustard-gas[41] and 2,000 high-explosive shells. While the high-explosive shells spewed shrapnel, the gas caused first- and second-degree burns on exposed skin, eyes, throat and lungs. The oily agent would hang in the air for hours or even days, and a Marine who jumped into a shell hole might find the gas waiting for him there. Victims often drowned as their tissue dissolved into liquid. During this bombardment, Gunnery Sergeant Fred Stockham removed his own gas mask and put it on a wounded Marine before continuing to help others. Stockham died a few days later in a field hospital. For his selfless and courageous act, he was awarded the Medal of Honor, although not until 21 years after the war in July 1939.

Holcomb's 2/6, Hughes's 1/6 and the machine gun battalion all reported heavy losses in their units. Nearly everyone in one of Holcomb's companies became a casualty. His battalion was reduced from 800 effectives to 300. The Marines spent much of the day in their gas masks, which were hot and uncomfortable to wear and limited their fighting ability. Catlin later compared wearing a gas mask in combat to "fighting with a clothespin on your nose and a bag over your head."[42]

Feuding between Wise and Hughes over each man's perceived failures to support the other led Harbord to put Lieutenant Colonel Logan Feland, second in command of Neville's 5th Regiment, in overall charge of the operation in the north wood and to replace Wise in command of the 2/5 with Major Ralph Keyser. About the same time, Hughes was evacuated for gas poisoning and replaced in command of the 1/6 by Major Franklin Garrett.

By the following day, June 15, fully half of the Marine brigade had been killed, wounded or gassed since launching the attacks on June 6. Inexperienced replacements now filled many of these gaps in the ranks. Late in the day, the Marine Brigade received word that they would be relieved by French and U.S. Army troops and moved to the rear to recover.

Thirteen—Belleau Wood

Reflecting on the losses, Wise later wrote: "It was enough to break your heart. I had left ... on May 31 with 965 men and 26 officers. Now, before me stood 350 men and 6 officers." Soon after, when asked by his wife, who was in Paris, "How are the Marines?" All Wise could say was, "There aren't any more Marines."[43]

The last Marine unit in the wood was relieved late the next day. Daly's 73rd Machine Gun Company was one of the last to come out. He and his men filed out of the blasted wood with red-rimmed eyes, shaggy beards and tattered uniforms after dark on June 17. That day, Daly and his Marines enjoyed their first hot meal in 12 days. They also got some mail from home after many weeks.

On June 21, Daly was ordered to a field hospital with a shrapnel wound to his left thigh that he had received before the relief.[44] Daly reportedly received the wound while repeatedly crawling out into no-man's-land between the battle lines as he had on June 10 and dragging wounded Marines to safety.[45] After his release from the field hospital on June 27, Daly was sent to a replacement camp to help train replacements while he continued his recovery. He returned to the 73rd Machine Gun Company in August.

While the Marines got some desperately needed rest, their successors, the U.S. Army's 7th Infantry Regiment, struggled without much success to gain any ground in Belleau Wood. This was the regiment's first outing in combat and it had taken 300 casualties in a little over a week.

On June 23, the Marines returned to the fight with 2,800 replacements.[46] The smell of rotting corpses hung in the hot, humid summer air beneath the shattered treetops and across the chewed up wheat fields. No one had been able to bury the dead. They still lay where they fell. Replacements could be forgiven if they wretched at the horrible stink. For veterans, the reek of death was an uncomfortable reminder of many other difficult days on other battle fronts.

"We lost the sense of emotion," recalled First Lieutenant Elliott D. Cooke of the 2/5's 55th Company. "Dull-eyed, resigned, lacking the courage to go forward or back, yet we clung desperately to that rocky edge of woods. It seemed to be all we had left in the world and we would not give it up. Not for Heinie, Kaiser Bill, nor the devil himself."[47]

Getting food and water up to the Marines on the front line was a great hazard throughout the battle. At one point, a detail of 30 Marines from Sibley's 3/6 were sent to the rear to obtain these necessities. Only 11 of the men returned. The other 19 had been killed or wounded.[48]

Major Shearer and the 3/5 were tasked with advancing from the high ground in the wood and clearing the northern portion of Germans. The attack began at 7 p.m., about 90 minutes before dark, without any artillery preparation. As before, the German machine guns took a toll on the attacking Marines. After each German machine gun was knocked out, the machine guns on either side opened up on the victorious Marines, adding to the casualties. Progress was agonizingly slow and heartbreakingly bloody.

Unable to push the last of the Germans out of the wood, Harbord and Bundy, the division commander, pulled Shearer and the 3/5 back a ways and pummeled the remaining portion of the wood with 14 hours of artillery fire to soften it up. The bombardment began at 3 a.m., June 25. It ceased at 5 p.m. and Shearer's 3/5 went forward, with Keyser's 2/5 in support.[49] What remained of the trees had been shelled to splinters.[50] Despite the extensive artillery preparation, the Germans put up a spirited defense and only the grim determination and individual heroism of the attacking Marines rooted out the defenders.

"The Germans opened up with machine guns, hand and rifle grenades, and trench mortars," recalled Private William A. Francis. "Just then we all seemed to go crazy for we gave a yell like a bunch of wild Indians and started down the hill running and cursing in the face of the machine gun fire. Men were falling on every side, but we kept going, yelling and firing as we went."[51]

Late in the day, Sibley's 3/6 moved up and joined the final push.

Fighting continued through the night, but by morning of June 26 Shearer was able to report: "WOODS NOW U.S. MARINE CORPS ENTIRELY." The 3/5 and 3/6, which Berry and Sibley had led into the killing ground of the wheat field on June 6, were there at the finish and helped write the final chapter in the Marines' capture of Belleau Wood.

Writing about the battle, historian Dick Camp, a retired Marine colonel who endured the siege at Khe Sanh in Viet Nam, said Belleau Wood "was the site of unequaled heroics and unspeakable horror.... [It] became more than a bloody battleground for the men of the Marine Brigade. It became hallowed ground, synonymous with valor and self-sacrifice, and a reference point by which to judge all other events in their lives."[52]

In a tribute to the Marines, General Jean Marie Joseph Degoutte,

Thirteen—*Belleau Wood*

commander of the French 6th Army, issued an order on June 30 changing the name of the Bois de Belleau to the "Bois de la Brigade de Marine." General Pershing also congratulated the Marines for this victory, calling the fight to capture the wood the "Gettysburg of the War."[53] It certainly marked the final turning of the tide. Many years later, General Bullard, no fan of the Marines after the Gibbons dispatch, wrote: "The Marines didn't 'win the war' here, but they saved the Allies from defeat. Had they arrived a few hours later I think that would have been the beginning of the end."[54]

Other notables, including French Premier Georges Clemenceau, added their own compliments on the Marines' achievement. In addition, the French Army awarded a unit citation to the 5th and 6th Marine Regiments, which entitled their members to wear the Fourragère, a braided cord in the green and red colors of the Croix de Guerre on their left shoulder.

The taking of Belleau Wood had been conceived by the senior commanders of the Allied corps, division and brigade as a minor affair, but it quickly had become so much more. On June 7, the commander of the German 7th Army issued a special order declaring any success by American forces would boost the morale of the Allies and prolong the war. "In the coming battles, therefore, it is not a question of the possession of this or that village or woods, insignificant in itself, it is a question of whether the Anglo-American claim that the American Army is the equal or even superior to the German Army is to be made good." A similar attitude took hold on the American side, from Pershing down to Harbord and his regimental commanders. Belleau Wood was no longer just a military objective; it was now a test of wills.[55]

While the achievement was great, so was the cost. The Marine brigade went into action at Chateau Thierry and Belleau Wood with 258 officers and 8,211 enlisted men. The butcher's bill for the battles around Chateau Thierry, Belleau Wood and Bouresches was 665 dead and 3,633 wounded for a total of 4,298 casualties.[56] In just three weeks of war, roughly half of all the Marines in France were either dead or wounded, including many veteran officers and NCOs. Many more battles lay ahead. Daly and the other "old timers" who remained would have to finish the job with replacements fresh from basic training.

The Marines also emerged from this battle with a reputation as ferocious fighters that neither the Army nor the Navy possessed, and a new nickname, "Devil Dogs." Legend has it that the Germans who

"Devil Dog" Dan Daly

fought at Belleau Wood referred to the Marines there as "Teufelhunde," in English "Devil Dogs." While some historians have continued to treat the legend as fact, others have dug deeper and debunked this story. They have pointed out that the Germans did not apply derogatory names to their adversaries in World War I. Historians also have noted that the term "teufelhunde" is not a common term in the German language. The closest one comes to the legend being fact is one German lieutenant who wrote in his diary that "the American Marines fought like devils." Some historians have suggested that the term originated in one of Floyd Gibbons' colorful dispatches, although no one has found that phrase in any of his dispatches. Other historians have said a more likely source is a Marine Corps recruiting poster created by artist Charles B. Falls around 1918 with the words "Teufel Hunden, German Nickname for U.S. Marines—Devil Dog Recruiting Station."[57]

Whatever the origins of this legendary phrase, it quickly became part of Marine Corps lore, and journalists and historians just as quickly attached it to "Devil Dog" Dan Daly.

Fourteen

The Third Medal of Honor

Reflecting on Daly's actions at Belleau Wood, his service record states: "[He] showed distinguished conduct in the face of the enemy at Lucy-le-Bocage; noted for his reckless daring and constant attention to [the] wants of his men; a peerless soldier of the old school."

Daly's superiors were so impressed by his heroic actions during the battle of Belleau Wood that they recommended him for an unprecedented third award of the Medal of Honor.[1] He was cited for four specific actions by Colonel Lee: "1st Sergeant Daly, 73rd (MG) Company, twice holder of the Medal of Honor, repeatedly performed deeds of valor and great service. On 5 June, he extinguished a fire in an ammunition dump at Lucy-le-Bocage. On 7 June, while the sector was under one of its heaviest bombardments, he visited all gun crews of his company, then posted over a wide portion of the front, cheering his men. On 10 June, singlehanded, he attacked an enemy machine-gun emplacement and captured it by use of hand grenades and his automatic pistol. On the same date, during enemy attack on Bouresches, he brought in wounded under fire. At all times, by his reckless daring, constant attention to the wants of his men, and his unquenchable optimism, he was a tower of strength until he was wounded by enemy shrapnel fire on 20 June."[2] General Bundy, the division commander, endorsed Lee's recommendation on 12 July.

Because the Marines were serving as part of the U.S. Army's 2nd Infantry Division, the recommendation was submitted through Army channels, per an order from Pershing to all AEF units serving in France, regardless of branch of service.

However, instead of the Medal of Honor, the Army presented Daly with the newly created Army Distinguished Service Cross. Daly's medal,

"Devil Dog" Dan Daly

DSC number 237, was pinned on during a parade and review ceremony behind the lines on Sunday, August 25, 1918. Some 5,000 troops were present, representing all U.S. divisions in France. Daly was one of 38 officers and men of the 4th Marine Brigade decorated with the DSC that day for actions taken at Belleau Wood in June and Soissons in July. Major General Hunter Liggett, commanding I Corps, was there as Pershing's representative and personally pinned on the medals. Major General Joseph Dickman, commanding IV Corps, also attended.[3]

The DSC had been authorized by Congress on July 9, at the request of Pershing, Secretary of War Newton Baker and President Wilson. They had seen a need to create heroes to sustain public support for the war. The awarding of medals for valor in battle would achieve this purpose. The same act of Congress, 10 U.S.C. Section 3741–3756, that established the DSC also created the Distinguished Service Medal and the Citation Star (also known as the Silver Star Citation, which later became the Silver Star Medal). The Navy followed suit the following year. The Navy Cross and Navy Distinguished Service Medal were created by an act of Congress (Public Law 65-253) on February 4, 1919. Eligibility for all of these decorations was made retroactive to April 6, 1917, the day Congress declared war.

The most frequently cited explanation for denying Daly a third Medal of Honor is that someone in the Army chain of command in France decided that no one should have three Medals of Honor.[4] If this was the basis for the decision, it contravenes the July 9 act of Congress, which specifically contemplated multiple awards of even this highest of medals. Section 3744 stated that no actual medal would be presented for any additional award, but any successive award would be recognized by "a suitable bar or other device" to be worn with the first medal. Today, multiple awards of a medal are recognized with an oak leaf cluster pinned to the medal's ribbon.

While it is plausible that some Army official thought a third medal would be unseemly and blocked it, there is another possibility. It seems likely that inter-service rivalry between the Army and Marines led the Army brass to deny Daly a third medal. This is where Gibbons' dispatch, sent off to the Army censors in Paris just before the attack on Belleau Wood, comes in.

Pershing had imposed strict regulations on press reports from the war zone. Among the restrictions was a ban on identifying any military unit in a dispatch. This meant the readers back home knew only that the

FOURTEEN—The Third Medal of Honor

AEF was engaged in a particular battle, but not which regiment, division or corps. The military purpose, of course, was to prevent the enemy from learning any useful information from press reports. It also had the effect of keeping the focus on the AEF as a whole and on Pershing. To ensure compliance, all dispatches had to be approved and, if necessary, edited by Army censors in Paris.

In his dispatch of June 6, Gibbons didn't name a specific unit, but he did write "I am up front and entering Belleau Wood with the U.S. Marines." Because there was only a single Marine brigade in all of France, this vague reference was actually quite specific, and thus would normally have been censored.

However, word of Gibbons' wounding spread quickly, including to the censors in Paris. One of them was an ex-newspaperman and old pal of Gibbons. When Gibbons didn't show up at any of the aid stations that afternoon, his friend the censor assumed he had been killed and let what he thought was Gibbons' last dispatch go out uncut. It was intended as a benign tribute to Gibbons, but it ignited a firestorm of jealousy that turned into a nasty feud between the Army and the Marine Corps. The headline that appeared above Gibbons' story in the June 6 *Chicago Daily Tribune* read: "U.S. Marines Smash Hun, Gain Glory in Brisk Fight on the Marne." The following day, the *Tribune* headline read: "Marines Win Hot Battle, Sweep Enemy from Heights Near Thierry." Other papers followed suit and suddenly stories about the Marines engaged in a desperate battle around Chateau Thierry flooded the newsstands nationwide. Because the censors cut any mention of any unit after that, no Army unit received any credit. Hence, when the battle was over, Americans were left with the mistaken impression that the Marines alone had saved Paris and won the battle. The Army was livid. From the soldiers in the trenches to the generals at headquarters, they blamed the Marines. They accused the Marines of being publicity hounds, even though it was the Army censor's fault for not editing the dispatch.[5]

As evidence of the Army's upset, when French Premier Georges Clemenceau later visited the 2nd Infantry Division's headquarters to commend the unit for saving Paris, none of the officers from the 4th Marine Brigade, including the Army's own General Harbord, were invited to attend the event. The next day, when Harbord learned of the snub, he protested but was ignored.

In addition, when French General Degoutte issued his order renaming the Bois de Belleau for the Marines, Pershing's headquarters tried,

"Devil Dog" Dan Daly

and failed, to have the order rescinded. Finally, when it came time after the war to write the official history of the AEF, the Pershing-led commission downgraded the fighting at Belleau Wood from a battle to a local engagement, merely a phase in the larger Aisne-Marne defense.[6]

The feud did not abate after the war but continued in large ways and small for decades. As an example, in 1942 General Douglas MacArthur declined to recommend the 4th Marine Regiment for a Presidential Unit Citation for its heroic stand in the Philippines. When President Franklin Roosevelt asked him why, MacArthur replied, "The Marines received enough credit during the last war."[7]

Given that back story, it seems not only plausible but probable that the feud played a role in denying Daly the third medal. In fact, it seems likely given the scarcity of Medals of Honor given to Marines for their epic fight at Belleau Wood. Only one Marine got the Army Medal of Honor for actions at or around Belleau Wood. Ernest Janson (aka Charles Hoffman) received it for repelling the 12-man counterattack on Hill 142. Although Hill 142 was part of the Belleau Wood battle, the words "Belleau Wood" do not appear in the citation, just the words "near Chateau Thierry."

Five days after the Armistice was signed on November 11, 1918, Pershing created a panel of officers from his headquarters to make recommendations on who should receive the Medal of Honor. The panel reviewed all recommendations for the Medal of Honor as well as all awards of the Distinguished Service Cross. The panel then compiled a list, with supporting material, of those individuals deemed worthy of the Medal of Honor and the DSC. This package was submitted to Pershing, who made the final selection.[8]

As someone who had already received the Distinguished Service Cross and been recommended for the Medal of Honor, Daly was among those whose actions were reviewed by the AEF panel.

By November 23, 1918, Pershing's headquarters had received 24 recommendations for award of the Medal of Honor and approved four. (The four awardees were Captain George C. McMurty, Private Thomas C. Neibaur, Major Charles Whittlesey and First Lieutenant Samuel Woodfill. All of these awards involved Army actions in the Meuse-Argonne offensive in October 1918. Whittlesey and McMurty led the "Lost Battalion.") Between November 1918 and July 1919, Pershing approved an additional 78 awards of the Medal of Honor. Of the 102 total, 95 went to Army personnel and seven to Marines.[9]

146

FOURTEEN—The Third Medal of Honor

Daly with Gunnery Sergeant Ernest Janson in 1919. Janson earned the Medal of Honor for his actions at Hill 142 the first day at Belleau Wood (Marine Corps History Division Archive).

Daly was not among the seven Marines selected to receive the Medal of Honor.

In addition to Ernest Janson, the following Marines received the medal for actions in World War I:

Louis Cukela, gunnery sergeant, 66th Company, 1st Battalion, 5th

"Devil Dog" Dan Daly

Regiment. Citation: "When his company, advancing through a wood, met with strong resistance from an enemy strong point, Sgt. Cukela crawled out from the flank and made his way toward the German lines in the face of heavy fire, disregarding the warnings of his comrades. He succeeded in getting behind the enemy position and rushed a machine-gun emplacement, killing or driving off the crew with his bayonet. With German hand grenades he then bombed out the remaining portion of the strong point, capturing 4 men and 2 damaged machineguns." The action took place on July 18, 1918, at Villers-Cotteret, south of Soissons. He also received a battlefield commission.

John J. Kelly, private, 78th Company, 2nd Battalion, 6th Marine Regiment. Citation: "For conspicuous gallantry and intrepidity above and beyond the call of duty, in action against the enemy at Blanc Mount Ridge, France, October 3, 1918. Private Kelly ran through our own barrage one hundred yards in advance of the front line and attacked an enemy machine-gun nest, killing the gunner with a grenade, shooting another member of the crew with his pistol, and returned through the barrage with eight prisoners." Pershing personally presented Kelly with the Army Medal of Honor while he was serving in the Army of Occupation.

Matej Kocak, sergeant, 66th Company, 1st Battalion, 5th Marine Regiment, Citation: "When the advance of his battalion was checked by a hidden machine-gun nest, he went forward alone, unprotected by covering fire from his own men, and worked in between the German positions in the face of fire from enemy covering detachments. Locating the machine-gun nest, he rushed it and with his bayonet drove off the crew. Shortly after this he organized 25 French colonial soldiers who had become separated from their company and led them in attacking another machine-gun nest, which was also put out of action." This action took place July 18, 1918, at Villers Cotteret, south of Soissons, France. He was killed in action October 4, 1918, in the battle for Blanc Mount Ridge.

John Henry Pruitt, corporal, 78th Company, 2nd Battalion, 6th Marine Regiment, Citation: "For conspicuous gallantry and intrepidity at the risk of his life above and beyond the call of duty in action with the enemy at Blanc Mont Ridge, France, October 3, 1918. Corporal Pruitt single-handedly attacked two machine-guns, capturing them and killing two of the enemy. He then captured 40 prisoners in a dugout nearby. This gallant soldier was killed soon afterward by shell-fire while he was sniping the enemy." Pruitt was killed in action on his 22nd birthday.

Rounding out the seven Marines who received the Medal of Honor,

Fourteen—The Third Medal of Honor

two Marine aviators, pilot **Ralph Talbot** and his gunner **Robert Guy Robinson**, were awarded the Medal of Honor for their actions over the Meuse-Argonne in October 1918.

While far more soldiers than Marines received the Medal of Honor in World War I, it must be noted that far more soldiers than the Marines engaged in combat in World War I. However, it is also noteworthy that only Janson received the Medal of Honor for Belleau Wood. The other four Marines who received the medal for ground combat all did so for actions elsewhere. Two occurred near Soissons on July 18, and the other two at Blanc Mount Ridge on October 3. Is it really possible that no other Marine's actions during the savage 21-day battle for Belleau Wood met Pershing's requirements for the medal? Or is it more likely that Pershing and his review panel allowed jealousy to cloud their judgment?

Other facts also raise questions about how Pershing and his panel went about this task. As previously mentioned, Daly received the Army DSC for his actions at Belleau Wood. Many other prominent individuals in the 4th Brigade also received the DSC. They included three of the seven battalion commanders at Belleau Wood: Benjamin Berry, Maurice Shearer and Julius Turrill. The Army presented the next highest decoration in the pyramid, the Distinguished Service Medal, to James Harbord, John Lejeune, Wendell Neville and Frederic Wise. However, the other three battalion commanders at Belleau Wood—Thomas Holcomb, John Hughes and Berton Sibley—received neither a DSC nor a DSM. Where is the logic in that? The omission of Sibley from either of these honors is particularly striking, given his vital role in the June 6 attack.

Such omissions led to complaints from senior Marine Corps and Navy officers up the chain of command. In response, Secretary of the Navy Josephus Daniels convened his own panel of officers to review the heroics by Navy and Marine Corps personnel during the war. The review panel of nine retired senior officers met for seven months before Secretary Daniels abruptly dissolved it in October 1919 before it had completed its work. Daniels largely ignored the recommendations he had received so far from the panel and drew up his own list. It was a disaster, particularly Daniels' intention to award the Navy's Distinguished Service Medal to the captain of every ship that had been sunk during the war, while passing over many of the captains whose ships had sunk *enemy* vessels. In the face of a public outcry, Daniels reconvened the panel he had dissolved but retained the final say. The panel made about 4,000 recommendations for medals, although in many cases for a lesser decoration than the one the man's commander had proposed. Daniels accepted most of the recommendations, raised some, reduced others.

This led to new complaints. During Congressional hearings on the issue in 1920, Marine Commandant Barnett testified that he did not recommend any Marine who served in France for any decorations. He said he believed he was barred by law from doing so because they had served under Army command.[10]

In the end, each of the five Marines listed above, who had been awarded the Army Medal of Honor for ground combat, received the Navy version of the medal as well. Some additional Navy officers and enlisted men also received the Navy Medal of Honor.

Daly was once again passed over for a third Medal of Honor. Instead, in late 1920 the retired Daly received the Navy Cross to go with his Army DSC. The wording of both citations is identical. There was no official explanation. Perhaps it was Washington politics this time. The Navy secretary may have felt it would look like a public rebuke of Pershing, who was now hailed as a national hero, if he gave Daly a higher decoration than he had already received from Pershing for the same actions.

The Navy did make up for the lack of any major decoration to the three battalion commanders at Belleau Wood who had not received a DSC or DSM. It awarded the Navy Cross to Holcomb, Hughes and Sibley. All three received the award for their actions at Belleau Wood.

In addition, the Navy awarded the Navy Cross to Berry, Shearer and Turrill, who had already received the Army DSC. Again, all three received this award for their actions at Belleau Wood. Wise was the only battalion commander at Belleau Wood who did not receive the Navy Cross. Instead, Wise received a Navy DSM to go with his Army DSM. However, both DSMs were for his performance at St. Mihiel with the Army's 59th Brigade, not at Belleau Wood with the Marines. Lejeune and Neville also received Navy DSMs to match their Army DSMs. The awards were for their overall performance during the war, not just Belleau Wood.

Finally, while no two acts of valor are identical, Daly's singlehanded attack on a machine gun emplacement and capture of several prisoners appears comparable to the actions of three of the five Marines who received the Army and Navy Medals of Honor. Likewise, his rescue of

Fourteen—The Third Medal of Honor

wounded Marines between the battle lines resembles the actions of five Navy medical aid men who received the medal. At this late date it is impossible to know with absolute certainty why Daly didn't receive his third medal. However, it appears such an award would have been fully justified.

Fifteen

Soissons

While Daly recovered from his wound and trained replacements, the 4th Marine Brigade was rushed into action once more. The destination this time was near the ancient crossroads town of Soissons, 62 miles northeast of Paris and 26 miles north of Belleau Wood. The result would be another "noble victory"[1] at another terrible cost.

On July 15, German Field Marshal Erich Ludendorff began two drives that would become the last German offensive of the war. The ultimate goal was to draw Allied reserves eastward toward Rheims in preparation for what Ludendorff hoped would be a final grand offensive far to the north in Flanders to win the war. The two drives began on either side of Rheims, a city 80 miles east-northeast of Paris where French kings had traditionally been crowned for 1,100 years. The eastern drive quickly ran into solid defenses and collapsed, but the western drive succeeded in pushing seven divisions across the Marne River east of Chateau Thierry. Only the stubborn defense of the U.S. 3rd Infantry Division, fighting in three directions, slowed the Germans. Allied reinforcements gradually brought the German drive to a halt.

The offensive had begun three days prior to a July 18 offensive French General Ferdinand Foch had planned to launch against the huge German salient created by the June offensive that had been halted at Chateau Thierry and Belleau Wood. Faced with this new German threat, Foch converted his offensive into a counteroffensive. Again, the objective was to reduce the German salient by pushing in on either side of the bowl and cut the main north-south road from Soissons to Chateau Thierry. If this main supply route could be cut, the Germans in the salient would be forced to beat a hasty retreat, hopefully triggering a broader withdrawal.

In preparation for the planned offensive, the U.S. 1st and 2nd Infantry Divisions had been assigned to the French 10th Army, headed by

FIFTEEN—Soissons

General Charles "The Butcher" Mangin, whose troops gave him the nickname after heavy losses during the 1917 Nivelle Offensive.[2] To preserve the element of surprise, Foch delayed sending the troops to their attack positions until the last minute. The 4th Marine Brigade was quartered about five miles southwest of Belleau Wood. On the evening of July 16, the Marines received orders to immediately move to the Forest of Retz, southwest of Soissons. Once again they endured a bone-jarring, sleepless night in the camions. Arriving late the following day in the old-growth forest, the Marines still had a 14-mile hike in preparation for the attack. They were given no time to rest but immediately began a march in three columns up a paved road for wheeled traffic and clay shoulders for those on foot. The clay shoulders turned to slippery slush in what became a steady downpour. Owing to the volume of vehicles and troops, the heavy rain and total darkness, which required each man to hold on to the coattail of the man in front of him, the march progressed at a dawdling pace of about one mile an hour. The Marines would later recall the agony of this march as a greater hardship than either Belleau Wood or Soissons.[3]

When they reached a staging area behind the front, they were told to wait there for further orders. They did not have long to wait. Just after midnight July 17–18, the 5th Regiment received orders to begin an immediate final march to get into attack position. It was still raining. As the time for the attack neared, the 5th Regiment had to double-time the last mile or so to be in position in time near Villers-Cotterêts. Some units went directly from double-timing in a column to deploying in attack formation and joining the assault. Tired after an all-day ride and all-night march, soaking wet, with empty bellies and nearly empty canteens, the Marines had one more cross to bear. By French Army directive, their machine guns were being transported as part of the regimental train. The guns were still somewhere in the rear and would not arrive in time for the attack. It would be July 19 before most of the machine guns could join the fight.[4]

The German salient into the Allied line was now a bowl stretching roughly 30 miles wide and 20 miles deep with its apex at Chateau Thierry. Soissons sat on the top left rim of the bowl. The 1st Infantry Division's starting position was on the upper left of the bowl, below Soissons. The 2nd Infantry Division was below the 1st with the 1st Moroccan Division sandwiched between them. The Moroccans were a highly regarded colonial unit both hated and feared by the Germans for their savage fighting ability. Several other American divisions were spread around the left side of the bowl, interspersed with French divisions of the French 6th, 9th and 10th armies. Both the 1st and 2nd Infantry divisions experienced the disorganized dash to the front. By contrast, the 1st Moroccan Division was already in place, this being their place in the Allied line before the offensive. The Moroccans simply had to pull in their flanks to make room for the Americans on either side of them for the attack.[5]

Adding to the muddle, a series of command changes had just occurred in the 2nd Division. Harbord had been promoted to major general on July 11 and replaced Bundy in command of the entire division on July 15.[6] With his elevation, Colonel Wendell Neville was named brigade commander, and his deputy, Lieutenant Colonel Logan Feland, took over the 5th Regiment. Lieutenant Colonel Harry Lee continued in command of the 6th Regiment.[7]

Harbord complained bitterly, both then and later, about being left out of the loop by the French planners and having to discover the whereabouts of his units in the 24 hours before the attack. "A division of twenty-eight thousand men…," he wrote in his memoir, "had been completely removed from the control of the responsible commander, and deflected by marching and by truck, through France to destination unknown to any of the authorities responsible either for its support, its safety, or its efficiency in the coming attack. The French Corps Commander and his staff were unable to state the points at which the division would be debussed or where orders could reach it which would move it promptly to its attack position. This was within thirty hours of a decisive battle. The only assistance the French Corps Headquarters was able to give was a liberal supply of maps and copies of the Corps Attack Order; though their Operations Officer offered to write my attack order for me, an offer which I declined with thanks, and perhaps a little ice in my voice. They said the division would undoubtedly be in place in the forest by Wednesday morning (July 17). I doubted it and said so."

At dawn on the 17th, Harbord began a hunt by motor car for the scattered units of his division. After finding part of the division's 23rd Infantry Regiment, he dispatched selected officers "in every direction to locate 2nd Division units and inform them where they should concentrate and where the division headquarters had been established."[8]

Sometime around dawn on the 18th (the exact time is in dispute; official accounts vary from 3:45 to 6:00 a.m.), the Allies unleashed a

FIFTEEN—Soissons

Marine Corps recruiting poster, 1918. "TeufelHunden" is German for Devil Dog. Legend has it that the Germans used the term at Belleau Wood to describe their Marine foes. However, many historians now discount this as the origin of this description of Marines.

rolling artillery barrage that moved forward at a rate of 100 meters every two minutes toward the German lines. The Allied troops moved out on a front two miles wide.⁹ The front line of the 2nd Division's advance consisted of Turrill's 1/5 and Keyser's 2/5 on the left, with Shearer's 3/5 in support; the Army's 9th Infantry Regiment in the middle and the Army's

23rd Infantry Regiment on the right. The 6th Marine Regiment was in reserve a mile and half to the rear.[10] Mostly they advanced in lines but here and there individual Marines ran ahead to take out machine gun emplacements singlehanded. Sergeants Louis Cukela and Matej Kocak of the 55th Company, 1/5, each performed this feat and received the Medal of Honor. The advance continued through the forest and onto a treeless plain with waist-high wheat, stone masonry villages and machine gun nests. There were no trenches but the plain was cut by four deep, marshy ravines that served as natural defenses.

The plan of attack called for the assault units to change direction after seizing various objectives as they advanced. On a map, this produced a planned route that looked like a slithering snake, meandering back and forth in an easterly direction. On the ground, however, this produced disorganization bordering on chaos as attacking units in all three 2nd Division regiments either advanced straight ahead when they should have turned, or else veered too far to the right or left. Soon, companies were straying into their neighboring units' routes of advance and becoming jumbled up. Compounding these challenges, the company commanders had no maps, just compass headings to direct their changes in direction.[11]

Despite these problems, all three regiments managed to keep advancing. Foch had indeed surprised the Germans and the advance proceeded quickly, although the Moroccan division found it difficult to keep pace with the American units on either side. This had the effect of leaving those neighboring American units exposed to enemy fire from their flanks. At times, the Allied troops found themselves taking fire from three sides at once, as well as a steady rain of German artillery shells from above. Given the troops' exhaustion after nearly 48 hours with no rest, no food and no clear idea of where they were, it is a wonder that the first day's attack achieved as much as it did. As they passed through the fields of mature wheat, many hungry Marines scraped the heads of the wheat through their fingers, caught the grain in their hands and downed the morsels. "It seemed to taste pretty good," recalled Merwin H. Silverthorn, a sergeant at Belleau Wood and a lieutenant at Soissons who became a lieutenant general during World War II.[12]

By the time the advance slowed to a halt for the night, the 2nd Division had gained more than five miles. It now held a line half a mile beyond the village of Vierzy, a major strong point located on one of the

FIFTEEN—*Soissons*

ravines that had been taken only after fierce fighting. In addition, the 2nd Division had bagged many German prisoners, machine guns and nearly all of the artillery of two German divisions.[13] That was in the plus column. On the negative side of the ledger, three of the division's four regiments had gone into the attack and by the end of the day none were fit to continue the fight. Their losses had been severe. As a result, a single regiment, the 6th Marines, would have to continue the attack on a front where three regiments abreast had advanced the day before. This time, there would be no element of surprise. The Soissons-to–Chateau Thierry road still lay at least two miles ahead.

Sizing up the first day's results with sardonic wit, First Lieutenant Elliott D. Cooke, leading a company in Keyser's 2/5, later wrote: "In one of the best-planned and most successful attacks of World War I, no two units jumped off at the same time. And once started, battalions crossed each other's boundaries, seized wrong objectives, and even broke up into small groups fighting wars of their own.... [I]f that was a sample of a coordinated attack, I feel sorry for anyone who has to lead men into an uncoordinated one."[14]

Overnight, the Germans brought up fresh troops, more machine guns and more artillery. At 7:30 a.m., the 6th Marines moved forward through the 5th Marines to prepare to advance. They passed bodies of dead Marines and Germans. Some looked like they were merely asleep; others more closely resembled "a heap of blood-soaked rags."[15] It was a harbinger of what was to come.

Hughes' 1/6 was on the right, Holcomb's 2/6 was on the left and Sibley's 3/6 was behind them in support. A rolling barrage was supposed to support the advance, but by 8:30 a.m. when the Marines began their attack, the barrage had already been fired. They had their machine guns now and a line of 28 slow-moving French tanks to lead them, but otherwise the Marines were on their own.[16] First Lieutenant Clifton Cates, leading a platoon in Holcomb's 2/6, would later recall: "It was a pretty sight to look out at that bunch of men in eight waves moving across the open wheat fields." However, he found the tanks more trouble than they were worth. Their sluggish pace slowed down the advance, and they were magnets for the enemy's big guns, which took an outsized toll of the Marines following close behind.[17]

The Germans wasted no time tearing into the waves of attackers. Historian George Clark described the scene in a nutshell. "As the Marines advanced, the 77s ate them up and the 105s tore up the ground,

Marines and tanks. Then the machine guns finished what the artillery hadn't accomplished."[18]

Private Carl Brannen in the 80th Company, 2/6, was in the midst of it. "I will never know how I went through that curtain of shells untouched," he later wrote. "I was black from the powder of the exploding shells. Most of my trousers was [sic] left in the barbed wire entanglements. At first I expected a counterattack and was prepared to come to my feet and sell myself as dearly as possible. The slaughter of my comrades had left a bad taste." No counterattack came but enemy machine guns kept him pinned down while enemy planes strafed anyone who moved. So Brannen played dead through the long hot afternoon until it was dark and he could slip away.[19]

The Marines had been ordered not to stop to aid any of their wounded comrades, lest the advance stall. As wave after wave moved forward, individual Marines stopped only long enough to pick up the rifle of one of the wounded and thrust it into the ground bayonet first to mark the location for the medical aid men behind them.[20] Soon a forest of upended rifles filled the field.

The Marines gained about a mile of ground during the first two hours of the attack, but there the advance sputtered to a halt as "men dropped like flies." A memorable message from Cates illustrates how dire the situation had become. All of the officers in the 96th Company, 2/6, had been wounded, including Cates, who nonetheless took command and continued the fight. "I have only two men out of my company and 20 out of some other company," he wrote. "We need support, but it is almost suicide to try to get it here as we are swept by machine gun fire and a constant barrage is on us. I have no one on my left and only a few on my right. I will hold."

The Marines had outrun their artillery support. They faced what one Marine later described as a "black curtain" of enemy shells 200 yards in front of the German lines. "The Germans had massed their artillery on a hill about three or four miles off in front of us," recalled Sergeant Gerald C. Thomas of Hughes' 1/6, a future general and assistant commandant of the Marine Corps. "It was all direct fire.... Our attack collapsed. The attack was over."[21]

The Germans also had air superiority over the battlefield and the planes of Hermann Goering's Flying Circus strafed the Marines as they flattened themselves on ground through the remainder of the day, unable either to advance or withdraw in daylight.

Fifteen—Soissons

At 3:45 p.m., Colonel Lee, leading the 6th Regiment, sent a message to his battalion commanders directing them to "dig in and hold our present line at all costs. No further advance will be made for the present." By this time, Lee was simply stating the obvious. He added his congratulations on the regiment's "gallant conduct in the face of severe casualties."[22]

Severe indeed. The 6th Marine Regiment began the battle with 2,450 officers and men, and ended 24 hours later with 1,300 of its men as casualties. Seventy percent of the two leading battalions, the 1/6 and 2/6, were dead, wounded or missing, as well as nearly 50 percent of the 3/6 in support. The 5th Marine Regiment fared somewhat better, but its casualties still totaled nearly 500.[23]

The 2nd Division was relieved by a French colonial division of Algerians during the night of July 19–20. As they pulled back, the Marines collected their wounded. They also buried their dead in shallow graves where they fell. They worked by moonlight, the flickering light from the burning tanks and the glare of German flares popping overhead. When the men reached the rear, they found the field kitchens waiting and had what for most of them was their first meal in four days.[24]

The 2nd Division came the closest to cutting the vital supply road between Soissons and Chateau Thierry. On July 19, two companies of Sibley' 3/6 were finally halted 700 yards shy of that objective.[25] The Germans could see the end game. Beginning that night, they pulled out of their bridgehead across the Marne River and began an orderly withdrawal out of the entire 30-mile-wide bowl above Chateau Thierry. The Allies kept the pressure on and by August 4 all of the gains made by the Germans since their May 27 attack across the Chemin des Dames had been erased. The planned final offensive in Flanders to end the war was canceled too.[26]

Once again the 2nd Division and its Marines were lavished with praise for their performance. Harbord issued a general order on July 21 passing along Pershing's "affectionate personal greetings," and noting the division's achievements: "Three thousand prisoners, eleven batteries of artillery, over a hundred machine guns, etc."[27]

Sixteen

St. Mihiel

Following the battle at Soissons, Harbord received a new assignment, to take charge and reorganize the poorly performing Service of Supply. Apparently Pershing could see that his former chief of staff's administrative ability outweighed his combat command skills.

Marine Corps Brigadier General John Lejeune, who had taken command of the 4th Brigade from Neville on July 26, succeeded Harbord as division commander on July 29 and Neville resumed command of the brigade. Lejeune had arrived in France on June 8 and briefly commanded an Army brigade in a quiet sector. On August 7, Lejeune was promoted to major general, Neville to brigadier general and Feland to colonel.

Feland continued to command the 5th Regiment. Turrill and Shearer remained in charge of the 1/5 and the 3/5, respectively, and Wise returned to lead the 2/5, replacing Keyser. Lee continued in command of the 6th Regiment. Holcomb and Sibley remained at the head of the 2/6 and 3/6, respectively, while Major Frederick A. Barker now led the 1/6 in place of Hughes.

"Johnny the Hard" Hughes was now in hospital. The effects of his gassing at Belleau Wood and broken bones from being shelled at Soissons, combined with an old wound from the Dominican Republic, had finally put him out of the war. He would be medically retired in July 1919.[1]

His replacement, Barker, had been serving as assistant provost marshal in Paris since arriving in France with the 3/5. Barker had joined the Marines in 1899 and risen to sergeant. Commissioned in 1904, he had fought at Haut de Cap and Fort Riviere in Haiti in 1915 and later been cited for valor at Las Trencheras and Guayacanes in the Dominican Republic in 1916.

There were a lot new faces in the brigade now. The brigade had

Sixteen—St. Mihiel

received 2,800 replacements after taking 4,300 casualties at Belleau Wood, and 1,000 replacements for the 2,000 casualties sustained at Soissons. That left the brigade short about 2,500 men.[2]

Some of the wounded began to return to help fill the ranks. One of them was Daly. Now recovered from his wound, he rejoined the 73rd Machine Gun Company on August 21.[3] Four days later he participated in the parade ceremony at which he received his DSC for Belleau Wood.

It would not be long before Daly and his fellow Marines were back in the thick of the action. The Allies had gone over to the offensive and they intended to keep it by hammering at multiple locations along the German defensive line. This created the opportunity that General Pershing had been seeking for months, a chance to show the Allies and the Germans that an American army could mount its own offensive, independent of the French or British. Pershing's target was the St. Mihiel Salient, a 25-mile-wide, 16-mile-deep bulge in the Allied line southeast of Verdun that had resisted reduction by the French since the early days of the war. Strategically, a successful attack on the salient could pose a threat to the German city of Metz, about 20 miles from the front line, and the vital rail supply line northwest to Sedan. Cutting that rail line would split the German armies in two.[4]

On July 24, General Foch, as Allied commander in chief, finally accepted Pershing's long-sought plan to wipe out the salient. After some further haggling between the Allied commanders, a revised plan was adopted on September 2. It called for erasing the salient using 15 American divisions totaling 550,000 men, and four French divisions with 110,000 men. Arrayed against them were about 100,000 German troops that the German high command rated as only second and third class.[5] They were adequate for holding a quiet sector, but not for repelling a sustained attack.

In the days leading up to the September 12 attack, the Marine Brigade had undergone a series of leadership changes. Turrill had been promoted to Feland's deputy at the 5th Regiment, and Lieutenant Colonel Arthur J. O'Leary had taken his place at the 1/5. O'Leary had joined the Marines during the Spanish-American War but Marine Corps muster lists don't show any combat assignment prior to World War I, just postings aboard the battleships *Oregon* and *West Virginia* and at various naval stations. He arrived in France in mid–1918 as a major with a replacement battalion and was promoted to lieutenant colonel shortly before taking command of the 1/5. Immediately after St. Mihiel, he was listed as "sick in hospital."

Major Robert E. Messersmith had taken over the 2/5 from Wise, who had been promoted to colonel and given command of the Army's 59th Infantry Regiment. Messersmith had been commissioned in the Marine Corps in 1909 and served in Cuba, Nicaragua and the Dominican Republic. As commander of the 78th Company, 2/6, he had been gassed at Belleau Wood and suffered a head wound at Soissons. Each time he had been hospitalized for about a month before returning to the brigade. In early September, he was promoted to major and took over the 2/5.

Lieutenant Colonel Holcomb became Lee's deputy at the 6th Regiment and handed over command of the 2/6 to Major Ernest C. Williams.[6] Williams was a difficult man and a hard drinker. He was known more for his aggressiveness than his judgment. He had earned the Medal of Honor in the Dominican Republic in 1916 for a daring but reckless attack. With only a dozen men, he had charged the fortress gate at San Francisco de Macoris. Eight of his men were shot down, but Williams pressed ahead with the remaining four men. He threw himself against the gate as it was being closed, forced his way in and within minutes he and his remaining men had subdued the garrison and freed about 100 prisoners.

Daly's 73rd Machine Gun Company also got a new skipper. Captain Swink, who had led the company through Belleau Wood and Soissons, was assigned as a machine gun school instructor at Langres. He had been awarded a Silver Star Citation and the Croix de Guerre. The new skipper was Captain George Shuler, the adjutant in the 3/5 under Berry and then Shearer. His tenure would be brief, from September 7 to 18, but it would encompass the 73rd's next battle.[7]

The Allies tried to conceal the movements of their troops into attack position around the St. Mihiel Salient. The troops marched by night and hid in woods during the day to escape detection by enemy aircraft. However, the Germans sleuthed out the planned attack and on September 11 began withdrawing their forces from the lightly defended salient.

Daly and the 73rd Machine Gun Company used mule-drawn carts to haul their guns, tripods and ammunition up to the jump-off line. Getting into position the final night was another nightmare for Daly and his men. A heavy rain turned the road into a quagmire, sucking at the men's boots and requiring them to lend their shoulders to keep the carts moving. Their assignment, along with the other machine gun companies in the division, was to add overhead fire to the artillery barrage at the moment the attack began. Once the infantry passed by them, each machine gun company was to link up with their respective battalion and join the advance.[8]

At 1 a.m., September 12, the Allied attack on the salient began with a heavy bombardment of the German frontline. At 5 a.m. the ground assault began and the machine gun companies each fired approximately 15,000 rounds to pave the way. Seven U.S. divisions charged into the east side of the salient between St. Mihiel on the left and Pont-a-Mousson on the right. The lead companies advanced in four waves at 50-yard intervals. At the same time, two U.S. divisions thrust into the upper west side of the salient with the goal of sealing the top of this pocket and bagging a bevy of prisoners. French forces attacked the nose of the salient to pin down the enemy troops there. The timing of the attack caught the Germans in an awkward position. They had begun pulling out their big guns and supplies, and they were thus deprived of vital artillery support at this critical moment.[9]

The 2nd Division was on the east side of the salient, in the very center of the seven U.S. divisions there. The 89th Division was on its left and the 5th Division on its right. This was the first major combat operation for either of these divisions. The 2nd Division's objective was Thiaucourt, a town about five miles from the front line in a horseshoe bend of and on the north bank of the Rupt de Mad River. A second objective was the high ground near Jaulny, a town a mile northeast of Thiaucourt.

The division's 3rd Army Brigade led the advance, with the 23rd Infantry Regiment on the left and the 9th Infantry Regiment on the right. The 4th Marine Brigade followed. Barker's 1/6, supported by Daly and the 73rd Machine Gun Company, followed the 23rd on the left to protect the left flank. Shearer's 3/5 followed the 9th and guarded the right flank. The other Marine battalions were instructed to stay a thousand yards behind the unit ahead of them.

The 2nd Division attack across rolling hills dotted with woods began on a mile-and-a-half front between Limey and Remenauville. The division was supported by 45 French tanks. As the attack developed the 5th Regiment had trouble keeping pace with the 23rd Infantry. This led Neville to push Feland to speed up, and Feland to likewise press Shearer. Adding to Shearer's problems, two of his companies became "lost" and ended up in advance of the two companies they were supposed to be behind in the advance. Barker and the 1/6 with Daly's 73rd Machine Gun Company encountered no such problems.[10]

By noon, the 3rd Brigade had advanced through Thiaucourt and by 5 p.m. it was nearing Jaulny. The attack halted for the night on its first-day's objective and the field kitchens came up to provide a hot meal to the troops.

The next morning, September 13, the advance continued as before and continued north of Jaulny. Later that day, the U.S. 1st and 26th Divisions linked up at Vigneulles, closing the top of the pocket. Despite the speed of the advance, many of the Germans in the salient had already fled north. For its part, the 2nd Division captured 118 guns and 3,300 prisoners.[11]

That night, the 4th Brigade passed through the 3rd Brigade and took over the lead. The next day the Marines continued pushing the Germans back. Neville directed the 5th and 6th Marines to send out company-size patrols to probe the woods ahead for the German defenses.

On September 15, two companies of Barker's 1/6 advanced through the Bois de la Montagne, a W-shaped wood roughly 2,000 yards wide and 1,500 yards deep, to its northern edge. Colonel Lee instructed Williams and the 2/6, to move to the southern edge of the woods to provide support for the two companies. Despite warnings from his scout officer that the woods had not been cleared of Germans, Williams advanced in a column of twos with himself at the head of the column on horseback and rode into a machine gun ambush in a ravine in the woods. The battalion became disorganized and split into two groups. The lead unit, the 80th Company, was cut off, surrounded and pinned down. German troops attacked it from two sides but were beaten back. Finally, other elements of the 2/6 advanced and rescued the 80th from the trap.[12]

Barker's 1/6 advanced to support Williams' 2/6 and both battalions became scattered in the foggy woods. In the resulting confusion, Barker's battalion found itself divided on either side of Williams' battalion, which was taking heavy fire and had to be reinforced by elements of Sibley's 3/6. The German resistance stiffened and Williams called in artillery to soft it up.

Daly and the 73rd Machine Gun Company were in the thick of the action. Advancing in support of Barker's 1/6, he and his men fearlessly exposed themselves to enemy fire to set up their guns in the open and deliver enfilade fire that broke up a powerful German counterattack within 100 yards of the American lines.[13] Two of Daly's gunners, Corporals Lyle C. Houchins and Casey V. Loomis,[14] earned both the DSC and the Navy Cross for their valor, while Sergeant Hildor B. Ellison received a Silver Star Citation and the French Croix de Guerre.

At dusk that evening, the Germans' bombarded the front line of the 6th Regiment and launched a ground assault on the left flank. Barker's 1/6 and Daly's 73rd Machine Gun Company beat back the attack. The 4th Brigade was then relieved and moved to the rear. From there, they moved by train to Chalons, 15 miles south of Suippes in the Champagne region between Rheims and Verdun to prepare for their next fight. Unfortunately, relief came too late for Major Sibley, leading the 3/6. He was wounded by shrapnel and gassed on September 16. His long recovery put him out of the war and he would soon be medically retired. In recognition of his exemplary service, he was promoted to colonel in retirement.

After St. Mihiel, Captain Shuler left the 73rd Machine Gun Company and Captain Reginald Carman MacKnight Peirce took command of the company. Peirce had been a lieutenant in the company since its inception back at Quantico. He had seen action at Belleau Wood, Soissons and St. Mihiel, and been awarded a Silver Star Citation. He was a wealthy adventurer with an interesting personal history. Born in 1887 in New York City, his stepfather, John Peirce, whose surname he took, was a prominent New Yorker whose family owned a granite quarry business in Maine. Known as "the granite king," his construction company built many large-scale infrastructure projects, including New York's first subway system. In 1906, he built a posh residence in a tony row of townhouses across from Manhattan's St. Patrick's Cathedral.[15] Reginald Peirce graduated from Yale University in 1909 and went to work on Wall Street as an insurance broker, although he listed his occupation as "contractor" on a 1914 passport application. On his 1917 draft registration form, he listed five years as a private in the New York National Guard. On his Marine Corps enlistment form, he included service in the Mexican Punitive Expedition in 1916 and the British Army in 1914–15, probably as an ambulance driver to avoid a conflict with U.S. neutrality laws. He joined the U.S. Marine Corps in July 1917, received a commission, and reported to the 73rd Machine Gun Company at Quantico that same month.[16]

The Marine casualties at St. Mihiel were light, at least compared to

"Devil Dog" Dan Daly

Belleau Wood and Soissons. The Marine Brigade suffered 132 dead and some 600 wounded. The majority of these were from Williams' firefight in the Bois de la Montagne.

Casualties for the 2nd Division were 195 dead, 1,041 wounded, 23 gassed and 292 missing for a total 1,552. This was only a third the toll at Soissons. The next battle would be more like the first two in cost and intensity.[17]

Seventeen

Blanc Mont Ridge

At an elevation of just 200 meters,[1] Blanc Mont Ridge is not an imposing terrain feature by itself. However, because the surrounding area is a gently rolling plain dotted with woodlots, the ridge dominates that part of the Champagne Region 110 miles northeast of Paris. From atop the ridge, the twin towers of Rheims Cathedral 26 miles to the west and the lofty pines of the Argonne Forest 20 miles to the east are visible through field glasses. It is a perfect artillery observation post. No attacking force could approach without being seen at a great distance. The southern approach slopes gently upward for more than a mile, providing the crescent-shaped ridge's defenders with unparalleled fields of direct and flanking fire. It is a killing ground, and a great many French soldiers died trying in vain to capture the two-mile-long massif.[2]

Blanc Mont in French means White Mountain. It is named for the chalky limestone subsoil of this region that becomes a gleaming white when the topsoil is scraped or blasted off. The ends of the ridge curve south toward the route of the American advance. Blanc Mont is on the left end of the ridge and Hill 210 is on the right end. Scrub pines cover parts of the ridge.

The Germans seized Blanc Mont Ridge in the first days of the war in 1914 and used the intervening four years to good advantage, honeycombing it with a network of tunnels, caves and dugouts capable of withstanding bombardment. Artillery lined the reverse slope, ready to pummel any attacker foolish enough to test the defenses. A maze of trenches, blockhouses, machine gun emplacements and barbed wire infested the forward slope.

Into this perfect hell stepped the AEF. As General Pershing prepared to launch his offensive between the Argonne Forest and the Meuse River in September 1918, the French high command asked him to lend them two American divisions for their attack in the Champagne Region,

"Devil Dog" Dan Daly

Pershing was in a buoyant mood, having finally secured a major separate offensive for his army, and readily agreed. He assigned the experienced 2nd Infantry Division and the untested 36th Infantry Division, a National Guard unit from Texas and Oklahoma, to the French 4th Army.

A rumor reached Major General Lejeune, commanding the 2nd Division, through his chief of staff that the French planned to break up the division and add its two brigades to two French divisions. Without confirming this rumor, Lejeune met with General Henri Gouraud, commander of the 4th Army, to learn if this was true. Gouraud took the opportunity to outline the problem he faced in his own offensive, namely the need to capture Blanc Mont Ridge. As he explained it, if the Allies could take the ridge and the town of St. Etienne 4,000 yards beyond it, the Germans would be forced to withdraw nearly 20 miles to the Aisne River. This would set up the Allies for an attack aimed at cutting the vital German rail supply line between Mézières, Sedan and Metz. Unfortunately, he said, the French 4th Army was too worn down to achieve this goal. Taking Gouraud's not-so-subtle hint, Lejeune said, "General, if the 2nd Division is kept together as a unit and is allowed to attack on a narrow front, I am confident it can take Blanc Mont Ridge in a single assault." It was only then that Gouraud informed Lejeune that he had no intention of breaking up the 2nd Division, but he would happily accept Lejeune's offer to attack Blanc Mont Ridge. Lejeune had been played and he knew it, but he couldn't withdraw the offer.[3]

General Gouraud and his staff proposed a frontal attack on the ridge by the 2nd Division with a supporting assault by the French 21st Division on the Americans' immediate left. Lejeune and his staff looked at the plan and concluded it was suicidal. Rather than a frontal attack on the center of the ridge, they came up with an eye-popping alternative. They would split the 2nd Division in two. Each brigade would advance on a one-mile front, with a mile-wide gap between the two brigades at the starting point. The 4th Brigade Marines would drive northeast against the left flank of the ridge while the 3rd Brigade soldiers would attack northwest against the right flank. This would allow each brigade to avoid the German strong-points in the center and reduce the effectiveness of flanking fire from the horns of the crescent. Once the two brigades linked up at the ridge, they would turn and wipe out the bypassed strong-points in the center. While the French were dubious, they accepted the plan. After all, it was the Americans who would be charging into a slaughterhouse.

SEVENTEEN—Blanc Mont Ridge

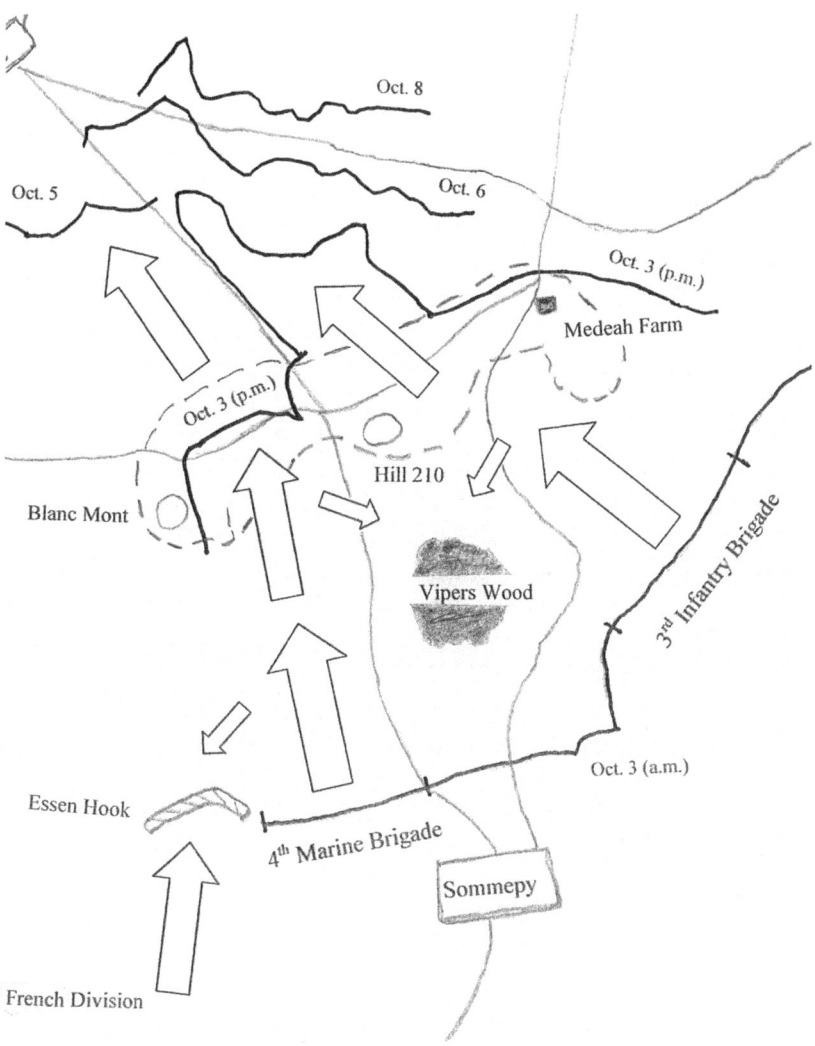

Map of the Marine battle for Blanc Mont Ridge, 1918. The Marine Brigade attack began on the lower left, the Army Brigade on the right. The dotted-line in the middle of the map indicates the position of the ridgeline, stretching from Blanc Mont to Medeah Farm. Once the American forces reached the ridge, they turned to seize the enemy defense between them, including Vipers Wood. The Marines also had to capture the enemy position at Essen Hook after a French division failed to do so, leaving the Marines exposed to flanking fire (author's map).

"Devil Dog" Dan Daly

As Lejeune prepared the 2nd Division for this battle, Neville continued to lead the Marine brigade; Feland, the 5th Regiment; and Lee the 6th Regiment. However, three battalions had new commanders. In the 5th Regiment, Major George Hamilton had replaced O'Leary[4] in charge of the 1/5. Hamilton had led the 1/5's 49th Company with great distinction through the fighting at Belleau Wood, Soissons and St. Mihiel. Messersmith still led the 2/5 while Major Henry Larsen took command of the 3/5, replacing Shearer, who was in school at Langres in October and then assigned to division headquarters as assistant chief of staff. Larson had been the battalion adjutant and had briefly led the 3/5 after Berry's wounding at Belleau Wood. In the 6th Regiment, Barker and Williams still led the 1/6 and 2/6, respectively. Major George Shuler, formerly the 5th Regiment's adjutant at Belleau Wood and Soissons and Daly's C.O. at St. Mihiel, had replaced the wounded Sibley at the helm of the 3/6.[5]

There was also a leadership change in Daly's 73rd Machine Gun Company. Captain Peirce, the company commander, was in school at Langres during the battle for Blanc Mont Ridge. First Lieutenant George R. Jackson would lead the company through the battle with Daly as his first sergeant. Jackson had been the adjutant in Sibley's 3/6 at Belleau Wood and had volunteered to help deliver a truckload of ammunition under fire to the Marines at Bouresches. He would receive the Crox de Guerre with star for his performance at Blanc Mont Ridge.

The French began their Champagne offensive between Rheims and the Argonne Forest on September 26, the same day Pershing launched his Meuse-Argonne offensive. In the Blanc Mont Ridge area, the French were assigned to capture the German trenches, known as the Essen Hook, on the Marines' left flank near the jump-off line. The Hook bent around a hill 500 yards inside the French division's sector. It was supposed to be taken before the U.S. assault began, but the Germans were still in place when the Americans launched their attack on the ridge.

As the regiments marched toward the jump-off trenches below Blanc Mont Ridge, Daly got a good look at the total devastation that four years of modern warfare had wrought on the French countryside. The previous battlegrounds at Belleau Wood, Soissons and St. Mihiel had been almost pristine at the outset compared to what lay before him now. The village of Sommepy, just south of the jump-off line, was reduced to charred rubble. Farther north, he saw a moonscape of craters, bleached bones and body parts jutting out of the ground, rotting carcasses of horses, shell-torn trenches reeking of gas and death, and seemingly endless coils of rusted barbed wire.[6]

The 2nd Division began its attack at 5:50 a.m., October 3. Each brigade attacked in column of battalions. In the 4th Brigade, the 6th Regiment was on the left and the 5th Regiment was on the right. Each of the regiments was supported by a company of 12 French tanks. Unfortunately, the tanks proved largely ineffective in this fight.

On the left, Williams' 2/6 led off, supported by the 81st Machine Gun Company, followed by Barker's 1/6 with Daly and the 73rd Machine Gun Company, and Larsen's 3/6 with the 15th Machine Gun Company. Each of Daly's company's three platoons was assigned to one of the 1/6's infantry companies. The 1st Platoon advanced with the 74th Company, the 2nd Platoon with the 75th Company, and the 3rd Platoon with the 78th Company.

On the right, Messersmith's 2/5 led off, supported by the 23rd Machine Gun Company, followed by Shuler's 3/5 with the 77th Machine Gun Company, and Hamilton's 1/5 with the 8th Machine Gun Company.[7]

As he prepared to lead his company forward in the first wave, Lieutenant Clifton Cates, in Williams' 2/6, recalled seeing a good omen loom out of the early morning mist. "It was a double rainbow and went from the eastern horizon to the western horizon." While the rainbow proved to be a good omen for Cates, it was the last pleasant sight many Marines would ever see.

Waiting in the trenches to go forward with Barker's 1/6, Daly did his best to buck up the spirits of his men, many of them replacements for whom this battle would be their first combat. No flowery speeches for Daly, just a few simple words to focus their minds for the task ahead. Things like: Remember your training. Make every shot count. Hit 'em hard.

A heavy artillery barrage pounded the German frontline positions for five minutes before the troops went over the top. Then a rolling barrage began. It moved forward at the slow pace of 100 yards every four minutes. Once the barrage moved 300 yards beyond each objective, the artillery would maintain a curtain of fire at that position for 30 minutes before moving on again. This would break up any counterattack.

The Germans responded with phosphorus shells, which showered the immediate area with fiercely flaming particles that ignited clothing and burned through flesh.

"Devil Dog" Dan Daly

All along the line, the sergeants blew their whistles, the officers shouted "Follow me," and the Marines and soldiers of the 2nd Division stepped off toward Blanc Mont Ridge.

"Wave after wave, the 6th went forward," recalled Lieutenant John Thomason, Jr., of the 5th Regiment. "For a moment the sun shone through the murk, near the horizon, a smoldering red sun, banded like Saturn, and all the bayonets gleamed like blood. Then the cloud closed again."[8]

The Marines walked as close behind the rolling barrage as they could without getting hit by it. This enabled them to fall upon the German defenders before many of them were able to climb out of their bunkers and man their machine guns. As the Marines closed in with their bayonets, many German gunners threw up their hands and surrendered. Those who fled to the rear tended to be chopped down by the rolling barrage.

Both brigades advanced nearly two miles behind the barrage and moved up to the sloping flanks of the ridge by 8:30 a.m. In less than three hours, the Yanks had done what the *Poilus* had found impossible to do for four years. As the Marines closed in on the ridge, they narrowed their front and the 5th Regiment fell in behind the 6th Regiment.[9]

However, the failure of the French to capture the Essen Hook subjected the Marines to flanking fire from that fortified position. As a result, the 6th Regiment took fire from both its left and front. The Marines went to work to knock down the fire from the left. At the same time, individual Marines exercised initiative to take out machine gun emplacements holding up the advance to the front. Private John Kelly ran through his own barrage, killed a gun crew and returned through the barrage with eight prisoners. Similarly, Corporal John Pruitt knocked out two machine gun emplacements and returned with 40 prisoners from an enemy dugout. Both Kelley and Pruitt would receive the Medal of Honor for their brave deeds. Sadly, Pruitt was killed an hour later by enemy shell-fire. Squads of Marines cleaned out other emplacements.

"We started over in a pretty formation," recalled Lieutenant James Sellers, skipper of the 78th Company, 2/6, that included both Kelly and Pruitt, "but the fight soon degenerated into a sort of free for all."[10]

Williams' 2/6, leading the advance, progressed beyond the tree-lined crest to the road along the ridge between Blanc Mont on the left and Medeah Farm on the right. Barker's 1/6 then slipped around to

SEVENTEEN—Blanc Mont Ridge

the right and linked up with the 3rd Brigade's 23rd Infantry Regiment after that regiment had passed through the 9th Infantry Regiment.

The 1/6, next in column behind the 2/6, arrived at Blanc Mont Ridge at 9 a.m. Daly and the officers of the 73rd Company organized a front line along the west fork of the St. Etienne–Sommepy Road. In addition to the 73rd's complement of machine guns, they deployed three machine guns and a *minnewerfer*, all captured from the enemy.[11] A *minnewerfer* was a type of short range mortar on wheels that was intended to be used by engineers to clear obstacles, such as blockhouses and barbed wire obstacles.

Within a short time on the ridge, Daly and his men looked like ghostly apparitions. The chalk soil clung to their clothes, cloaking the men in a sticky white powder from helmet to boots.[12]

While the Marines on the right flank were in a good position, the same could not be said of those on the left. The French 21st Division had not even left its trenches and the Marines were still taking heavy fire from their exposed left flank.

One section of Daly's 73rd Machine Gun Company was sent to cover the 6th Regiment's exposed left flank until the 5th Regiment's 43rd Company arrived at 4 p.m. to assume this role.

Hamilton's 1/5, the tail-end unit in the Marine column of battalions, now went to work to eliminate the threat from the Essen Hook. Captain Leroy Hunt led his 17th Company through a covered trench to within 800 yards of the Hook. He then deployed machine guns to suppress fire from the German guns in the Hook while he moved closer with two platoons. They then charged across the final 300 yards from two different directions to finally silence this deadly outpost.[13]

Hunt's 17th Company stormed the Essen Hook, capturing it around 10:30 a.m. The Marines then handed over their prisoners to the French, who had finally come up, and joined the fight for the ridge. That afternoon, the French lost the Essen Hook to a German counterattack and the enemy fire on the Marines' left resumed.[14]

Although the 6th Regiment Marines were on the ridge, they did not control it. The Germans' defensive network allowed them to pop up out of caves and tunnels to fire at the Marines from all directions. Throughout the day, various Marine unit commanders reported that they had reached their objectives and taken the ridge. However, confusion about their locations meant it would be more days before the entire ridge would truly be in Allied hands.

With the French continuing to lag behind, the Marine regiments had to contend with a mile-and-a-half of their left flank exposed to enemy fire.[15] Adding to this problem, Messersmith had orders to link up with the French. As he shifted the 2/5 southwest trying to find the French, he opened a gap between his battalion and Williams 2/6 on his right. The Germans moved into this gap, increasing the pressure on the flanks of the two Marine battalions. Shuler's 3/6 moved up to close this gap even as Messersmith's situation became more precarious.

Meanwhile, Larsen's 3/5, second behind Messersmith's 2/5 in the column of battalions, continued its advance up the slope, and Hamilton's 1/5, bringing up the rear of the column, shifted northwest, extending the 2/5's line even farther to the left. As a result of these dislocations caused by the absence of the French, the 2nd Division's front extended one-third of a mile into the French zone. Finally, the French corps commander gave up waiting for the French 21st Division to move up and ordered the French 170th Division to advance and support the Marines' left flank, which it did.

Despite this infusion of French firepower on the Marines' left, by early afternoon neither the 4th Brigade nor the 3rd Brigade was in any position to advance further that day. This situation was apparently lost on headquarters. Lieutenant Colonel Earl Ellis, the 4th Brigade adjutant, issued orders for the 5th Regiment to pass through the 6th Regiment and continue the advance. The 5th was to move up the road that ran northwest toward St. Etienne, which was located about 4,000 yards beyond Blanc Mont Ridge. The immediate objective was a line of trenches about 600 yards southeast of St. Etienne.[16]

Determined to follow orders, Feland ordered Messersmith and the 2/5 to lead this new advance. However, Messersmith was in the midst of a firefight on the Marines' left flank and in no position to launch a fresh attack northward. At about 3 p.m., Messersmith sent a desperate message to Feland, advising him that he had lost contact with two of his four companies. Nor was Messersmith the only battalion commander who didn't know where some of his units were. Given the general confusion, the proposed continuation of the attack on October 3 was cancelled.

Meanwhile, the 3rd Brigade's 23rd Infantry Regiment had outrun all other units and was now within a few hundred yards of St. Etienne. However, the Germans fought back fiercely with artillery and machine gun fire, inflicting heavy casualties. The 23rd's attempt to advance further stalled after 300 yards and the lead battalion was forced to

SEVENTEEN—Blanc Mont Ridge

withdraw to a trench line where its last assault began. Even this pullback left them way out front in an exposed position.

The first day's battle ended with the Marines holding part of the ridge, having secured a salient roughly one mile wide at the bottom, one-and-a-half miles deep, and 500 yards wide at top. They also had taken many prisoners and guns. However, the battle was just beginning. The Germans spent the night turning St. Etienne and its cemetery into strong points with fresh troops.[17]

The 4th Brigade planned to renew its attack at 6 a.m., October 4, with Larsen's 3/5 in the lead, moving up the road to St. Etienne. Hamilton's 1/5 and Messersmith's 2/5 were to follow in column of battalions. Once again the objective was the line of trenches on the left side of the road, 600 yards from St. Etienne. Larsen's men stepped off on time and immediately came under heavy machine gun fire from the left end of Blanc Mont Ridge as well as their front and flanks. Unlike the day before, there was no artillery preparation or rolling barrage to support the advance. Larsen's battalion soon had to halt and hunker down for a time.

Five hours later, Larsen's 3/5 had managed to push forward and link up with the 23rd Infantry's point battalion near St. Etienne, but they were still taking heavy fire. So were the 2/5 and 1/5 behind them. At this point, Larsen sent messages to Messersmith and Hamilton pleading with them to come up and support him, as he was taking fire from three sides.[18] They advanced with considerable difficulty and took up positions on either side of Larsen's 3/5. Casualties in all three battalions were now estimated at 60 percent or more.

As Hamilton prepared to lead an assault up a nearby unpaved road toward St. Etienne, he observed "numbers of men were running to the rear," including several officers that he named, Major Messersmith among them. Hamilton said Messersmith told him "he had lost all of his officers, but [Messersmith] didn't show any initiative or leadership."[19] Hamilton reported that he and other officers had to draw their pistols and threaten the fleeing men to halt the panic. Messersmith was relieved of his command on October 10 for failing to report this rout and was assigned to paymaster duties.

Once this stampede had been halted, Hamilton's 1/5 began its advance toward a strongpoint below St. Etienne. The other two battalions of the 5th Regiment formed up and kept pace. As they approached a fortified hill known as Ludwig's Rucken, the Marines came under

175

intense enemy fire from high-explosive, shrapnel and gas shells as well as machine gun and rifle fire. The Marines would later dub this area "The Box." Despite the torrent of enemy fire, Hamilton's 1/5 fought its way up the slope. At the summit, they were met with German bayonets and the Marines responded in kind. Before long, the surviving German defenders fled down the reverse slope. Although Hamilton's battalion had lost about 75 percent of its men, he and his men beat back a counterattack with well-aimed rifle fire to hold the ground they had won.

However, as night approached, Hamilton concluded that, with barely more than 100 men, he could not continue to hold his position. With no chance of support reaching them, what remained of the 1/5 retraced their steps under enemy shelling to join the rest of the 5th Regiment dug in on the road to St. Etienne.

At 10 a.m., October 4, Daly's 73rd Company moved to the forward slope of the Blanc Mont Ridge to support the infantry there and repelled two powerful enemy counterattacks.

The 6th Regiment spent the day making several attempts to drive the Germans out of their defenses on the ridge, but each effort failed with heavy losses. By now, Williams' 2/6 was down to a few more than 300 men out of the 800 or so he began the battle with just the day before.

That night, the 3rd Brigade withdrew a battalion of the 23rd Infantry Regiment because its right flank was unprotected by any other unit. This left the 4th Brigade's 5th Regiment with no unit on either side of it, exposed to attack on three sides. Despite this precarious situation, Neville ordered the 4th Brigade to remain in place. Overnight, the 5th Regiment fought off two counterattacks and Barker's 1/6 moved up from reserve to reduce pressure on the 5th's left flank. The next day the 3rd Brigade returned to its previous position on the 5th Regiment's right flank.

On October 5, the 6th Regiment broke through the ring of fire around the 5th Regiment to clear the Germans from the 5th's rear and end its encirclement. The attack by Shuler's 3/6, supported by a French division, began at 6:15 a.m. By 9 a.m., the joint effort had finally wrested the last portion of Blanc Mont Ridge from the enemy.[20] By then, however, the 5th Regiment was no longer an effective fighting force, having suffered 1,120 dead and wounded. The 6th Regiment was not in much better shape.[21]

Nevertheless, there was still St. Etienne to be taken. The next phase of the battle began at 6:30 a.m., October 6. This time the French

SEVENTEEN—Blanc Mont Ridge

Division assigned to the Marines' left flank advanced behind an artillery barrage with Shuler's 3/6 and the Army's 23rd Infantry Regiment. In addition, two regiments of the Army's 36th Division moved up to support the advance.

During the night of October 6–7, the shattered 5th Regiment and two battalions of the 6th Regiment were relieved by the 36th Division.[22] Only Barker's 1/6, supported by Daly's 73rd Machine Gun Company, remained at the front with the 36th Division to instruct the new arrivals.

On October 8, Barker's 1/6 joined an attack by a brigade of the 36th Division to capture St. Etienne. The inexperienced soldiers proved no match for the German defenders and were driven back. Despite heavy losses, Barker's 1/6 took the town. Supported by Daly's 73rd Company, they held it in the face of repeated counterattacks.

Daly and the 73rd Company set up four guns in the front line north of St. Etienne with the 76th Company, 1/6. Four more guns were placed in shell holes with the 75th Company, 1/6, covering a gap on the right of the cemetery. A machine gun nest was established in the cemetery northeast of St. Etienne. Three guns commanded an enemy position on a nearby hill and the road to St. Etienne.[23]

During the night of October 8, the guns of the 73rd broke up two determined enemy counterattacks with heavy losses. While engaged in repelling these counterattacks, Daly was wounded, not once but twice in separate events. One wound was in the left shoulder and the other to his left upper thigh, although some entries in his service record say the second wound was to his left knee. Regardless of their location, Daly's medical records classified his injuries as "severe." These wounds put the old warrior into a hospital and, ultimately, out of the war. Unlike so many of his comrades who were dead or disabled, he would recover and return once more to his unit. But not before this war, the Great War, the war to end all wars, finally came to an end.

Daly's service record states that he was wounded on October 8, while the October 1918 muster roll for the 73rd Company says it was October 6. Whatever the date, Daly was treated in an evacuation hospital and then sent to Base Hospital 41,[24] located at the L'Ecole de la Legion d'Honneur. It is a large classical set of buildings and gardens in a walled compound in southeast Paris that was created by Napoleon as a school for the offspring of Legion of Honor winners. Daly spent almost two months here.

On October 9, Barker's 1/6 was relieved by a battalion of the 36th

"Devil Dog" Dan Daly

Division. The following night, the machine gun units, including Daly's 73rd Company, were pulled out too. The 2nd Division's battle for Blanc Mont Ridge was over.[25]

In a week of almost continuous fighting, the 2nd Division had taken the seemingly impregnable fortress of Blanc Mont Ridge and captured nearly 2,000 prisoners, 25 artillery pieces and 332 machine guns. In the process, its members had taken heavy losses. More than 700 of its officers and men were dead, some 3,600 were wounded, and nearly 600 were missing for a total of almost 5,000 casualties out of 8,000 troops engaged.[26]

The Marine Brigade lost 494 dead and 1,864 wounded for a total of 2,358. Battalions had been reduced to reinforced companies, and some companies were now led by sergeants because all of their officers were gone. The final toll from Belleau Wood had been higher but October 4 at Blanc Mont Ridge had exceeded even the horrific single day loss of June 6.[27]

The 5th and 6th Marines each received a third citation of the Croix de Guerre; the first two citations were for Belleau Wood and Soissons. They are the only American regiments in World War I to receive three citations. This entitles their members even today to wear the red and green *fourragère* cord on their left shoulder and the Croix de Guerre with two palms and one gilt star, symbolizing two citations in Orders of the Army and one in Orders of the Corps.

Foch, the Allied commander in chief, added his only personal commendation, saying, "The taking of Blanc Mont Ridge is the greatest single achievement of the 1918 campaign."

Those who fought there had their own estimate of the battle's worth. For Lieutenant Lemuel Shepherd, a future Marine Corps commandant, "October 3 at Blanc Mont was the toughest day of the war. And I think most of the men with me agreed."[28] Perhaps the only disagreement among Marines was over the date. For many, the 4th at Blanc Mont Ridge was even worse than the 3rd. The price paid in blood that day was certainly higher.

Eighteen

Meuse-Argonne

After being withdrawn from Blanc Mont Ridge on October 10, the 2nd Division went into reserve for some much needed rest and refitting. The division also received about 1,500 replacements to fill the yawning gaps in its ranks. On October 21, the 4th Brigade's Marines marched to an area northeast of St. Etienne where they were to support the continuing French offensive toward the Aisne River. The following day that order was canceled and the brigade retraced its steps to Chalons, where it rejoined the 2nd Division. From there, the division marched north and east about 65 miles over four days, mostly in the rain, to Exermont. They were there to join Pershing's Meuse-Argonne offensive, which had begun on September 26.

The Meuse-Argonne battleground was essentially two parallel valleys, running north between the Aire and Meuse rivers, 135 miles east of Paris. The valleys were separated by a broken ridge line with high points at Montfaucon, Romagne, Cunel and Barricourt. Overlooking these valleys on the west was a wide, rugged series of steep hills topped by the Argonne Forest and bristling with machine guns. On the east, a line of hills on the far side of the Meuse River, known as the Heights of the Meuse, enabled German artillery to put plunging fire into the valleys. The French Army had learned this the hard way in 1914. After the initial German advance had been halted, the French had counterattacked here and suffered considerable pain for no gain. The French Army had not tried any more major assaults here since 1914.[1]

In the intervening four years the Germans had constructed a defensive network in this sector 12 miles deep. Now the Allies intended to throw the full weight of the American First Army, plus the French 4th Army, against this 25-mile-wide section of the German line. At the same time, British and French forces would launch attacks in the northwest. The objective of all of these drives was to sever the German supply line that ran between Lille in Flanders and Strasbourg on the Rhine River. The Meuse-Argonne offensive was aimed like a dagger at the rail hub at Sedan. Cutting that line would force either a general withdrawal or a complete collapse of the German center. This was a worthy goal, but there was little room to maneuver in the Meuse-Argonne sector. The assault forces would have to attack straight ahead into the best natural and man-made defenses almost anywhere on the Western Front.

At 3:30 a.m., September 26, 10 American and French artillery brigades, totaling 2,775 guns, began the offensive with a thunderous two-hour preparatory barrage. There were 156 guns per mile, standing practically wheel to wheel, across the entire front.[2] At 5:30 a.m. the guns shifted the shelling north so the assault forces could advance behind a rolling barrage, and nine American divisions, with six more divisions in reserve, went over the top.

By November 1, when the 2nd Division entered the front line north of Sommerance, the offensive was in its fifth week. It had already gone through two phases and was about to launch a third. In the first phase, from September 26 to October 4, some U.S. divisions achieved their objectives while others failed to take theirs, and one badly mauled division barely repulsed a counterattack. In the second phase, from October 4 to 28, frontal attacks gained 10 miles and breached the eastern portion of the Hindenburg Line, but at great cost. It was during the second phase that the so-called "Lost Battalion" of the 77th Division outran the units on either side of it and became surrounded for nearly a week. It had to be rescued by an attack by the 82nd Division that forced a German withdrawal from the Argonne Forest.

As the offensive progressed, seven more U.S. divisions joined the fray. To better manage this huge number, Pershing reorganized his forces into the First Army on the left, under Major General Hunter Liggett, and the Second Army on the right, under Major General Robert Bullard. The 2nd Division was assigned to Liggett's V Corps, led by Major General Charles Summerall.

Summerall was the son and grandson of preachers from Florida. After graduating from West Point in 1892, he entered the artillery. He served in Reilly's Battery when it helped relieve the besieged legations in Peking during the Boxer Rebellion. He was in charge of the artillery brigade at Cantigny and was credited with perfecting the rolling barrage to support the infantry. Promoted to commander of the 1st Infantry Division, he performed well at Soissons and St. Mihiel. When Liggett moved up to command of First Army, he took over V Corps. Summerall was pious, ambitious and hard-driving; a highly respected commander and a gifted tactician. One war correspondent described him as "daring and careful, ruthless and inspiring ... a twentieth century Stonewall Jackson."[3]

Summerall did not countenance anything less than success. When he met with Lejeune, he made clear that he had relieved unit commanders in the past who failed to achieve the results he expected. The implication was clear. Failure to reach objectives would result in removal.[4]

The third phase of the offensive began November 1 with nine U.S. divisions on the front line plus two in ready reserve. Arrayed from left to right, the divisions were the 26th and 79th (French XVII Corps), the 5th and 90th (III Corps), the 89th and 2nd (V Corps), and the 80th, 77th and 78th (I Corps). The three divisions in the center, the 90th, 89th and 2nd, would make the main thrust aimed at driving a deep wedge through the German defenses that would force a general retreat. The 1st and 42nd divisions were positioned behind the three center divisions ready to exploit any breakthrough.[5] All five of these divisions were battle-hardened now.

All of the senior commanders of the 4th Brigade, except one from the battle for Blanc Mont Ridge, were still in place. Messersmith had been replaced as commander of the 2/5 by Captain Charley Dunbeck. Dunbeck had joined the Marines in 1903, and arrived in France as a gunner before receiving a commission. He had been wounded at Belleau Wood and again at Blanc Mont Ridge as the skipper of the 43rd Company, 2/5. He earned the DSC and Navy Cross at Blanc Mont Ridge plus four Silver Star Citations by the end of the war.

The Marine battalions began the attack with an average of 850 men each, down from a full complement of 1,000. However, the 4th Brigade was supported by extra artillery and nine tanks. In addition, Allied aircraft were assigned to support the advance.

As the divisions under his command prepared to go over the top, Summerall visited each battalion in the 4th Brigade and threatened to remove every field grade officer if the Marines failed to capture the objectives set for them. He also reminded Lejeune that he had relieved unit commanders in the past who failed to carry out his orders.[6] This could hardly have endeared Summerall to his subordinates who would actually have to do the fighting.

The attack began at 5:30 a.m., November 1, under a cover of fog and a rolling artillery barrage. The division's machine gun companies also added their fire to the opening salvo. All of this enabled the assault divisions to make good progress. The Marine regiments of the 2nd Division led the way. Together with the 89th Division, they made the day's deepest penetration. Observers noted that the lines of Marines advancing toward Barricourt Ridge weren't as "pretty" as Cates had noted in a previous assault. Clambering over trenches and through woods broke up the neatly spaced waves but they nonetheless swept up the slope like an irresistible tidal surge.

The ground over which the Marines advanced offered little cover amid the barbed wire entanglements and woodlots studded with German machine guns. In the initial attack, Marines went down like ninepins before enemy machine guns. Those who survived dove for cover in underbrush. New replacements, including officers in their first combat, sometimes froze. In those instances, seasoned veterans took charge. Advancing in rushes, the Marines engaged in fire and maneuver to close on an enemy machine gun nest and kill its crew with grenades, rifle fire and bayonets.

One example of the fierceness of the fighting is the following citation for the DSC to a Marine in the 76th Company, 1/6: "When his platoon was held up by barbed-wire entanglements within 30 yards of an enemy machine-gun nest, Private First Class [David E.] Depue took an automatic rifle from a dead gunner near him and, firing [from the hip] as he advanced, charged through the wire. He fell twice [from wounds], but reached the enemy position after his ammunition was exhausted, swinging his rifle above his head as a club upon the enemy defenders. When the platoon reached the enemy nest, Private Depue was found lying mortally wounded among four enemy dead."[7]

Nearly 1,400 Marines were killed or wounded in the first two days of the offensive. However, after they overran the first line of machine gun nests, German resistance melted away for a time before stiffening again. The 2nd Division advanced six miles the first day to the western slope of Barricourt Ridge. Meanwhile, the 90th Division on its left advanced two miles to the eastern slope of the ridge. By 4 p.m., the 89th Division on its right also had reached the crest of the ridge.

Two men in the 89th would receive the Medal of Honor for singlehandedly knocking out machine gun nests in the day's drive. When a hidden machine gun nest held up his company's advance, Sergeant Arthur Forrest advanced to a point within 50 yards of the nest, before

Eighteen—Meuse-Argonne

charging into it and routing the gun crews. Similarly, Lieutenant Harold Furlong crossed several hundred yards of open ground to get behind the line of enemy machine guns and with his rifle put four guns out of action and took 20 prisoners.[8] Although several Marines accomplished similar feats during this offensive, no Marine received the Medal of Honor for any actions during the Meuse-Argonne Offensive.

The 3rd Brigade took the lead on the second day and advanced seven more miles, besting their Marine counterparts by a mile. Competition between the Marines and soldiers of the 2nd Division seemed to propel both units to excel.

On the night of November 3–4, the German high command concluded that the American offensive could not be stopped and ordered a general withdrawal behind the Meuse River. The American forces pursued them vigorously. What had begun as a confrontation became a chase, with the Germans trying to stay ahead of the American advance and escape across the Meuse.

By November 5, the 5th Regiment had reached the Meuse River north of Beaumont, and began making preparations to cross it under fire. At this point, the Germans were falling back across the river along the entire front.

As American units moved up to the Meuse, they had to contend with casualties not only from combat but also the Spanish flu. Commanders reported that cases of exhaustion, diarrhea and influenza were sapping the effective strength of their units. Private Carl Brannen in the 6th Regiment recalled, "The men were nearly all affected with dysentery from the scanty, unfit food and polluted water.... We were all weak and exhausted."[9] Colonel Lee reported that the 6th Regiment was down to 1,800 effectives, from 3,000.

On November 6, the 5th Regiment moved to a wood two miles west of Beaumont while the 6th Regiment moved farther west to a wood near Villemontry. The enemy occupied a tall, steep, wooded ridge facing each of the regiments, although, as it turned out, not in great strength.

By this point, the men in the ranks were sick and worn out. They also were aware that an end to the fighting was close at hand. No one wanted to be the last casualty in this dreadful war. What sense did it make to continue to risk death in a river crossing so late in the game? However, the negotiations to end the war dragged on and the generals insisted on advancing.

The 6th Regiment, including Daly's 73rd Machine Gun Company, plus Larsen's 3/5, was chosen to spearhead the 2nd Division's crossing. The plan called for the 6th Regiment to move north three miles to Mouzon on the evening of November 10. Once there, they were to cross the river on two footbridges made of duckboards laid over boats tied side by side.[10] They were then to seize two hills. Major Shuler, leading the 3/6, was in overall charge. Enemy artillery slowed the march that night and the regiment did not arrive in position until an hour after the scheduled jump-off time. It was then they learned that only one footbridge had been built. Enemy fire had thwarted the engineers trying to construct the second footbridge. Shuler concluded that two bridges were essential and he set his men to work with the engineers to try to build it. However, by 4 a.m. the next morning, the bridge wasn't complete and, with daylight approaching, the 6th Regiment had to abandon the crossing.

The plan had called for the 5th Regiment to make a crossing farther south near Letanne and then move north along the river to join the 6th. While the 6th was held up, the 5th made the crossing as scheduled, using two footbridges. Despite numerous casualties from enemy artillery and machine gun fire, the 5th Regiment made it across. Major Hamilton was in charge of the crossing. The 1/5 was now led by Captain LeRoy Hunt. Commissioned in 1917, Hunt led the 17th Company, 1/5, at Belleau Wood, Soissons, St. Mihiel and Blanc Mont Ridge. He earned the DSC and Navy Cross at Blanc Mont Ridge and three Silver Star Citations during the war. During World War II, he led the 5th Marine Regiment at Guadalcanal until relieved of command for operational failures. He later commanded the 2nd Marine Division during the occupation of Japan.

The 1/5 was the first across the river, but by the time it assembled on the far side, only about 100 men remained of the battalion. After seeing the heavy losses suffered by Hunt's battalion, Dunbeck's men balked. "I am going across the river," Dunbeck announced to his men, "and I expect you to go with me." They did.[11] An hour later, around 11:30 p.m., Dunbeck's 2/5 completed its crossing.

Despite their depleted condition, the two 5th Regiment battalions moved out to try to secure their objectives. They took out numerous machine gun nests but there were simply too few Marines left in action to take larger objectives by themselves. As two battalions of the 89th Division and a battalion of the 3rd Brigade made it across the river, the Marines went forward with them. At 11:45 a.m., November 11, word reached these units that an armistice had taken effect at 11 a.m. The war had officially ended 45 minutes earlier.

Eighteen—Meuse-Argonne

Daly's 73rd Machine Gun Company, minus the hospitalized Daly, was in the thick of the action during the final days of the war as it accompanied Barker's 1/6. Lieutenant George R. Jackson was in command on November 1. Each of his three platoons was attached to an infantry company in the battalion. However, within minutes of the start of the attack[12] the platoon accompanying the 76th Company had three of its four guns and most of their crews put out of action. When its lieutenant also was wounded, a sergeant took charge of the platoon. Undaunted, the men of the 73rd Machine Gun Company pressed ahead. The platoon accompanying the 74th Company was instrumental in the capture of Imécourt, a village northwest of Landres et St. George. This attack netted 350 prisoners and 20 machine guns.

On November 2, Lieutenant Jackson was evacuated suffering from both a wound and the flu, which was ravaging both sides in this battle and inflicting as many casualties as combat. Lieutenant John L. Hunt, the company's last officer, took command until he was succeeded by Major Louis E. Fagan Jr., later in the day. Fagan had been dispatched from Shuler's 3/6 to take over the 73rd. A Naval Academy graduate, Fagan had received his Marine Corps commission in 1913 and served in the Haitian Constabulary under Smedley Butler in 1916. Since arriving in France, he had fought with the 4th Brigade at Blanc Mont Ridge. He would remain with the 73rd through the end of this offensive.

The depleted 73rd Company spent the next three days in woods with the 1/6. During this time, battalion commander Barker was evacuated with the flu and the lingering effects of being gassed. He was replaced by Major George Stowell, who would command the 1/6 through the end of the war.

Stowell had been thrust into such situations before. He had been skipper of the 76th Company at Belleau Wood until Major Hughes sacked him in a fit of pique. At Blanc Mont Ridge, he had been rushed in to command the 75th Company when all of its officers were lost. In preparation for the Meuse-Argonne Offensive, he had taken charge of a cobbled together detachment consisting of the 95th Company of the 1/5, a platoon from the Daly's 73rd Machine Gun Company and an infantry company from the 80th Division. Their assignment was to provide a reliable liaison between the two divisions as they advanced. Stowell's ad hoc unit also was the liaison between I Corps and V Corps. Now he was rushed in to take charge of the 1/6.

Stowell moved the 1/6, together with the 73rd Company, to another wood on November 5, and to yet another wood on November 6. Each move brought the unit closer to the Meuse River. That night, Lieutenant Hunt was evacuated with the flu and Lieutenant David Duncan, who had been at school, rejoined the company. This gave Fagan one officer besides himself. By this time, the company was down to just four guns and barely enough men to crew them.

The 73rd Company, along with the 6th Regiment, spent three anxious days preparing to cross the Meuse on the night of November 10–11. When their crossing was abruptly canceled, they avoided the heavy casualties suffered by the 5th Regiment that night. At 11 a.m. the Armistice took effect and the guns finally fell silent.

The 4th Brigade's combat losses during the Meuse-Argonne Offensive were relatively light compared to previous battles: 185 Marines killed and 1,233 wounded. However, historian George Clark grimly noted that 31 Marines died and 148 were wounded crossing the Meuse in the war's final hours. Most of the final night's casualties fell on the 5th Regiment.[13]

At a Congressional hearing after the war, General Pershing was asked why he had pressed ahead with the river crossing on November 11 when he knew the Armistice was imminent. He said he was following General Foch's orders to keep up the pressure because no one really knew until the shooting stopped whether the Germans would actually stop fighting.[14]

During all of its time in combat in World War I, the 2nd Division lost 4,478 killed and 17,752 wounded. Of these, Marines accounted for slightly more than half of the 2nd Division's losses: 2,461 (55 percent) killed and 9,520 (53 percent) wounded.[15]

However, such big picture statistics don't adequately convey the human toll. In their history of the Marines in World War I, Edwin Simmons and Joseph Alexander provided a small picture example that is more telling: "Although more than seven hundred men had served in the [1/6's 75th] company since June, only six men … remained of the pre–Belleau Wood roster."[16] Only six out of the 250 Marines who began the war were there at the end.

A similar picture emerges from muster lists for Daly's 73rd Machine Gun Company. Only 10 of the 115 men who were on the roster before Belleau Wood were still listed as effectives with the 73rd after Meuse-Argonne. In addition to the combat casualties, almost every other member of the company had become a casualty of the flu.

EIGHTEEN—Meuse-Argonne

A few, such as Major Shearer and Captain Swink, had left for other assignments. But most of those not killed in action were in a hospital with either wounds or influenza. The 73rd lost 12 killed in action and 24 wounded at Belleau Wood; two killed, 17 wounded and four missing at Soissons; four wounded and one missing at St. Mihiel; six killed and 11 wounded at Blanc Mont Ridge; and 13 killed and 23 wounded at Meuse-Argonne. That's a total of 117 dead and wounded in a company that started with 115 men. By the war's end, the original roster had been reduced to a single squad.

One of the 10 still in the 73rd was Lieutenant Peirce. He had been at Belleau Wood, Soissons and St. Mihiel, but missed Blanc Mont Ridge and Meuse-Argonne while serving as an instructor at Langres. Promoted to captain, he rejoined the company four days after the Armistice. Colonel Lee recommended him for the DSC for Soissons but it was reduced to a Silver Star Citation. Another one of the 10 was Albyn A. Wilcox. A corporal at Belleau Wood, he had been commissioned after that battle and ended the war as a first lieutenant with a Silver Star Citation. Hildor Ellison, promoted to gunnery sergeant on November 1, was also still on the roster at the end. He had fought in every battle and earned three Silver Star Citations. The seven other men from the original roster were a sergeant, two corporals, three privates and a drummer.[17]

The 2nd Division emerged from the war as one of the most celebrated divisions in the AEF, and the Marines earned a permanent place in the nation's pantheon of heroes.

Nineteen

Final Years

On December 27, 1918, Daly was finally recovered sufficiently from his wounds to be released from the hospital in Paris. He returned to what was left of the 73rd Machine Gun Company after its mauling in the Meuse-Argonne offensive.[1]

By then, the defeated German forces had withdrawn into Germany, trailed by those Allied units designated as the Army of Occupation. Allied forces occupied Germany's western border region stretching from The Netherlands to Switzerland. The Allies were concerned that if negotiations broke down over the final peace treaty, Germany might resume the war. The presence of Allied troops was meant to prevent this. Longer term, the occupation was intended to create a demilitarized buffer between Germany and its neighbors to the west.

The U.S. occupation forces, totaling 250,000 men, included the 2nd Division. Although the Marines didn't have to fight their way into Germany, the march there was no picnic. It was three weeks of cold, rain and occasional snow, which turned the roads to mud. Adding to the misery, every man in the 2nd Division carried 75–80 pounds of equipment.[2]

Beginning November 27, the 2nd Division marched about 90 miles through Belgium and Luxembourg in eight days. Each day's march ended with sore and blistered feet. After the Armistice, the men had all been issued new English shoes that were "stiff as a board." Some men resorted to marching in their socks. While they had new shoes, the troops began the march in the same filthy, tattered uniforms they had worn since before Blanc Mont Ridge. When they halted briefly at the German border, they were issued new uniforms. This eliminated the cooties that had been their constant companions. There were two meals a day. Whenever the kitchens caught up, the men received a hot meal. As they marched, village residents along the way lined the streets. They waved American flags and handed the passing troops food and wine.

Occasionally, a young woman would "break into the ranks and shower a kiss or so on some lucky fellow."[3]

The division entered Germany on December 1. Sullen faces now greeted the men. Twelve days later, after marching about 100 miles into Germany, the division crossed the Rhine River and settled into the area around the town of Neuwied, 13 miles up the Rhine from the city of Coblenz (now spelled Koblenz), where the Moselle River flows into the Rhine.

Upon his return to the 2nd Division, Daly learned that he had been awarded the Medaille Militaire, the French Army's highest decoration, and the Croix de Guerre with palm for his actions at Belleau Wood. Although the French president's decision to award Daly the Medaille Militaire was announced on December 22, 1918, the actual presentation did not take place until August 1919 in the Marine Corps Recruiting Office in New York City, where Daly was then posted.[4]

Daly was one of 304 American servicemen to receive the Medaille Militaire for World War I, and one of 10 awarded to Marines in the 4th Brigade. The Croix de Guerre is presented with a device attached to its ribbon that denotes the level of the award. A bronze star is for mention at regiment or brigade level; a silver star for division level, a gold star for corps level, and a bronze palm denotes mention at the army level. Daly's bronze palm was thus the highest level of the medal.

Occupation duty quickly proved boring. The division patrolled its sector, and there was always drill practice. But there wasn't much else to do. So sports and marksmanship competitions, amateur theatrical productions and educational programs were held. The 2nd Division posted the highest aggregate score among 12 divisions in the rifle competition. The 73rd Machine Gun Company, now reconstituted with replacements, took the division football championship with six wins against two losses.[5]

Most of the American troops were quartered in the homes of German civilians. The U.S. command established a no fraternization policy, but given the living arrangements the policy proved unenforceable.

On March 14, 1919, General Pershing came to inspect the 2nd Division. Nearly 20,000 men assembled in an open field that day. Pershing walked up and down the rows of soldiers and Marines, inspecting each unit. He also pinned medals on several men. The division then marched past Pershing and the other dignitaries in a formal review while a 300-piece band played.

First Sergeant Daly receiving the Medaille Militaire in August 1919. The ceremony took place in the Marine Corps recruiting office in New York City. The officer making the presentation and the enlisted men observing are not identified.

Ten days later, Daly said goodbye to the 73rd Machine Gun Company and headed for America by way of a train to the port of Marseilles and a ship to New York City. Captain David Bellamy of the 3/6 stated in his published diary that on March 24 "[Dan] Daly and 600 marines left for home, the best representatives of our regiments that may ever go back together. A sad leaving. The Colonel made a speech and the band played at Neuwied Station. Generals and Colonels to see them off."[6]

Daly set sail on April 21 aboard the Italian steamship *America* and arrived in New York City on May 7. The ship carried 28 nurses and 2,274 troops, including 700 Marines. The *New York Tribune*[7] reported that "Daly had a real grouch on as he strode down the gangplank. Categorically, he protested first, against prohibition; second, against American soldiers in France marrying what he termed 'bamboo girls,' and third, because he missed the Giants' first game of the season.... Daly has been a friend of [New York Giants' Manager John] 'Muggsy' McGraw for twenty years, and was also well acquainted with the late Mayor [William Jay] Gaynor and the late Senator Patrick H. McCarren."[8]

The day after his arrival in New York, Daly was among a group of Marines honored at an afternoon memorial service for the war dead in Central Park and a theatrical production by Marine recruiters at the Republic Theater that evening.[9]

The Treaty of Versailles was finally signed June 28, officially ending the war. The 2nd Division began coming home in July. The last contingent arrived on August 8 and that afternoon the 2nd Division, now 27,000 strong, marched in a ticker-tape parade up Manhattan's 5th Avenue to the deafening cheers of New Yorkers lined several rows deep along the five-mile route. The parade began at 6th Street (Washington Square). Along the route, the troops paraded through a huge, white, Roman-style Victory Arch[10] at 24th Street (Madison Square). Built expressly to honor returning servicemen, the arch was a magnificent, albeit temporary, structure made of wood and plaster. It was topped by a chariot drawn by six horses meant to symbolize the Triumph of Democracy. The troops also passed through the Arch of Jewels at 60th Street (southeast corner of Central Park), which were columns linked by cables festooned with sparkling prisms. The parade ended at 110th Street, in a meadow at the northern end of Central Park. As division commander, Lejeune led the way on horseback along with Neville,[11] as brigade commander. Feland[12] and Lee,[13] also on horseback, rode at the head of their regiments.

On August 12, Neville led the 4th Brigade in a parade down Pennsylvania Avenue in Washington, D.C., where they were reviewed by President Wilson and Marine Commandant Barnett. Many parades were held over several months as divisions returned from Europe. In addition to New York City and Washington, D.C., cities around the country held parades for returning local units.[14]

"Devil Dog" Dan Daly

That same day, Secretary of War Newton Baker sent a letter to Secretary of the Navy Josephus Daniels restoring the 4th Marine Brigade to the Navy Department and commending the brigade's "unconquerable tenacity and dauntless courage." He added, "Throughout this long contest the Marines, both by their valor and their tragic losses, heroically sustained, added an imperishable chapter to the history of America's participation in the World War."[15] The following day, the two Marine regiments were demobilized at Quantico.

Such compliments did not prevent the Army from trying to disband the Marine Corps shortly after the war, arguing that the nation did not need a large land-fighting force besides the Army. The feud between the branches fueled by Gibbons' Belleau Wood dispatch was a significant factor in this effort.

Upon his return, Daly was assigned to the Marine Barracks at Quantico. He then went on furlough, spending time with family members in New York and taking in baseball games with his long-time friend, John McGraw, the manager of the New York Giants from 1907 to 1932. Like Daly, McGraw was small in size, just 5-foot-7 and 155 pounds, but a fierce competitor. When Daly returned to duty, he was posted to the Eastern Recruiting Division Headquarters in Philadelphia. He retained his rank of first sergeant.

Having completed over 20 years of active service, Daly requested transfer to inactive status. On September 11, 1919, he was transferred to inactive status in the Fleet Marine Corps Reserve. He was recalled to active duty on

Daly wearing his many medals following the award of the Medaille Militaire, 1919. Missing from his many medals is the Navy Cross, which was not awarded to him until 1920.

NINETEEN—Final Years

December 1, 1919, and promoted to sergeant major on December 30. A month later, he returned to inactive status.[16] Daly retired with the rank of sergeant major after 30 years of service in the Marine Corps on February 6, 1929.[17] Daly was only 48, but his many years of hard service had aged him beyond the mere fact of his age.

Daly's request to retire was formally approved in a letter from the office of Major General Commandant John Lejeune on January 31, 1929. "The records show that upon the day of your retirement you will have completed thirty years and ten days service in the Marine Corps and in the Fleet Marine Corps Reserve. You have served your country long and faithfully in a manner which has reflected credit to yourself and to the Corps, and it is my sincere hope that the coming years may bring you much happiness."

Daly's pension in 1929 was $119.70 per month (the equivalent of $1,813 in 2020). Not a princely sum, but more than he made as a first sergeant a decade earlier. Daly's pension was comparable to the average income of a New York City taxi driver at that time. As a Medal of Honor recipient, he received an extra $10 per month ($152 in 2020 dollars). Correspondence between Daly and the Marine Corps indicate he tried to collect every dollar to which he was entitled. This included requesting recalculations of added pay for overseas and combat duty. Some of his efforts were successful while others were not. He lived simply and frugally.

After leaving active duty, Daly lived with his sister Mary's family in a two-story rented house at 1290 Rockaway Avenue, in the Canarsie section of southeast Brooklyn. It was a crowded household with eight people: Mary, her husband, William Loeb, their two daughters, a niece, a nephew, and Daly's widowed mother, Ellen.[18] Before long, the family moved to a duplex at 335 McComb Place (now 73rd Street) in the Glendale section of Queens. A son had been added to the Loeb family and the niece and nephew, now adults, had moved out.[19] By 1925, the Loebs had moved to a single-family home on a tree-lined street in Glendale, Queens, 7845 Slocum Street (now 78–45 64th Place). Ellen died in 1928 but Daniel continued to live with his sister and her family.[20]

A week after he left active duty in September 1919, an article appeared in the *New York Tribune* stating that Daly had "applied at the Reemployment Bureau for Soldiers, Sailors and Marines for work as a special guard, special agent or any other outside position." It suggested

"Devil Dog" Dan Daly

he would have no trouble finding one with his 21 years of military service and 11 medals.

Daly took a job as a guard at Brown Brothers & Co., a prominent, private Wall Street bank established in 1832.[21] In 1930, it merged with Harriman Brothers & Co., and became known as Brown Brothers Harriman & Co. In addition to being a financial powerhouse, the firm is notable for the number of influential American politicians and high government officials who have worked there. They include W. Averell Harriman, the son of railroad tycoon E.H. Harriman who became governor of New York and U.S. ambassador to Great Britain and the Soviet Union; George Herbert Walker, a Democratic power broker, and his son-in-law, U.S. Senator Prescott Bush, the father of President George H.W. Bush and grandfather of President George W. Bush.

Daly spent 17 years as a bank guard at Brown Brothers Harriman, which is located in the granite columned edifice at 59 Wall Street. (Coincidentally, it was adjacent to National City Bank, the same bank involved in Haiti's financial crisis that led to Daly and the Marines landing there in 1915.) At his request, he served as captain of the night guard so he could indulge his passion for attending major league baseball games during the day.[22]

Having his days free also allowed time for playing catch with his nephew, which led to meeting other children in the neighborhood. Daly acquired quite a following among them. Of course, it didn't hurt that he always seemed to have nickels in his pocket for ice cream cones. In a 1960 article in the *Marine Corps Gazette*, Edward Dieckmann related a conversation he had with one of these children. "I remember him well," she said. "I've never met a quieter, more thoughtful man. So kind, so cheerful, and [he] loved all of us children and we all loved him."

That scene would have dumbfounded some of the men who shook in their boots as he approached them for inspection.

On Armistice Day, November 11, 1921, Daly participated in ceremonies at Arlington National Cemetery for the internment of the Unknown Soldier of World War I. Eight noncommissioned officers (five Army, two Navy, and one Marine Corps) were chosen as body bearers to handle the casket.[23] The Marine Corps representative was Gunnery Sergeant Ernest Janson, who had won the Medal of Honor at Hill 142 in the battle for Belleau Wood. Nine general officers and three flag officers, all of whom had served in the war, served as honorary pallbearers. The body bearers carried the casket down the steps of the Capitol, where it had lain in state, and placed it on a horse-drawn caisson. The large procession of dignitaries and military units then made its way down Pennsylvania Avenue and across a bridge over the Potomac River to the Memorial Amphitheater at the cemetery, three hours after leaving the Capitol.

All living recipients of the Medal of Honor were invited to march in the procession. They marched eight abreast, arranged in ranks based on the dates of their medals with the oldest first. At the cemetery, Daly and the other Medal of Honor recipients were among those seated in the amphitheater to hear President Warren G. Harding's remarks. The Marine Band played and hymns were sung. The participants then moved outside to the tomb. Cannons fired three salvos while the casket was lowered into the crypt. The ceremony ended after a bugler played taps.[24]

Daly declined most invitations to public events. However, he did attend the 2nd Division's annual convention in June 1934. It was held at the posh Hotel Astor, just off Times Square in Manhattan. More than 1,200 veterans of the division attended a dinner in the main ballroom with their families. After several major generals had spoken to the crowd, including James Harbord and Logan Feland, and other generals were waiting to speak, a chant began: "Dan Daly."

A reluctant Daly was prodded to the dais and stepped up to the microphone. "We was in Belleau Wood one day" he began, "when General Harbord came up. He was on a horse. Yeah, a horse! The orders had been for the men to clean up their guns and horses and such. He came up and he asked me where my company was. I said 'carrying out their orders, sir.' 'Fine,' said he and he rode off. Now the fact was the whole company was over to one of the canteens. So that was one time anyway when the marines put one over on the army. And so, with all due respect to the generals, I think we should give a hand to the enlisted men." The crowd roared with delight and Harbord not only joined in the applause but slapped Daly on the back for good measure.

Daly's remarks were featured in the next day's *New York Times* under the headline: "Sergeant Is Hero at Veteran Dinner; 1,200 Cheer as He Tells Joke on General Harbord; Victim Also Gives Him a 'Hand.'" None of what the generals said in their speeches got even a mention in the story.[25]

Daly did agree to serve on the executive committee of the 2nd Division Association when it was formed in 1920.[26] He also accepted a gold medal from the Joseph A. Wynn[27] Post, Veterans of Foreign Wars shortly after retiring from the Marine Corps. The occasion was a patriotic rally at the Williamsburg Bridge Plaza in Brooklyn in honor of President Washington's birthday.[28]

Daly's fame also had a darker side. In March 1936, a man "claiming to be Fighting Dan Daly" and seriously ill from a heart attack, sought help from an American Legion post in Bakersfield, California. The post commander became suspicious and wired the Navy Department asking if this man could be Daly. The Marine Corps checked with Daly who advised that he was in Queens, not California, and "my physical condition is good." Daly's personnel file doesn't reveal what happened to the imposter.

In 1937, Daly accepted an invitation to march in the parade at President Franklin D. Roosevelt's second inauguration as the official flag-bearer for the Veterans of Foreign Wars. This was the first inauguration held on January 20 instead of March 4. The 20th Amendment to the U.S. Constitution had been adopted to reduce the time between the election and the swearing in of the president and the new Congress.

Unfortunately, January 20, 1937, turned out to be by far the wettest and one of the coldest inaugurations in U.S. history. The temperature was just one degree above freezing. Heavy rains, totaling 1.77 inches that day, drenched the capital city. More than two-thirds of an inch of rain fell between 11 a.m. and 1 p.m. The swearing-in began at 12:23 p.m. on the east portico of the Capitol, followed by Roosevelt's inaugural address.[29]

Afterward, Roosevelt returned to the White House and took his place in a reviewing stands to watch the parade as it passed by on Pennsylvania Avenue. Inauguration day parades involve numerous marching units, bands and floats. Some parades have lasted as long as three hours. On this day, it took an hour and a half for all of the parade units to pass the president's reviewing stand. Of course, all of the parade units had spent hours waiting to march. They had then marched the mile and a half to the White House, before making their way back to their transport. All of this occurred in a near-freezing downpour.

Daly caught a severe cold that turned into pneumonia and weakened his already damaged heart. His condition gradually deteriorated and he died of a heart attack at the Loeb home at 9:15 a.m., April 27, 1937, a rainy Tuesday. The official cause of death was cardiac decompensation,[30] a long-term worsening of the heart's functioning characterized

NINETEEN—Final Years

by difficulty breathing, swelling of the arms and legs, and fatigue, ending in heart failure. Based on his Marine Corps enlistment papers, he was 63 years old. However, based on the census records from his youth and other evidence, it appears he was 66.

As preparations were being made for Daly's funeral, A.J. Cincotta of the 2nd Division Association sent a telegram to Marine Corps Commandant Thomas Holcomb. "The body of the late Sargent [sic] Dan Daly lies in state at funeral parlor at Glendale Queens County New York City being viewed by hundreds of people. Body unattended. Request honor guard details at least for this afternoon and evening. His funeral tomorrow such request made to Navy Yard Brooklyn denied."[31] This got immediate action.

Upon learning of Daly's death, Holcomb, who had served with Daly in France, wrote Mary Loeb a personal letter of condolence. "Sergeant Major Daly was truly an outstanding Marine. On a number of occasions in active combat, he had demonstrated the highest qualities of leadership and bravery. His record brought glory to the Corps he loved, and will live in the hearts of his fellow comrades long after his remains have been laid to eternal rest."[32]

Like Holcomb, Cincotta had a personal connection to Daly. As a 26-year-old private, Angelo J. Cincotta joined Headquarters Company, 6th Marine Regiment in August 1918 as a replacement after Soissons. He certainly was aware of Daly, a legend in the corps, and probably had contact with him during this time. Cincotta served with the 6th Regiment until he was shipped home after the war. He was one of the 600 Marines who left the 2nd Division with Daly on March 24, 1919, and arrived in New York City with him aboard the *America*. After the war, Cincotta was commissioned in the Marine Corps. When Daly died in April 1937, Cincotta was a captain assigned to the New York Navy Yard in Brooklyn. He retired in the 1950s as a full colonel.

It had been Daly's wish that he be buried at Cypress Hills National Cemetery, just four blocks from the Loeb family home. At the time of his death, the cemetery was closed to new burials. Daly's sister fired off an appeal to Marine Corps Headquarters on April 28 to intercede on her brother's behalf. The Marine Corps made it happen. Daly was buried there on May 1, a sunny Saturday morning, with full military honors.[33]

In addition to Daly, there are 23 other Medal of Honor recipients buried at Cypress Hills. The cemetery was established in 1862 to honor

"Devil Dog" Dan Daly

Civil War veterans. Today, Union and Confederate soldiers lie side by side there. Among the 21,000 graves are those of veterans of every American conflict, from the Revolution and Indian Wars to World War II, Korea and Vietnam. The legendary Dan Daly rests for eternity among a company of heroes.

Twenty

Daly's Legacy

"Devil Dog" Dan Daly[1] was a legend in his own time, and he remains a larger-than-life figure even today. Long before his immortal battle cry was carved into a wall of the National Museum of the Marine Corps, his two Medals of Honor and daring deeds at Peking, Vera Cruz, Haiti and Belleau Wood made him a subject of awe and veneration. The following story illustrates this point. During World War I, a young Marine replacement, upon being told that Daly was his first sergeant, exclaimed, "My God! Do you mean he's real? I thought he was somebody the Marines made up, like Paul Bunyan."[2]

Seven decades later, a 1988 article in *Leatherneck* magazine stated "Every Marine, old or young, knows his name and maybe one or two stories about him. His valorous exploits are so tightly woven into the fabric of the Marine Corps' tradition he'll never be forgotten.... Dan Daly was a legend in his own time and remains a hero in ours."[3]

In 2005, nearly a century after World War I, the U.S. Postal Service selected four Marines to honor with a set of commemorative postage stamps. The four were "Chesty" Puller, "Manila John" Basilone,[4] John Lejeune and Dan Daly. The USPS said it receives about 50,000 suggestions annually for commemorative stamps. Of these, 30 are selected for review by a citizen advisory committee. The USPS said the panel chose these four individuals because they "best represented the spirit and tradition of the Marine Corps."

Dan Daly has been remembered, revered and rewarded in many ways, both big and small.

The most significant honor, at least in size, came in 1942 when the Navy named a new Fletcher-class destroyer after Daly. His niece, the daughter of his sister Mary, christened the warship. The *Daly* (DD-519) earned eight battle stars in World War II and one in the Korean War before being decommissioned in 1960. During combat at Cape

"Devil Dog" Dan Daly

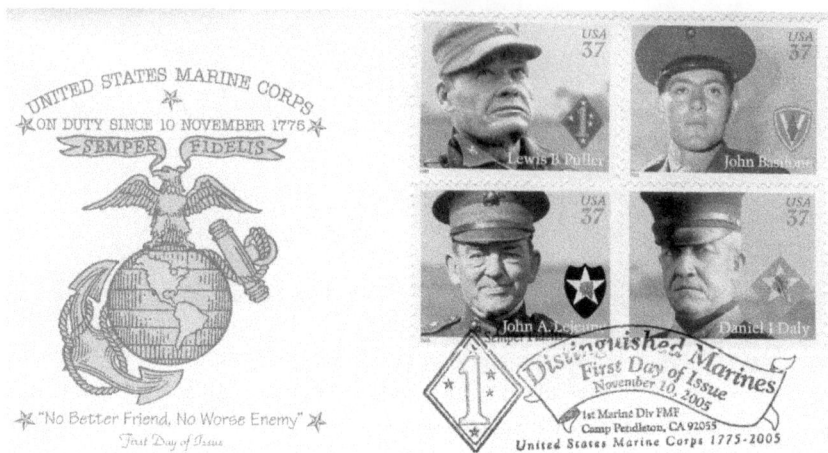

In 2005, the U.S. Postal Service issued a set of commemorative stamps honoring four legendary Marines (clockwise from upper left): John Lejeune, Chesty Puller, Dan Daly and John Basilone (Marine Corps History Division Archive).

Gloucester, her gunners shot down two Japanese bombers and rescued 168 sailors from a destroyer despite exploding depth charges coming from the sinking ship. In the epic naval battle of Surigao Strait, the *Daly* was one of the "tin cans" that took on Japanese battleships and cruisers with torpedoes and five-inch guns. She also saw action at Iwo Jima, where her crew rescued 11 men from an aircraft carrier struck by a kamikaze. During the battle for Okinawa, the *Daly* splashed an enemy dive bomber just 25 yards off the port beam, but a bomb from that plane struck the ship, killing three of her sailors and injuring 16. She was a warrior just like her namesake.

Some years later, the Marine Corps paid tribute to Daly by naming the multistory building at Quantico that houses the Enlisted Men's Club and Marine Corps schools Daly Hall.

A much more modest honor came in 2014, when the City of Glen Cove renamed the northern portion of New York Route 107 for the one-time resident. The four-lane arterial highway runs north across the midsection of Long Island from Massapequa to Glen Cove. It is a fitting local tribute. The route passes near where the church and school Daly attended once stood, and ends at Glen Cove Creek, adjacent to where the starch works once employed Daly's father and housed the Daly family upon their arrival in America.

Twenty—Daly's Legacy

Daly's heroics earned him fame, but he rose steadily in rank based on his everyday performance. After enlisting in 1899, he was promoted to corporal in 1906, sergeant in 1909, and gunnery sergeant in 1915, all before the relatively minuscule Marine Corps mushroomed in size for World War I. Those who served with Daly described him as a strict disciplinarian but not a martinet. He demanded strict obedience to orders, plenty of spit and polish, and immaculate maintenance of weapons. He was considered imminently fair, and had a well-earned reputation for always looking out for the welfare of his men.[5] He was a soft-spoken man by nature, but he could make himself heard when he wanted to, whether on the parade ground or the battlefield.

His attention to detail was both a gift and a curse to the men he led. It saved lives in combat, but some found it daunting in quieter times. In his memoir, Marine PFC James Draucker recalled a classic example one day at the Washington Navy Yard. About 75 Marines were assembled for inspection. Daly went up and down the rows of men. He stopped in front of Draucker and put him on restriction for not having a freshly pressed uniform. "I'm mixed with 75 men and he could spot a little thing like that," said Draucker. "He sure was a 'Giant of the Corps' in more ways than one."[6]

During World War I, Daly was offered an officer's commission. He declined. "Any officer can get by on his sergeants," he once said. "To be a sergeant, you have to know your stuff. I'd rather be an outstanding sergeant than just another officer."[7]

Many stories have been told about Daly. Some are true, some are embellished, and some appear to be apocryphal. A 1960 article in the *Marine Corps Gazette* by Edward A. Dieckmann, Sr., cited some of these tales: "He is described as a rough, tough, unsmiling NCO who was always ready and eager to use his fists at the least excuse. He is also described as having been the most prolifically profane man in the history of the armed services. He could curse in seven languages it is said, never repeating himself once. He is credited by the blood-and-guts, wildly imaginative writers with deeds, both in and out of combat, that make Superman look like a kindergarten freshman." In Dieckmann's view, these stories do a disservice to Daly, who he concluded was a model of modesty, courage, and self-sacrifice, not a fire-breathing, swashbuckling, uber-warrior.

Dieckmann appears well-qualified to evaluate Daly's character. He spent 21 years in the Navy, retiring as a boatswain's mate in 1930. He

"Devil Dog" Dan Daly

then spent 23 years as a San Diego policeman, rising to lieutenant and head of the homicide bureau. Finally, he turned to writing, penning articles about ancient Greece and Rome, hardboiled detective fiction, and military history.

One of the stories about Daly that Dieckmann did not include in his roundup seems best consigned to the apocryphal file. Supposedly, some Marines were being held captive in a Haitian jail awaiting execution. Acting alone, Daly tunneled under the wall of the jail, shot the guards, and rescued the captives.[8] (There is no support for this yarn in Daly's service record.)

Arguably the most reliable sources of information about Daly's actions, character and personality are those who served with him.

Lieutenant General John Lejeune, who led the 4th Marine Brigade in France and later served as commandant of the Marine Corps, called Daly "the outstanding Marine of all time."

"It was an object lesson to have served with him," recalled Major General Smedley D. Butler, who personally witnessed Daly's heroism in Haiti and is the only other Marine to receive two Medals of Honor for separate actions. "He was the fightin'est Marine I ever knew."

Lieutenant Colonel Frank E. Ellis, adjutant of the 6th Regiment, said of Daly: "I came into close and practically daily contact with him. He and the Regimental Sergeant Major [John Quick], in my opinion had more to do with the fighting spirit of the regiment than any other two officers or men. Daly's influence on new officers and men was remarkable. He enjoyed the respect, confidence and admiration of every man in the regiment. For loyalty, spirit, and absolute disregard of fear, he was almost unique in the entire brigade and his devotion to his officers and to the men of his company was demonstrated time after time."[9]

"He was quiet, unassuming, with never a thought of publicity or fame," said General Allen H. Turnage, who served with Daly in Haiti and would command the 3rd Marine Division in World War II and rise to four-star rank. "I can see him now upon receipt of each of his many medals stowing them away and saying to himself: 'Just another job.' He was a man of excellent habits and conduct. His nearest approach to profanity was an occasional emphatic damn. Of all the Marine NCOs whom I knew well during 35 years of active service, Dan Daly was the most outstanding."[10]

Major General William P. Upshur, Daly's company commander in Haiti and eyewitness to his heroism in the ambush, called him "The finest soldier any captain could wish to have."

Twenty—Daly's Legacy

According to Lieutenant Colonel James McB. Sellers, who served in France with the 2/6, Daly's talents included storytelling and scrounging, both of which were appreciated by those with whom he served. In his memoir, Sellers told how Daly held gullible young officers spellbound at Quantico with stories of "the old days." When one of the officers mentioned a rumor that nurses and telephone operators would sail with the Marines to France, Daly launched into a personal anecdote. "I don't want to shipmate with no women," he said. Asked if he had had a bad experience with women, Daly said, "I was going to shipmate with a woman once upon a time and I saved up $800 and give it to her. Then she run off with a coxswain of a trolley car."[11] As for his talent for scrounging whatever his unit needed, Sellers wrote, "Dan was so skillful at thievery that when he went to the Quartermaster for supplies, all hands would drop everything in an attempt to keep Dan from stealing them blind."

In his later years Daly reportedly shunned strong drink, which had blackened his service record on occasion early in his career, but he enjoyed smoking a pipe filled with cut plug tobacco. He also shunned the limelight. In fact, Daly did his best to avoid publicity.

Over the years, when reporters asked how he got so many medals, Daly often replied, "I got all these medals for minding my own damn business."[12] Pressed for details, he said, "I got my DSC at Belleau Wood. I was out pickin' pansies for my girl in Brooklyn one day when all of a sudden a car drove up loaded with brass hats. One of the officers said, 'Hey, lookut the Marine pickin' flowers all by himself. Let's give the poor guy a medal.' Well, sir, they pinned the DSC on me before I could stop 'em."

When a reporter asked what the most exciting thing the famous war hero had seen during the war in France, Daly replied, "Well, pretty much the most exciting thing I ever saw was Paris when the Armistice was signed and everybody went crazy. The French girls went crazy. They kissed everybody."[13]

Daly disliked nosy reporters but the people who really got his Irish up were proselytizers. "France was full of well-meaning folks," he remarked once, "who wanta give you somethin' for nothin' just for the opportunity to save your soul. Most Marines ain't got souls, but them that has don't need to be told how to take care of 'em."[14]

His disdain for what he called "a lot of foolishness" about medals reportedly continued to the grave. As they prepared for his funeral, it took his sister's family an hour of searching their home to locate all of his medals for a memorial display, so casual had he been about them.[15]

Sergeant Major Daniel J. Daly's Medals and Citations

Medal of Honor (First Award)

The President of the United States of America, in the name of Congress, takes pleasure in presenting the Medal of Honor (First Award) to Private Daniel Joseph Daly (MCSN: 73086), United States Marine Corps, for extraordinary heroism while serving with the Captain Newt Hall's Marine Detachment, 1st Regiment (Marines), in action in the presence of the enemy during the battle of Peking, China, 14 August 1900, Daly distinguished himself by meritorious conduct.

Medal of Honor (Second Award)

The President of the United States of America, in the name of Congress, takes pleasure in presenting the Medal of Honor (Second Award) to Gunnery Sergeant Daniel Joseph Daly (MCSN: 73086), United States Marine Corps, for extraordinary heroism in action while serving with the 15th Company of Marines (Mounted), 2d Marine Regiment, on 22 October 1915. Gunnery Sergeant Daly was one of the company to leave Fort Liberte, Haiti, for a six-day reconnaissance. After dark on the evening of 24 October, while crossing the river in a deep ravine, the detachment was suddenly fired upon from three sides by about 400 Cacos concealed in bushes about 100 yards from the fort. The Marine detachment fought its way forward to a good position, which it maintained during the night, although subjected to a continuous fire from the

Sergeant Major Daniel J. Daly's Medals and Citations

Cacos. At daybreak the Marines, in three squads, advanced in three different directions, surprising and scattering the Cacos in all directions. Gunnery Sergeant Daly fought with exceptional gallantry against heavy odds throughout this action.

Distinguished Service Cross

The President of the United States of America, authorized by Act of Congress, July 9, 1918, takes pleasure in presenting the Distinguished Service Cross to First Sergeant Daniel Joseph Daly (MCSN: 73086), United States Marine Corps, for repeated deeds of heroism and great service while serving with the Seventy-Third Company, Sixth Regiment (Marines), 2d Division, A.E.F., on 5 June and 7, 1918, at Lucy-le-Bocage, and on 10 June 1918 in the attack on Bouresches, France. On June 5, at the risk of his life, First Sergeant Daly extinguished a fire in an ammunition dump at Lucy-le-Bocage. On 7 June 1918, while his position was under violent bombardment, he visited all the gun crews of his company, then posted over a wide portion of the front, to cheer his men. On 10 June 1918, he attacked an enemy machine-gun emplacement unassisted and captured it by use of hand grenades and his automatic pistol. On the same day, during the German attack on Bouresches, he brought in wounded under fire.

Navy Cross

The President of the United States of America takes pleasure in presenting the Navy Cross to First Sergeant Daniel Joseph Daly (MCSN: 73086), United States Marine Corps, for repeated deeds of heroism and great service while serving with the 73d Company, 6th Regiment (Marines), 2d Division, A.E.F., on June 5 and 7, 1918, at Lucy-le-Bocage, and on 10 June 1918 in the attack on Bouresches, France. On June 5, at the risk of his life, First Sergeant Daly extinguished a fire in an ammunition dump at Lucy-le-Bocage. On 7 June 1918, while his position was under violent bombardment, he visited all the gun crews of his company, then posted over a wide portion of the front, to cheer his men. On 10 June 1918, he attacked an enemy machine-gun emplacement unassisted and captured it by use of hand grenades and his automatic pistol.

Sergeant Major Daniel J. Daly's Medals and Citations

On the same day, during the German attack on Bouresches, he brought in wounded under fire.

Silver Star Citation

By direction of the President, under the provisions of the act of Congress approved July 9, 1918 (Bul. No. 43, W.D., 1918), First Sergeant Daniel Joseph Daly (MCSN: 73086), United States Marine Corps, is cited by the Commanding General, SECOND Division, American Expeditionary Forces, for gallantry in action and a silver star may be placed upon the ribbon of the Victory Medals awarded him. First Sergeant Daly distinguished himself while serving with Machine Gun Company, Sixth Regiment (Marines), 2d Division, American Expeditionary Forces at Chateau-Thierry, France, 6 June–10 July 1918.

(In 1918, Congress created the Silver Star Medal, replacing the Silver Star Citation. In 1932, all personnel who had been awarded the Silver Citation Star were authorized to wear the Silver Star, the nation's third highest decoration for combat heroism.)

Three letters of commendation
Good Conduct Medal with two bronze stars denoting second and third awards
China Relief Expedition Medal
Philippine Campaign Medal
Expeditionary Medal with one bronze star
Mexican Service Medal
Haitian Campaign Medal
World War I Victory Medal with Aisne, St. Mihiel, Meuse-Argonne and Defensive Sector clasps
French Medaille Militaire,
French Crox de Guerre with Palm
French Fourragere

Chapter Notes

Preface

1. Anne Skelly. "Dan Daly: Legendary Marine 'Devil Dog.'" *Leatherneck*, November 1988.
2. "Daniel Daly, Hero of the Marine Corps; Sergeant Major Who Twice Won Congressional Medal of Honor, Dead at 63," *New York Times*, April 28, 1937.

Chapter Two

1. Daly's Marine Corps service record in the National Personnel and Records Center, St. Louis, Missouri.
2. *The New York Times*, weather report, November 12, 1873.
3. Ireland birth and baptism records, Familysearch.com. https://www.familysearch.org/ark:/61903/1:1:FRQX-8XJ.
4. U.S. census record dated June 11, 1880 and the New York State Census dated February 16, 1892 at Ancestry.com.
5. Paul Kleppner, "The Greenback and Prohibition Parties," *History of U.S. Political Parties: Volume II: 1860–1910, The Gilded Age of Politics*, edited by Arthur M. Schlesinger Jr. New York: Chelsea House/R.R. Bowker Co., 1973, 1556.
6. Birth-marriage-death records for Ireland on Ancestry.com; Familysearch.com marriage record states John was age 27 and Ellen was 20 at the time of their marriage in January 1865.
7. Ancestry.com and Familysearch.com records.
8. Records on Familysearch.com.
9. Martin Scorsese's 2002 movie *Gangs of New York* offers a vivid portrait of life in the squalid Five Points neighborhood of Manhattan.
10. Castle Garden opened in 1855 and closed in 1890. It was replaced by Ellis Island in 1892.
11. The 1880 U.S. Census for Glen Cove lists John as working at the starch works. The census lists only John, David and Daniel living there. John arrived in the 1870s with David and Daniel. Ellen and Julia joined them in June 1880.
12. Joan Harrison. *Glen Cove*. Charleston, SC: Arcadia, 2008.
13. Antonia Petrash, Carol Stern and Carol McCrossen. "History of Glen Cove." Glen Cove Public Library website, https://www.glencovelibrary.org/local-history/history-of-glen-cove/.
14. Joan Harrison. *Glen Cove Revisited*. Charleston, SC: Arcadia, 2010, 99.
15. Daniel E. Russell. "The Bells of St. Patrick's," http://www.glencoveheritage.com/legacy_site/stpatsbells.pdf.
16. 1892 New York State Census on Ancestry.com.
17. The 1888 annual report of the New York Authority for Improving the Conditions of the Poor.
18. WikiTree research by Eric Daly, posted 2013. https://www.wikitree.com/wiki/Daly-434.
19. Stephen O'Connor. *Orphan Trains*. Boston, New York: Houghton Mifflin Company, 2001, 88–90.
20. O'Connor, 88–90.
21. "Daniel Daly, Hero of the Marine Corps." *New York Times*. April 28, 1937; "Dan Daly." *Leatherneck*. March 1949.
22. http://boards.ancestry.com/surnames.ransweiler/1.2/mb.ash. Message

209

board comment posted June 18, 2014, William L. Daly wrote that his grandfather got Daly, a cousin, the job at "Devoe Oil" and he worked there in the 1890s.

23. James W. Gould. *Americans in Sumatra*, The Hague: Martinus Nijhoff, 1961; "Fire Destroys Devoe Oil Works," *New York Herald*, May 26, 1869.

24. Anthony Hamboussi and Paul Parkhill. *Newtown Creek: A Photographic Survey of New York's Industrial Waterway.* Princeton: Princeton Architectural Press, 2010.

25. E.E. Lippincott. "Newtown Creek, Sounding a Death Knell for a Long-Forsaken Waterway," *New York Times.* February 10, 2002.

Chapter Three

1. Daly's Marine Corps enlistment papers in the National Archives.
2. Diana Preston. *The Boxer Rebellion,* New York: Berkley Publishing Group, 1999, xxiii.
3. http://claver.gprep.org/sjochs/labor.htm.
4. https://www.reference.com/history/much-did-things-cost-1900-9e40559daa251473.
5. Preston, xxiii.
6. Daly's Marine Corps service record.
7. Robert Pendleton. Spanish-American War Centennial Site, http://www.spanamwar.com/1stmarineroster.html; Besides Hall, other notable Marines who saw action in Cuba with the 1st Marine Battalion were future Marine Commandants George Elliot and Wendell Neville and Sergeant John Quick. Another notable Marine, newly minted Second Lieutenant Smedley Darlington Butler, joined the battalion in Cuba in July 1898, after the unit's combat. Butler, the son and grandson of congressmen, had lied about his age to enlist. He was just 16.

Chapter Four

1. Raymond J. Tassin, *Double Winners of the Medal of Honor.* Canton, OH: Daring Books, 1986, 129.

2. Oscar Upham. "Log of Siege of Pekin." 1900. U.S. Marine Corps Historical Center, Washington, D.C., 64–65.
3. Upham, 2.
4. Upham, 4.
5. Diana Preston, 6.
6. Preston, 7
7. Upham, 7.
8. Preston, 63.
9. Tassin, 131.
10. Upham, 8.
11. Upham, 10.
12. Preston, 74–75.
13. Upham, 11.
14. Preston, 84.
15. Preston, 82, and Peter Fleming, *The Siege at Peking, The Boxer Rebellion.* New York: Dorset Press, 1959, 107.
16. Tassin, 133.
17. Preston, 83.

Chapter Five

1. Tassin, 133.
2. Preston, 131–132.
3. Upham, 16.
4. Upham, 18–20.
5. Tassin, 133.
6. Edward A. Dieckmann Sr. "Dan Daly, Reluctant Hero," *Marine Corps Gazette,* March 1960.
7. Chester M. Biggs Jr. *The United States Marines in North China, 1894–1942.* Jefferson, N.C.: McFarland, 2010, 83–84.
8. Biggs, 81.
9. Tassin, 137.
10. Upham, 28–29.
11. Preston, 152.
12. Upham, 30, and Tassin, 134.
13. Upham, 65.
14. Dieckmann.
15. Upham, 32; Preston, 161; http://www.standingwellback.com/home/2016/2/8/improvised-artillery.html.
16. Dieckmann.
17. Upham, 33.
18. Upham, 36, and Preston, 166.
19. Dieckmann; Tassin, 142.
20. Tassin, 143.
21. Tassin, 142–143.
22. Dieckmann.
23. Upham, 37.

Notes—Chapter Six

24. Upham, 41.
25. Preston, 195.
26. Upham, 47–48.
27. Upham, 50.
28. Preston, 196–197.
29. Upham, 52.
30. Upham, 53–54.
31. Robert Coltman, Jr. *Beleagured in Peking: The Boxer's War Against the Foreigner.* Philadelphia, PA: F.A. Davis Company, 1901, 139. Coltman was an American physician and medical professor based in Peking.
32. Upham, 55.
33. Fleming, 204.
34. Army Private Calvin P. Titus, Co. E, 14th Infantry, opened the way for the American forces by scaling the Tartar Wall, using niches in the wall as footholds. He received the Medal of Honor for his daring as well as an appointment to the U.S. Military Academy, from which he graduated in 1905.
35. Upham, 58.
36. Preston, 243.
37. Preston, 247.
38. Upham, 65.
39. Upham was one of five Marines in Peking awarded the Medal of Honor for helping to erect barricades on the Tartar Wall under heavy enemy fire. Daly and the other 12 recipients were simply cited for "meritorious conduct." Born in Ohio in 1871, Upham joined the Marine Corps in 1896, and saw action in the Spanish-American War aboard the *Oregon*. After the Marines, he worked for the U.S. Postal Service and died in Oklahoma in 1949.
40. H. W. Houk. "Dan Daly Retires," *Leatherneck Magazine,* March 1929.
41. Author's note: The date of Daly's heroic stand is in dispute. It varies in different accounts. His citation says August 14, the day the siege ended. Hall's letter says it took place "the night of July 15." Private Upham's journal indicates it was the night of July 14–15. Given that Hall's letter was written much later while Upham's journal was written at the time, I believe Upham's date is the most reliable.
42. Among the officers in the relief force, First Lieutenant Smedley Darlington Butler was brevetted to captain. He was cited for twice rescuing wounded men and holding off a large force of Chinese.
43. Resolution attached to an August 20, 1900 letter from Edwin Conger to Major William P. Biddle in the National Archives, entry 26, Record Group 127. Biddle saw action with the Peking relief force and went on to be commandant of the Marine Corps, 1911–1914.
44. Houk.
45. Edward A. Dieckmann Sr., "Dan Daly," *Marine Corps Gazette,* November 1960.

Chapter Six

1. Passport application at the U.S. Embassy in London, July 21, 1891, on Ancestry.com.
2. Coltman, 219 (photo).
3. Dr. Paul Campiche. "Notes sur la cariere d' Auguste Chamot" (Notes on the Career Path of Auguste Chamot). *Revue Historique Vaudoise,* 1955.
4. Campiche.
5. Coltman, 220.
6. Larry Clinton Thompson. *William Scott Ament and the Boxer Rebellion.* Jefferson, NC: McFarland, 2009, 149.
7. Coltman, 218.
8. Coltman, 218.
9. Fleming, 67.
10. Preston, 57.
11. Fleming, 67.
12. Fleming, 94.
13. Preston, 75–76.
14. Thompson, 198.
15. Thompson, 197.
16. Lanxin Xiang. *The Origins of the Boxer War.* Abingdon-on-Thames, U.K.: Routledge, 2014, 47.
17. Campiche, 30.
18. *Washington Post.* March 11, 1907. "Dowager's Jeweled Cap Part of Bankruptcy Evidence." Associated Press, Oct. 3, 1907.
19. Preston, 325.
20. "Heroes of Peking Lose Heavily by the Earthquake." *San Francisco Call.* May 19, 1906.
21. "Chamot Accuses Beautiful Wife." *San Francisco Call.* February 23, 1908.

22. "Affinity Turmoil Ends in Divorce." *San Francisco Call.*, May 19, 1908.
23. Preston, 325.
24. Associated Press, June 3, 1909.

Chapter Seven

1. Daly's service record.
2. The six Marine privates named in Biddle's letter of commendation along with Daly were Lewis F. Eads, Arthur S. Fowler, George H. Garretson, Fred R. Petherick, Edward P. Vadnay and Frank Youmans.
3. George B. Clark, *Battle History of the United States Marine Corps, 1775–1945*. Jefferson, NC: McFarland, 2014, 98–99.

Chapter Eight

1. Jack Sweetman. *The Landing at Vera Cruz: 1914*. Annapolis, MD: Naval Institute Press, 1968, 13.
2. James Brown Scott. " Mediation in Mexico," *The American Journal of International Law*, 1914, 589–582.
3. Sweetman, 35.
4. Scott, 590.
5. Sweetman, 44.
6. Sweetman, 52–53.
7. Sweetman, 52.
8. Sweetman, 58.
9. Sweetman, 59.
10. Sweetman, 60.
11. Sweetman, 62.
12. Alan Bevilacqua, Major, USMC (Ret.). "Johnny the Hard Settles for Nothing Less Than the Best," *Leatherneck*, June 2013, 16–20.
13. Tassin, 146.
14. Sweetman, 63.
15. Sweetman, 65.
16. Sweetman, 71.
17. Sweetman, 72–73.
18. Sweetman, 73.
19. Sweetman, 75.
20. Sweetman, 78.
21. Sweetman, 85.
22. Sweetman, 89.
23. Sweetman, 106.
24. Tassin, 148.

25. Lowell Thomas, *Old Gimlet Eye: The Adventures of Smedley Darlington Butler*, New York: Farrar & Rinehart, 1933, 179.
26. Sweetman, 123.
27. Sweetman, 136.
28. Sweetman, 139.
29. Daly's service record.
30. Act of Congress, March 3, 1915, 38 Stat. 928, 931.
31. Thomas, 180.
32. Letter from Daniels to Butler, dated August 3, 1916, in the Navy Department files of the National Archives.
33. *The Congressional Medal of Honor.* Bellevue, WA: Sharp & Dunnigan, 1984, 555–563.
34. Catlin, 106.
35. *New York Times*, April 28, 1937. The *New York Times* also reported on June 9, 1918, during the battle for Belleau Wood, that Daly had twice received the Medal of Honor and added, "The third award, which is now under consideration, has been recommended because of gallantry in the face of fire at Vera Cruz in 1914."

Chapter Nine

1. Patrick Bellegarde Smith, Alex Dupuy, Robert Fallon, Jr., Mary Renda, Emitte St. Jacques and Jeffrey Sommers. "Haiti and the Occupation by the United States in 1915: Antecedents and Outcomes." *Journal of Haitian Studies*. Special Issue, Fall 2015, 17.
2. Excerpt from a speech by Major General Smedley Butler to the Federation of American Scientists, 1933. https://fas.org/man/smedley.htm.
3. Hans Schmidt. *The United States Occupation of Haiti, 1915–1934*. New Brunswick, NJ: Rutgers University Press, 1995. 43.
4. Schmidt, 48.
5. Boot, 159.
6. Boot, 160.
7. George Marvin, "Assassination and Intervention in Haiti," *The World's Work*, New York: Doubleday, Page, & Co., 1916, 405.
8. Marvin, 408.

Notes—Chapter Nine

9. "U.S. Occupation of Haiti, 1915–1934," Naval History and Heritage Command website, https://www.history.navy.mil/research/library/online-reading-room/title-list-alphabetically/u/us-occupation-of-haiti-1915–1934.html; Marvin, 409.

10. Lowell Thomas. *Old Gimlet Eye: The Adventures of Smedley D. Butler*, New York: Farrar & Rinehart, 1933, 182.

11. Thomas, 182.

12. Thomas, 183.

13. Max Boot. *The Savage Wars of Peace: Small Wars and the Rise of American Power*. New York: Basic Books, 2014, 162.

14. Thomas, 186.

15. Mark Strecker. *Smedley D. Butler, USMC: A Biography*. Jefferson, NC: McFarland, 2014, 62.

16. Accounts vary as to the size of this patrol, ranging from 27 to 44. The number 40 used here is based on Butler's report recommending Daly for the Medal of Honor, which states that Butler, Captain Upshur, First Lieutenant Edward A. Ostermann, First Lieutenant Adolph B. Miller, Assistant Surgeon John T. Borden and 35 enlisted men participated in the patrol. (The report is in Daly's file in the National Personnel Records Center in St. Louis.) However, the October 1915 muster list for the 15th Marine Company contains a note next to the names of 38 enlisted Marines identifying them as having participated in the October 24–25 patrol and capture of Fort Dipitie. Adding Butler, Upshur, Ostermann, Miller and Borden to the list of 38 enlisted men makes it 43. (The muster list was accessed on Ancestry.com.)

17. Thomas, 190.

18. Thomas, 191.

19. Thomas, 191.

20. David Zabecki. "Paths to Glory: Medal of Honor Recipients Smedley Butler and Dan Daly." *Military History* magazine, December 26, 2007.

21. Thomas, 194.

22. Thomas, 195.

23. Annual Report of the Secretary of the Navy, 265.

24. Butler's report in Daly's personnel file recommending him for the Medal of Honor.

25. Annual Report of the Secretary of the Navy, 266.

26. Thomas, 197.

27. Smedley Darlington Butler and Anne Cipriano Venzon. *General Smedley Darlington Butler: The Letters of a Leatherneck, 198–1931*. New York: Praeger, 1992, 158.

28. Ivan Muscant. *The Banana Wars: A History of United States Military Intervention in Latin America from the Spanish-American War to the Invasion of Panama*. New York: Macmillan, 1990, 194.

29. Daly unit diaries. Togetherweserved.com. https://marines.togetherweserved.com/usmc/servlet/tws.webapp.WebApp?cmd=ShadowBoxProfile&type=EventExt&ID=135930.

30. Robert Heinl and Nancy Heinl. *Written in Blood: The History of the Haitian People, 1492–1971*. New York: Houghton Mifflin, 1978.

31. Edward A. Dieckmann Sr. "Dan Daly, Reluctant Hero." *Marine Corps Gazette*, November 1960.

32. Upshur's letter in Daly's service record.

33. Strecker, 64.

34. Samuel M. Harrington, Major, USMC. "The Strategy and Tactics of Small Wars," *The Marine Corps Gazette*, 1921, 484.

35. Muscant, 198.

36. Heinl, 413.

37. Franklin D. Roosevelt. "Trip to Haiti and Santo Domingo, 1917." University of Florida George A. Smathers Libraries, Latin American and Caribbean Collection.

38. Boot, 164.

39. Michael Clodfelter. *Warfare and Armed Conflicts: A Statistical Encyclopedia of Casualty and Other Figures, 1492–2015*. Jefferson, NC: McFarland & Co., 2017, 378.

40. Extract from the Navy secretary's letter of commendation to Daly contained in his service record. Daly actually received his second Medal of Honor on October 1, 1917, while serving in France, based on a letter from Commandant Barnett and acknowledgment of its receipt by Daly contained in his service record.

41. Annual Report of the Secretary of the Navy, 266.
42. Boot, 165.
43. Graham A. Cosmas. "*Cacos* and *Caudillos*: Marines and Counterinsurgency in Hispaniola, 1915–1924." *U.S. Marines and Irregular Warfare, 1898–2007*. Quantico, VA: Marine Corps University Press, 2008, 136; "Inquiry into Occupation and Administration of Haiti and Santo Domingo. Testimony before the Senate Select Committee on Haiti and Santo Domingo, 1922, 1808–1809.
44. *Congressional Record*, May 26, 1934, 9606.
45. Mark R. Folse. "The Impact of Great War on the Marines in Hispaniola, 1917–1919. Temple University James A. Barnes Graduate Student History Conference, 2014, 9.
46. "Lessons from another forgotten American occupation." *Progressive Historians* website. http://www.progressivehistorians.com/2008/04/lessons-from-another-forgotten-american.html; Harry A. Franck. "The Death of Charlemagne." *The Century Illustrated Magazine*. Scribner & Co., May-October, 1920, 23–24.
47. "An Iconic Image of Haiti Liberty." *The New Yorker*. July 28, 2015. https://www.newyorker.com/culture/photo-booth/haiti-u-s-occupation-charlemagne-peralte.
48. Clodfelter, 378.
49. Schmidt, 232.
50. Daly's service record.
51. Daly's service record.
52. Schmidt.

Chapter Ten

1. Daly's service record.
2. "Dominican Republic—Ulises Heureaux, 1882–99". Library of Congress, Federal Research Division. http://countrystudies.us/dominican-republic/8.htm.
3. Stephen M. Fuller and Graham A. Cosmas. "Marines in the Dominican Republic." Marine Corps History and Museums Division, 1974, 3–4.
4. Fuller, 6.
5. G. Pope Atkins. *The Dominican Republic and the United States: From Imperialism to Transnationalism*. Athens: University of Georgia Press, 1998, 46–47.
6. Atkins, 48.
7. Fuller, 7.
8. Fuller, 9.
9. Edwin N. McClellan, Major, USMC. "Operations Ashore in the Dominican Republic." *United States Naval Institute Proceedings*, 1921, 239.
10. Samuel M. Harrington, Major, USMC. "The Strategy and Tactics of Small Wars," *The Marine Corps Gazette*, December 1921, 478.
11. Fuller, 11.
12. Harrington, 490.
13. Marine Corps muster roll for 8th Marine Company, June 1916, accessed on Ancestry.com.
14. Marine Corps muster roll for 8th Marine Company, July 1916, accessed on Ancestry.com.
15. Holland M. Smith. *Coral and Brass*. New York: Charles Scribner's Sons, 1949, 40.
16. Kenneth W. Condit and Edwin T. Turnbladh. *Hold High the Torch, A History of the 4th Marines*. Quantico, VA: Historical Division, U.S. Marine Corps Headquarters, 1960, 42.
17. Fuller, 13.
18. Harrington, 479–480.
19. *United States Naval Institute Proceedings*, 241.
20. Fuller, 14.
21. Smith, 41.
22. Condit, 47.
23. Holland M. Smith. *Coral and Brass*. New York: Charles Scribner's Sons, 1949, 41.
24. Condit, 50.
25. Harrington, 482–483; Condit, 49.
26. *United States Naval Institute Proceedings*, 242.
27. Winans' Medal of Honor citation.
28. Condit.
29. Winans' Medal of Honor citation.
30. Fuller, 20.

Chapter Eleven

1. Edwin H. Simmons, Brigadier General, USMC (Retired). *The United States*

Notes—Chapter Twelve

Marines, the First Two Hundred Years, 1775–1975. New York: Viking Press, 1976, 108.

2. Clyde H. Metcalf, Lieutenant Colonel, USMC. *A History of the U.S. Marine Corps*. New York: G.P. Putnam's Sons, 1939, 449.

3. *120 Years of American Education: A Statistical Portrait*. U.S. Department of Education, National Center for Education Statistics, 1993, 26.

4. *Handbook of the Hotchkiss Machine Gun, Model of 1914*. U.S. War Department, Office of the Chief of Ordnance, November 1917. Reprinted by Normont Technical Publications, Wickenburg, Arizona, 1973.

5. Don V. Paradis. *The World War I Memoirs of Don V. Paradis, Gunnery Sergeant, USMC*. N.p.: Lulu.com, 2010.

6. Frank O. Hough, Lieutenant Colonel, USMCR. "Dan Daly." *Marine Gazette*, November 1954.

7. Anne Skelly. "Dan Daly: Legendary Marine 'Devil Dan.'" *Leatherneck*, November 1988.

8. Hough.

9. Edwin N. McClellan, Major, USMC. *The United States Marine Corps in the World War*. Washington, D.C.: Marine Corps Historical Branch, 1920, reprinted 1968, 32.

10. William K. Jones, Lieutenant General, USMC (Retired). *A Brief History of the 6th Marines*. Quantico, VA: History and Museum Division, U.S. Marine Corps Headquarters, 1987, 21.

11. Edward Lengel. "A Story Teller Hiking Through History," 2018 http://www.edwardlengel.com/tag/omar-bundy/.

12. "History of the 6th Regiment, United States Marines." U.S. Marine Corps Reference Branch, 1972, 8.

13. Albertus W. Catlin. *With the Help of God and a Few Marines, The Battles of Chateau Thierry and Belleau Wood*. New York: Doubleday, Page & Company, 1919. Reprinted 2016. 23.

14. Catlin, 31.

15. Jones. *A Brief History of the 6th Marines*. 3.

16. Lengel.

17. Mark Mortensen. *George W. Hamilton, America's Greatest World War I Hero*. Jefferson, NC: McFarland, 2011, 240.

18. Catlin, 43.

19. Catlin, 43.

Chapter Twelve

1. Martin Gilbert. *The First World War*. New York: Henry Holt and Company, 1994, 425.

2. "Marines Won High Place in Glory of War." *The Sun*, New York. December 9, 1918.

3. Levi E. Hemrick. *Once a Marine*. New York: Carlton Press, 1968; reprinted, Clarion Publishing, 2013.

4. Catlin, 53.

5. Catlin, 70.

6. Alan Axelrod. *The Miracle at Belleau Wood*. New York: Lyons Press, 2007, revised edition 2018, 136.

7. Edwin N. McClellan, Major, USMC. "Operations of the Fourth Brigade of Marines in the Aisne Defensive, *Marine Gazette*, March 1920, 190.

8. McClellan. "Operations of the Fourth Brigade," 191.

9. Catlin, 58.

10. "History of the 6th Regiment, United States Marines," 11; Catlin, 61.

11. Edwin Howard Simmons, Brigadier General, USMC (Retired) and Joseph H. Alexander, Colonel, USMC (Retired). *Through the Wheat: The U.S. Marines in World War I*. Annapolis, MD: Naval Institute Press, 2008, 89–90.

12. McClellan, *The History of the United States Marine Corps in the World War*, 41.

13. Catlin, 66.

14. McClellan. "Operations of the Fourth Brigade of Marines in the Aisne Defensive," 207.

15. "Marines Won High Place in Glory of War." *The Sun*, New York. December 9, 1918.

16. Gilbert, 427–428.

17. Edwin N. McClellan, Major, USMC. "Operations of the Fourth Brigade of Marines in the Aisne Defensive," *Marine Gazette*, March 1920, 195.

18. Catlin, 64.

19. Catlin, 59.

Notes—Chapter Thirteen

20. Catlin, 68.
21. McClellan, "Operations of the Fourth Brigade of Marines in the Aisne Defensive," 208.
22. McClellan, "Operations of the Fourth Brigade of Marines in the Aisne Defensive," 199.
23. Catlin, 70.
24. McClellan, "Operations of the Fourth Brigade of Marines in the Aisne Defensive," 213.
25. Tassin, 155.

Chapter Thirteen

1. The 1,300 casualties at Soissons on July 19 would top the one-day record of 1,087 Marine casualties at Belleau Wood. Not until the Marines invaded Tarawa in World War II would those records be eclipsed. The Marines had to wade half a mile through the atoll's lagoon to get at the entrenched defenders and suffered 1,500 casualties.
2. Catlin, 72–73.
3. Janson (1878–1930) served in World War I under the name Charles F. Hoffman. It was under this name that he received the Army Medal of Honor. He later received the Navy Medal of Honor for this same action, although this was issued under his real name, Janson. In addition, he received the Silver Star Citation, the French Médaille Militaire and the Croix de Guerre with palm for this action. Janson served for nearly 10 years in the U.S. Army under his real name before enlisting in the Marine Corps in 1910 under the name of Hoffman. Why he changed names is a matter of conjecture. Some sources suggest he got into trouble in the Army and sought to avoid the consequences. In 1921, Janson served as the Marine Corps pallbearer at the dedication of the Tomb of the Unknown Soldier at Arlington National Cemetery. He was promoted to sergeant major upon retirement in 1926. He died in 1930. His headstone reads "Ernest August Janson" and "AKA Charles E. Hoffman."
4. George B. Clark. *Devil Dogs, Fighting Marines of World War I.* Annapolis, MD: Naval Institute Press, 1999, 108.
5. Catlin, 11.
6. An infantry battalion in the A.E.F. consisted of four companies, each comprised of six officers and 250 enlisted, for a total of a little over 1,000 men. www.worldwar1.com/dbc/squarediv.htm. However, only half of them could be used in the first rush. Clark, *Devil Dogs: Fighting Marines in World War I*, 116; Simmons and Alexander, *Through the Wheat*, 106.
7. Catlin, 74; James Carl Nelson. *I Will Hold*, New York: Caliber, 2016, 93.
8. Catlin, 74.
9. Camp, 97.
10. Floyd Gibbons. *And They Thought We Wouldn't Fight.* New York: R.R. Donnelly & Sons Co., 2014 (first published 1919), 245.
11. Gibbons, 251.
12. Gibbons, 253–254.
13. Gibbons, 252, 257
14. Catlin, 77.
15. Axelrod, 145.
16. Catlin, 76.
17. Dick Camp, Colonel, USMC (Ret.). *The Devil Dogs at Belleau Wood.* Beverly, MA: Zenith Press, 2008, 85.
18. Simmons and Alexander, 108; Catlin later wrote that he believed his wounding was "a chance shot and not the result of good marksmanship, for the bullet must have come some 600 yards." Catlin, 79.
19. Camp, 88.
20. Simmons and Alexander, 110; Nelson, 101–103.
21. Axelrod, 188.
22. Quoted by Edward A. Dieckmann Sr., in "Dan Daly: Reluctant Hero," *Marine Corps Gazette*, November 1960.
23. Gibbons, 241–242.
24. Gibbons, 240.
25. Simmons and Alexander, 268n3.
26. Axelrod, 146.
27. Clark, *Devil Dogs*, 213n76.
28. Catlin, 83–84.
29. J.E. Rendinell and George Pattullo. *One Man's War, The Diary of a Leatherneck.* New York: J.H. Sears & Company, 1928, 103.
30. Rendinell, 107.
31. One of four incidents cited in Daly's award of the Distinguished Service Cross and Navy Cross.

Notes—Chapters Fourteen, Fifteen

32. Clark. *Devil Dogs,* 140; Axelrod, 193.
33. Tassin, 156.
34. Citation for the Distinguished Service Cross and Navy Cross.
35. Stephen W. Scott. *Sergeant Major Dan Daly, The Most Outstanding Marine of All Time.* Baltimore, MD: PublishAmerica, 2009, 107.
36. Clark. *Devil Dogs,* 144.
37. Camp, 108.
38. Axelrod, 201–202.
39. Simmons and Alexander. 114–115; Axelrod, 212.
40. Camp, 113.
41. On pages 28 and 29 in his book, *Miracle at Belleau Wood,* historian Alan Axelrod provides a vivid description of the horrible effects of the different types of poison gas used during World War I—chlorine, phosgene and mustard.
42. Simmons and Alexander, 76.
43. Axelrod, 221
44. Daly's service record; also Addendum to Muster Roll, July 1919. After initial treatment, he was taken to Base Hospital 18, located in a French estate at Bazoilles-sur-Meuse south of Nancy, 150 miles southeast of Belleau Wood. Later, he was moved to American Base Hospital 20 in Chatel-Guyon, near Vichy in Central France.
45. Tassin, 157.
46. Simmons and Alexander. 120.
47. Camp, 117.
48. Rendinell, 124.
49. Clark. *Devil Dogs.* 197–198.
50. Simmons and Alexander, 122.
51. Camp, 122.
52. Camp, 124.
53. Edwin N. McClellan, "The Aisne-Marne Offensive," *Marine Gazette,* March 1921, 68.
54. Axelrod, 227.
55. John S.D. Eisenhower. *Yanks, The Epic Story of the American Army in World War I.* New York: Simon & Schuster, 2001, 146.
56. George C. Clark. *Devil Dogs, Fighting Marines of World War I.* Annapolis, MD: Naval Institute Press, 1999, 64, 434.
57. For more on the legend, see Simmons and Alexander, *Through the Wheat,* footnote 8 on page 269; also see https://www.thoughtco.com/german-myth-teufelshunde-devil-dogs-1444315 as well as https://www.stripes.com/blogs-archive/the-rumor-doctor/the-rumor-doctor-1.104348.

Chapter Fourteen

1. George B. Clark. *Battle History of the United States Marine Corps, 1775–1945.* Jefferson, NC: McFarland, 2014, 240.
2. Colonel Lee's letter of 24 June 1918 to the brigade commander is part of Daly's service record.
3. Clark. *Devil Dogs,* 264; Simmons and Alexander, 184.
4. Clark, *Devil Dogs.* 213n76; A search of Army, Navy and Marine Corps records in the National Archives in Washington, D.C., Silver Spring, Md., and St. Louis, Mo., failed to locate any documents that shed light on the reason for downgrading the recommendation for a third Medal of Honor to a DSC.
5. Simmons and Alexander, 108–109.
6. Axelrod, 226.
7. Clark. *Devil Dogs,* 213, n75.
8. *The Congressional Medal of Honor: The Names and The Deeds,* Bellevue, WA: Sharp & Dunnigan Publications, 1984, 13.
9. *The Congressional Medal of Honor,* 957.
10. *Awarding of Medals in the Naval Service*: Hearing Before a Subcommittee on ... on Naval Affairs, https://books.google.com/books?id=qv08AAAAYAAJ&printsec=frontcover#v=onepage&q&f=false.

Chapter Fifteen

1. Lieutenant Clifton Cates of Keyser's 2/6 described the outcome at Soissons as "a noble victory." Nelson, 184.
2. Simmons and Alexander, 145.
3. Simmons and Alexander, 148.
4. Clark, *Devil Dogs,* 225.
5. Clark, *Devil Dogs,* 232.
6. In his memoir, Harbord complained that when he arrived from Paris, he had to wait all day July 15 for Bundy to pack

up and move out of division headquarters instead of being already gone. In a sign of his peevish nature, Harbord added: "Poor old General Doyen cramped my style by lingering for three days when I took over the Marines at Verdun and General Bundy stayed until after dinner the day of his relief, forgetting several times that he was no longer in command. I finally moved into the room just before bedtime." James G. Harbord, Major General. *Leaves from a War Diary,* New York: Dodd, Mead & Company, 1925, 315.

7. Clark, *Devil Dogs,* 223; Simmons and Alexander, 144.
8. Harbord, 318–321.
9. Simmons and Alexander, 146–147.
10. Clark, *Devil Dogs,* 226.
11. Simmons and Alexander, 152.
12. Simmons and Alexander, 158.
13. Clark, 244.
14. Nelson, 158.
15. Nelson, 169.
16. The advance on July 19 had been scheduled to begin at 7 a.m. The rolling barrage had begun at that hour but the Marines did not begin their advance until 8:30 because they were waiting for the tanks and Sibley's 3/6 to arrive.
17. Nelson, 167.
18. Clark, *Devil Dogs,* 248.
19. Brannen, 32.
20. Nelson, 169.
21. Simmons and Alexander, 168.
22. Clark, *Devil Dogs,* 251.
23. Clark, *Devil Dogs,* 253–254.
24. Simmons and Alexander, 173.
25. Nelson, 185.
26. *The West Point Atlas of American Wars,* New York: Frederick A. Praeger, Publishers, 1959, 66.
27. Clark, *Devil Dogs,* 254.

Chapter Sixteen

1. Simmons and Alexander, 178.
2. Simmons and Alexander, 184.
3. Daly's service record.
4. Simmons and Alexander, 185.
5. Brannen, 38; Simmons and Alexander, 185.
6. Clark, *Devil Dogs,* 268.

7. The 73rd Machine Gun Company muster list for September 1918 accessed on Ancestry.com.
8. Simmons and Alexander, 190; Brannen, 38.
9. *The West Point Atlas of American Wars,* 68.
10. Clark, *Devil Dogs,* 275.
11. Simmons and Alexander, 194.
12. Brannen, 40.
13. Clark, *Devil Dogs,* 282.
14. Houchins was killed in action on the first day of the Meuse-Argonne Offensive. Loomis survived the war, became a naval aviator and retired with the rank of lieutenant commander.
15. "John Peirce Residence, 11 East 51st Street, Manhattan." Landmarks Preservation Committee, June 23, 2009.
16. Peirce's Marine Corps service record, National Personnel Records Center; New York Abstracts of World War I Military Records, accessed on Ancestry.com.
17. Simmons and Alexander, 194; Nelson, 214.

Chapter Seventeen

1. Blanc Mont Ridge is described in various histories as either 200 feet high or 200 meters in elevation. Hill 210, at the east end of the ridge, is named for its elevation in meters above sea level, or 689 feet. Blanc Mont, at the west end of the ridge, is 201 meters, or 659 feet. The elevation of the Essen Trench, where the Marines began their advance, is 139 meters, or 456 feet. The difference in elevation between the trench and the ridge is 233 feet. So both claims about its height (200 feet vs. 200 meters) are essentially accurate. Peter F. Owen, Lieutenant Colonel, USMC (Ret.) and John Swift, Lieutenant Colonel, USMC (Ret.). *A Hideous Price: The 4th Brigade at Blanc Mont, Oct. 2–10, 1918.* Quanitco, VA: History Division, U.S. Marine Corps, 2019, 7. Romain Cansière, Ed Gilbert. *Blanc Mont Ridge, 1918: America's Forgotten Victory.* Oxford: Osprey Publishing, 2018.
2. *American Armies and Battlefields In Europe,* Washington, DC: American

Notes—Chapters Eighteen, Nineteen

Battlefield Monuments Commission, 1931, 351.

3. John Lejeune, Major General, USMC, *The Reminiscences of a Marine*. Philadelphia: Dorrance and Co., 1930, 342.

4. O'Leary took command of the 1/5 on August 29 and departed on September 19, immediately after the second day's battle at St. Mihiel. Marine Corps muster records show him "sick in hospital" followed by non-combat duties through the end of the war. He retired as a colonel in 1931.

5. Clark, *Devil Dogs*, 292.
6. Nelson, 222.
7. Clark, *Devil Dogs*, 292.
8. Nelson, 229.
9. Simmons and Alexander, 207.
10. Nelson, 231.
11. *Records of the Second Division (Regulars)*. U.S. Army, 1918.
12. Edwin N. McClellan, Major, USMC. "The Battle of Blanc Mont Ridge." *Marine Gazette*, 1922.
13. Simmons and Alexander, 209.
14. Clark, *Devil Dogs*, 302–303.
15. Clark, *Devil Dogs*, 304.
16. Clark, *Devil Dogs*, 307.
17. Simmons and Alexander, 210.
18. Clark, *Devil Dogs*, 311.
19. Clark, *Devil Dogs*, 314.
20. Simmons and Alexander, 212.
21. Clark, *Devil Dogs*, 332.
22. Simmons and Alexander, 215.
23. McClellan, "The Battle for Blanc Mont Ridge."
24. Addendum to the Muster Roll, July 1919.
25. *Records of the Second Division*.
26. Simmons and Alexander, 217.
27. Simmons and Alexander, 217.
28. Edward G. Lengel. *To Conquer Hell, The Meuse-Argonne, 1918*, New York: Henry Holt and Company, 2008, 255.

Chapter Eighteen

1. Esposito, 70.
2. Lengel, 76–77.
3. Thomas M. Johnson. *Without Censor*, Indianapolis: Bobbs-Merrill Company, 1927, 257.

4. Simmons and Alexander, 221.
5. Lengel, 387.
6. Simmons and Alexander, 223.
7. Clark, 349; also DSC citation: https://homeofheroes.com/distinguished-service-cross/service-cross-world-war-i/world-war-i-distinguished-service-cross-recipients/distinguished-service-cross-wwi-marines/.
8. *Congressional Medal of Honor*, 514–515.
9. Brannen, 55.
10. Clark, 369; Brannen, 55.
11. Simmons and Alexander, 236.
12. Clark, 358–359. Clark used the 73rd Machine Gun Company to describe what happened to a company engaged in the Meuse-Argonne Offensive. The account presented here draws heavily upon Clark's excellent telling of this tale.
13. Clark, 381. Simmons and Alexander put 4th Brigade losses in this final offensive at 323 killed and 1,109 wounded. The difference between their total casualties and Clark's is 14. To put these numbers in perspective, American casualties in the seven-week Meuse-Argonne Offensive were 122,000 (26,277 dead and 95,786 wounded).
14. For a fuller discussion of Pershing's response to questions from Congress about why last minute attacks were made, please see an article by Joseph E. Persico in the Winter 2005 edition of *MHQ (Military History Quarterly)* at https://www.historynet.com/world-war-i-wasted-lives-on-armistice-day.htm.
15. U.S. Marine Corps History Division.
16. Simmons and Alexander, 240.
17. The 73rd's seven other effectives were Sergeant Joseph A. Rankin, Corporal Elmer A. Archbold, Corporal William J Swiatkowski, Private Arthur J. Belisle, Private William A. Biharry, Private Harry King and Drummer Edward J. Allgor.

Chapter Nineteen

1. Daly's service record.
2. Jones, 18; Simmons and Alexander, 243.
3. Brannen, 57.

Notes—Chapter Nineteen

4. Letters from Marine Corps headquarters in Daly's service record.

5. Clark, 385–386; Simmons and Alexander, 248.

6. Clark, 386.

7. "War Hero Returns with Deep Grouch Against Dry Wave," *New York Tribune,* May 8, 1919.

8. Gaynor was a state Supreme Court justice elected mayor of New York in 1909 to clean up corruption. He was shot in the neck in 1910 by a recently fired dock worker. Gaynor survived for three years with the bullet lodged in his throat before dying at age 64. McCarren was a state senator and the boss of Brooklyn's Democratic organization. He died of natural causes at age 60 in 1909. It is unclear how Daly knew these men.

9. "Marines Give Show To-Night," *The Sun and New York Herald,* May 9, 1919.

10. The Victory Arch was 125 feet long, 40 feet wide and 100 feet tall. It cost $1 million in today's dollars and was designed by renowned New York architect Thomas Hastings, who also designed the Tomb of the Unknown Soldier at Arlington National Cemetery, the New York Public Library building, and the American Monument at Meaux, France, commemorating the Second Battle of the Marne, which included the 2nd Division's attack at Soissons. The Victory Arch was torn down in the summer of 1920.

11. Neville was promoted to major general in 1920, served as assistant to the commandant, and commanded the Fleet Marine Force. He succeeded Lejeune as commandant in 1929 but died suddenly in that post the next year.

12. Feland ended the war as a colonel with the DSC, both the Army and Navy DSM, the Legion of Honor, five Silver Star Citations and the Croix de Guerre with bronze star, gold star and four palms. In the late 1920s he commanded the Marines in Nicaragua during the hunt for rebel leader Cesar Sandino and received a second Navy DSM. He retired as a major general.

13. After the war, Lee commanded the Marine brigade in the Dominican Republic and served as military governor there. Later, he commanded the Marine Barracks at Parris Island and at Quantico.

14. For more information on the parades, see: https://www.archives.nyc/blog/tag/Ticker-tape+Parades and https://www.green-wood.com/2017/nycs-parade-at-the-end-of-world-war-i/.

15. Simmons and Alexander, 249.

16. Daly's service record.

17. Daly's service record.

18. 1920 U.S. Census. The niece (Catherine Daly, 21) and nephew (John Daly, 17) were most likely the children of Daniel and Mary's only other surviving sibling, brother David, 53. Some of Daly's correspondence with Marine Corps offices following his retirement have a return address of 32 Pulaski Street, Middle Village, Long Island, New York. That address today is 60–32 68th Avenue, a two-unit, two-story row house built in 1910. Some of the Marine Corps' replies are addressed to the same address, but in Brooklyn, three miles west of the other address. This correspondence is from 1921, 1922 and 1924. Daly himself listed the Middle Village address in an April 1922 letter. A July 1, 1925, Marine Corps document lists the McComb Place address while a December 1, 1925, document lists the Slocum Street address. All correspondence after that date used the Slocum address, the Loeb home, which is consistent with the 1930 U.S. Census.

19. 1925 New York State Census.

20. 1930 U.S. Census.

21. 1930 U.S. Census.

22. Although many of the firm's records have been preserved as historical documents, the same unfortunately is not true for any documents related to personnel at Daly's level, according to the records' archivist.

23. The other body bearers were Chief Gunner's Mate James Delaney, a U.S. Navy gun crew captain on board the merchant ship SS *Campana* that fought a gun battle with a U-boat; Field Artillery Color Sergeant James W. Dell who fought at Soissons; Chief Water Tender Charles Leo O'Conner, who risked his life to save fellow sailors during a U-boat attack; Coast Artillery First Sergeant Louis Razga, who was wounded in

a gas attack two days before the end of World War I; Corporal Thomas D. Saunders, a Native American combat engineer who with one other man captured 63 prisoners; First Sergeant Harry Taylor, who led a "suicide" charge at Gesnes in the Meuse-Argonne; First Lieutenant Samuel Woodfill, a Medal of Honor recipient who single-handedly destroyed three enemy machine-gun nests while suffering the effects of a mustard gas attack near Cunel in the Meuse-Argonne.

24. https://history.army.mil/books/Last_Salute/Ch1.htm.

25. *New York Times*, June 10, 1934.

26. "2d Division Forms a Post," *New York Times*, January 29, 1920.

27. Wynn was a Brooklyn-born machine gunner with the 27th Infantry Division, a New York-based National Guard unit. He was killed in action October 17, 1918 in a British 4th Army attack across the Selle River near Cambrai.

28. *New York Times*, February 23, 1929.

29. The National Weather Service reported the temperature at noon that day was 33 degrees, with sleet and freezing rain. The coldest inauguration was President Ronald Reagan's 1985 inauguration at a frigid 7 degrees above zero.

30. Daly's service record.

31. Telegram in Daly's service file, National Personnel Records Center, St. Louis, Mo.

32. Holcomb's April 29, 1937 letter is in Daly's service record.

33. Daly's grave is in Section 5, Grave Number 70 (40°41'17.9"N 73°52'55.9"W). The cemetery's website has a link to a map showing the location of Section 5: https://www.cem.va.gov/CEM/cems/nchp/cypresshills.asp.

Chapter Twenty

1. This nickname for Daly appeared repeatedly in articles during and after World War I. A headline in The *New York Tribune* on August 21, 1918 stated "'Devil Dog' Dan Daly Wins Another War Medal of Bravery."

2. Jack W. Jaunal, Sergeant Major, USMC (Ret.). "Devil Dog Dan," *Over There!* Vol. 8, No. 4; Edward A. Dieckmann Sr., "Dan Daly: Reluctant Hero," *Marine Corps Gazette*, November 1960.

3. Anne Skelly, "Dan Daly: Legendary Marine 'devil dog,'" *Leatherneck* magazine, September 1988.

4. Gunnery Sergeant Basilone earned the Medal of Honor at Guadalcanal and the Navy Cross (posthumously) at Iwo Jima.

5. Frank O'Hough, Lieutenant Colonel, USMC (Ret.). "Dan Daly," *Marine Corps Gazette*, November 1954.

6. Skelly.

7. O'Hough.

8. "Giants of the Corps," *Marine Corps Gazette*, March 1975. The author of the article is not identified.

9. Edward A. Dieckmann Sr. "Dan Daly: Reluctant Hero." *Marine Corps Gazette*, November 1960.

10. Dieckmann.

11. James McB. Sellers, *World War I Memoirs of Lieutenant Colonel James McBrayer Sellers, USMC*, Pike, NH: The Brass Hat, 1997.

12. O'Hough.

13. Dieckmann.

14. "Dan Daly," *Leatherneck* magazine, March 1949. The author is anonymous.

15. "Giants of the Corps," *Marine Corps Gazette*, March 1975.

Bibliography

Books

Atkins, G. Pope. *The Dominican Republic and the United States: From Imperialism to Transnationalism*. Athens: University of Georgia Press, 1998.
Axelrod, Alen. *Miracle at Belleau Wood, The Birth of the Modern U.S. Marine Corps*. Guilford, CT: Lyons Press, 2010.
Biggs, Chester M., Jr. *The United States Marines in North China, 1894–1942*. Jefferson, NC: McFarland, 2003.
Boot, Max. *The Savage Wars of Peace: Small Wars and the Rise of American Power*. New York: Basic Books, 2014.
Brannon, Carl Andrew. *Over There: A Marine in the Great War*. College Station: Texas A&M University Press, 1996.
Camp, Dick. *The Devil Dogs at Belleau Wood, U.S. Marines in World War I*. New York: Zenith Press, 2008.
Cansière, Romain, and Ed Gilbert. *Blanc Mont Ridge, 1918: America's Forgotten Victory*. Oxford: Osprey Publishing, 2018.
Catlin, Albertus W. *With the Help of God and a Few Marines: The Battles of Chateau Thierry and Belleau Wood*. New York: Doubleday, Page & Company, 1919. Reprinted 2016.
Clark, George B. *Battle History of the United States Marine Corps, 1775–1945*. Jefferson, NC: McFarland, 2014.
Clark, George B. *Devil Dogs, Fighting Marines of World War I*. Annapolis, MD: Naval Institute Press,1999.
Clark, George B. *The Fourth Marine Brigade in World War I: Battalion Histories Based on Official Documents*. Jefferson, NC: McFarland, 2014.
Coltman, Robert Jr. *Beleaguered in Peking: The Boxer's War Against the Foreigner*. Philadelphia: F.A. Davis Company, 1901.
Condit, Kenneth W., and Edwin T. Tunrbladh. *Hold High the Torch: A History of the 4th Marines*. Quantico, VA: Historical Division, U.S. Marine Corps Headquarters, 1960.
The Congressional Medal of Honor. Bellevue, WA: Sharp & Dunnigan, 1984.
Cummings, Constance Frederica Gordon. *Wanderings in China*. New York: W. Blackwood & Sons, 1900.
Esposito, Vincent J. *The West Point Atlas of American Wars*. New York: Frederick A. Praeger, 1959.
Fleming, Peter. *The Siege at Peking, The Boxer Rebellion*. New York: Dorset Press, 1959.
Ford, Walter G. *Reducing the Saint-Mihiel Salient, September 1918*. Quantico, VA: History Division, U.S. Marine Corps, 2018.
Fuller, Stephen M., and Graham A. Cosmas. *Marines in the Dominican Republic (1916–1924)*. Quantico, VA: Marine Corps History and Museums Division, 1974.

Bibliography

Gibbons, Floyd. *And They Thought He Wouldn't Fight.* New York: George H. Doran Company, 1918.
Gilbert, Martin. *The First World War.* New York: Henry Holt and Company, 1994.
Handbook of the Hotchkiss Machine Gun, Model of 1914. Washington, DC: U.S. War Department, Office of the Chief of Ordnance, November 1917. Reprinted by Normont Technical Publications, Wickenburg, Arizona, 1973.
Harbord, James C. *Leaves from a War Diary.* New York: Dodd, Mead & Company, 1925.
Jones, William K. *A Brief History of the 6th Marines.* Washington, DC: History and Museums Division, Headquarters, U.S. Marine Corps, 1987.
Keegan, John. *The First World War.* New York: Random House, 1998.
Lengel, Edward G. *To Conquer Hell: The Meuse-Argonne, 1918.* New York: Henry Holt and Co., 2008.
Lord, Walter. *The Good Years.* New York: Harper and Brothers, 1960.
Mackin, Elton E. *Suddenly We Didn't Want to Die: Memoirs of a World War I Marine.* Novato, CA: Presidio Press, 1993.
McClellan, Edwin N. *The United States Marine Corps in the World War.* Quantico, VA: Historical Branch, G-3 Division, Headquarters, U.S. Marine Corps, 1920.
Metcalf, Clyde H., Lieutenant Colonel, USMC. *A History of the U.S. Marine Corps.* New York: G.P. Putnam's Sons, 1939.
Mortensen, Mark. *George W. Hamilton, America's Greatest World War I Hero.* Jefferson, NC: McFarland, 2011.
Muscant, Ivan. *The Banana Wars: A History of United States Military Intervention in Latin America from the Spanish-American War to the Invasion of Panama.* New York: Macmillan, 1990.
Nelson, James Carl. *I Will Hold: The Story of USMC Legend Clifton B. Cates, from Belleau Wood to Victory in the Great War.* New York: Caliber, 2016.
Nelson, James Carl. *The Remains of Company D: A Story of the Great War.* New York: St. Martin's Griffin, 2009.
O'Connor, Stephen. *Orphan Trains.* New York: Houghton, Mifflin Company, 2001.
Owen, Peter F., Lieutenant Colonel, USMC (Ret.), and John Swift, Lieutenant Colonel, USMC (Ret.). *A Hideous Price: The 4th Brigade at Blanc Mont, Oct. 2–10, 1918.* Quantico, VA: History Division, U.S. Marine Corps, 2019.
Preston, Diana. *The Boxer Rebellion.* New York: Berkley Books, 1999.
Records of the Second Division (Regulars): 9th-23rd Infantry. 5th-6th Marines. 2nd Engineers. Arlington, VA: United States Army Division, 2d, 1918.
Rendinell, J.E., and George Pattullo. *One Man's War: The Diary of a Leatherneck.* New York: J.H. Sears Company, Inc., 1928.
Schmidt, Hans. *Maverick Marine: General Smedley D. Butler and the Contradictions of American Military History.* Lexington: University Press of Kentucky, 2014.
Scott, Stephen W. *Sergeant Major Dan Daly: The Most Outstanding Marine of All Time.* Baltimore: Publish America, 2009.
Simmons, Edwin H., and Joseph H. Alexander. *Through the Wheat: The U.S. Marines in World War I.* Annapolis: Naval Institute Press, 2008.
Simmons, Edwin H., Brigadier General, USMC (Retired). *The United States Marines, 1775–1975.* New York: Viking Press, 1976.
Skylark, Holly. *Washington's War on Nicaragua.* Boston: South End Press, 1988.
Strecker, Mark. *Smedley D. Butler, USMC: A Biography.* Jefferson, NC: McFarland, 2014.
Sweetman, Jack. *The Landing at Veracruz 1914.* Annapolis: Naval Institute Press, 1968.
Tassin, Raymond J. *Double Winners of the Medal of Honor.* Canton, OH: Daring Books, 1986.
Thomas, Lowell. *Old Gimlet Eye: The Adventures of Smedley D. Butler.* New York: Farrar & Rinehart, 1933.
Thompson, Larry Clinton. *William Scott Ament and the Boxer Rebellion: Heroism, Hubris and the "Ideal Missionary."* Jefferson, NC: McFarland, 2009.

Bibliography

Articles

Alexander, Joseph H. "The U.S. Marines in World War I." *Leatherneck,* November 2008.
Becker, Josh. "Devil Dogs, the Battle of Belleau Woods," http://www.beckerfilms.com/DevilDogs-p1.htm, April 17, 2000.
Bevilacqua, Alan, Major, USMC (Ret.). "Johnny the Hard Settles for Nothing Less Than the Best," *Leatherneck,* June 2013.
"The China Marines." http://chinamarine.org/peking.aspx.
Cosgrove, Neil. "Dan Daly, The Fightinest Marine." http://thewildgeese.irish/profiles/blogs/dan-daly-the-fightinest-marine, November 10, 2014.
Cosmas, Graham A. "*Cacos* and *Caudillos*: Marines and Counterinsurgency in Hispaniola, 1915–1924." *U.S. Marines and Irregular Warfare, 1898–2007.* Marine Corps University Press, 2008.
"Dan Daly." *Leatherneck,* March 1949.
"Dan Daly Award Nominations." *Leatherneck Line,* April 1996.
"Daniel 'Dan' Daly (1873–1937), Legendary Marine." Together We Served website. http://marines.togetherweserved.com/usmc/servlet/tws.webapp.WebApps?cmd=ShadowBoxProfile&type=Person&ID=6555.
"Daniel Daly, Hero of the Marine Corps, Sergeant Major Who Twice Won Congressional Medal of Honor is Dead at 63." *New York Times,* April 28, 1937.
Danticat, Edwidge. "The Long Legacy of Occupation of Haiti." *The New Yorker.* July 28, 2015.
"'Devil Dog' Dan Daly Wins Another War Medal for Bravery." *New York Tribune,* August 21, 1918.
Dieckman, Edward A., Sr. "Dan Daly: Reluctant Hero." *Marine Corps Gazette,* November 1960.
"Former Marine, Holder of 11 Medals, Seeks Job." *New York Tribune,* September 19, 1919.
Franck, Harry A. "The Death of Charlemagne." *The Century Illustrated Magazine.* Scribner & Co., May-October, 1920.
"Giants of the Corps: Dan Daly." *Leatherneck,* March 1975.
Hammer, Trygve. "Marine Sergeant With Near Suicidal Courage was Awarded Two Medals of Honor and Nominated for a Third!" https://www.warhistoryonline.com/war-articles/dontforget-remaining-m1911s-hand-guns-to-be-sold.html**,** November 12, 2015.
Harrington, Samuel M., Major, USMC. "The Strategy and Tactics of Small Wars," *The Marine Corps Gazette,* 1921.
Henderson, Jeanne. "The History of Glen Cove, NY." www.longislandgenealogy.com/community.html#glencove.
"History of the 6th Regiment, United States Marines." U.S. Marine Corps Reference Branch, 1972.
Houck, H.W. "Dan Daly Retires." *Leatherneck,* March 1929.
Hough, Frank O. "Dan Daly." *Marine Corps Gazette,* November 1954.
"An Iconic Image of Haiti Liberty." *The New Yorker.* July 28, 2015. https://www.newyorker.com/culture/photo-booth/haiti-u-s-occupation-charlemagne-peralte.
"Lessons from another forgotten American occupation." *Progressive Historians* website. http://www.progressivehistorians.com/2008/04/lessons-from-another-forgotten-american.html.
"Marines Give Show To-night; Renowned Fighters Here on Recruiting Duty Will Entertain." *The Sun and New York Herald,* May 9, 1920.
"Marines Won High Place in Glory of War. *The Sun,* December 9, 1918.
McClellan, Edwin N., Major, USMC. "The Battle of Blanc Mont Ridge." *Marine Gazette,* 1922.
McClellan, Edwin N., Major, USMC. "The Fourth Brigade of Marines in the Training Areas and the Operations in the Verdun Sector." *Marine Gazette,* 1920.

Bibliography

McClellan, Edwin N., Major, USMC. "Operations Ashore in the Dominican Republic." *United States Naval Institute Proceedings,* 1921.

McClellan, Edwin N., Major, USMC. "Operations of the 4th Brigade of Marines in Aisne Offensive." *Marine Corps Gazette,* March 1920.

Miller, J. Michael. "Battle Atop Tartar Wall, Boxer Rebellion." *Leatherneck,* August 2000.

Plante, Trevor K. "U.S. Marines in the Boxer Rebellion." *Prologue* magazine, National Archives. Winter 1999.

Rentfrow, Frank H. "Devil Dog Dan Daly, Hero of Marines Dies." *Leatherneck,* June 1937.

Scott, James Brown. "Mediation in Mexico." *The American Journal of International Law,* 1914.

"Sergeant Major Dan Daly, USMC, The Fightin'est Marine." http://irishamericanheritage month.com/, January 7, 2011.

"Sergeant Major Daniel 'Dan' Daly, USMC." http://www.usmarinesbirthplace.com/DALY. html.

"SgtMaj Dan Daly, USMC." U.S. Marine Corps History Division, https://web.archive. org/web/20150922191021/https://www.mcu.usmc.mil/historydivision/Pages/ Who%27s%20Who/D-F/Daly_DJ.aspx.

Siggurdsson, "Death of Sergeant Major Daniel Daly, USMC, Recipient of 2 Medals of Honor." http://burnpit.us/2016/04/death-sergeant-major-daniel-daly-usmc-recipient-2-medals-honor, April 27, 2016.

Skelly, Anne. "Dan Daly: Legendary Marine 'Devil Dog.'" *Leatherneck,* November 1988.

Smith, Patrick Bellegarde, Alex Dupuy, Robert Fallon, Jr., Mary Renda, Emitte St.Jacques and Jeffrey Sommers. "Haiti and the Occupation by the United States in 1915: Antecedents and Outcomes." *Journal of Haitian Studies.* Special Issue, Fall 2015.

Thompson, Ben. "Sgt Dan Daly." http://www.badassoftheweek.com/daly.html.

Upham, Oscar. "Journal." U.S. Marine Corps Historical Center, Washington, D.C.

"U.S. Occupation of Haiti, 1915–1934," Naval History and heritage Command website, https://www.history.navy.mil/research/library/online-reading-room/title-list-alphabetically/u/us-occupation-of-haiti-1915–1934.html.

Waller, Littleton W.T., Jr., Major, USMC. "Machine Guns of the 4th Brigade." *Marine Corps Gazette,* March 1920.

"War Hero Returns with Deep Grouch Against Dry Wave." *New York Tribune,* May 8, 1919.

Zabecki, David T. "Paths to Glory: Medal of Honor Recipients Smedley Butler and Dan Daly." *Military History,* December 26, 2007.

Government Documents

"Awarding of Medals in the Naval Service: Hearing Before a Subcommittee on Naval Affairs," United States Senate, Sixty-sixth Congress, Second Session, on S. Res. 285. U.S. Government Printing Office, 1920.

Daniel Daly's Marine Corps service record, National Personnel Records Center, National Archives and Records Administration, St. Louis, Missouri.

"Inquiry into Occupation and Administration of Haiti and Santo Domingo. Testimony before the Senate Select Committee on Haiti and Santo Domingo, U.S. Government Printing Office, 1922. https://books.google.com/books?id=L7MyAQAAMAAJ&dq=%22clark+h+wells%22+and+usmc&source=gbs_navlinks_s.

120 Years of American Education: A Statistical Portrait. Washington, DC: U.S. Department of Education, National Center for Education Statistics, 1993.

"Siege and Relief of the Legations at Pekin." *Papers Related to the Foreign Affairs of the*

Bibliography

United States. Washington, DC: U.S. Government Printing Office, 1902. https://books.google.com/books?id=jkRUAAAAIAAJ&pg=PA968&lpg=PA968&dq=peking+siege+and+swiss+consul&source=bl&ots=2--TQgI57y&sig=P6gfe_JCJkypnVzk7cKaL-URX5E&hl=en&sa=X&sqi=2&ved=0ahUKEwi8gZL3uYTVAhVM4GMKHQ9aB3gQ6AEIRzAG#v=onepage&q=peking%20siege%20and%20swiss%20consul&f=false.

Index

Alexander, Joseph 134, 186
Alexis, Pierre-Nord 73
Arias, Desiderio 93, 94, 101
Axelrod, Alan 134, 137

Badger, Charles J. 65
Baker, Newton 144, 192
Barker, Frederick A. 160, 163–165, 170–172, 176 177, 185
Barnett, George 84, 88–90, 104, 150, 191
Basilone, John 199
Batraville, Benoit 87
Bearss, Hiram 101, 104
Bellamy, David 190
Berry, Benjamin S. 120, 126–130, 136, 140, 149, 150, 162
Biddle, William P. 52
Bobo, Rosalvo 73–75, 77
Brannen, Carl 158, 183
Brown Brothers Harriman 194
Buchanan, Allen 60
Bullard, Robert 141, 180
Bundy, Omar 109, 111, 121, 137, 140, 154
Bush, George H.W. 194
Bush, George W. 194
Bush, Prescott 194
Butler, Smedley Darlington 7, 65, 66, 68, 72, 75, 77–85, 87–90, 185, 202
Button, William R. 86

Caceras, Ramon 92, 93
Camp, Dick 190
Canada, William W. 59, 60
Caperton, William B. 74, 88–90, 94, 95, 101, 107
Carranza, Venustiano 56, 57, 68
USS *Castline* 94
Cates, Clifton B. 131, 132, 157, 158, 171, 182

Catlin, Albertus W. 65, 68, 69, 85, 105, 112, 114–116, 118–120, 123, 125, 127, 130, 131, 134, 138
Chamot, Annie (nee McCarthy) 40–46
Chamot, Auguste 40–46
USS *Chester* 85
Cincotta, Angelo J. 197
Citation Star (aka Silver Star Citation, Silver Star Medal) 144, 207
Cixi, dowager empress of China 19, 37
Clark, George B. 54, 157, 186
Clemenceau, Georges 141, 145
USS *Cleveland* 50
Cole, Eli K. 75, 78, 82, 88, 89
Coltman, Robert 41, 42
Conger, Edwin 20, 25, 30, 34, 38
USS *Connecticut* 75, 82, 83
Conze, Jean-Baptiste 86
Cooke, Elliott D. 139, 157
Cukela, Louis 147, 156
Custer, George Armstrong 14

USS *Daly* 199, 200
Daly, Daniel Joseph: "America's 'Fightin'est' Marine" 7, 202; bank guard 194; birth 7; as boxer 13; burial 197, 198; as corporal 50, 51, 201; compared to Paul Bunyan 199; Croix de Guerre 189, 207; death 196, 197; disciplinary actions against 18, 47–51, 53; Distinguished Service Cross 2, 143, 144, 146, 150, 151, 161, 203, 206; enlistments 16, 17, 50, 51, 53, 91; factory worker 13; as first sergeant 101, 192; Good Conduct Medal 51, 53, 207; as gunnery sergeant 75, 201; health issues 49, 101, 196, 197; imposter claiming to be Daly 196; Medaille Militaire 189, 190; 207; Medal of Honor, First 2, 37–39, 48, 199, 225; Medal of Honor, Second 2, 81, 84, 88, 90, 199, 205; Medal of Honor, Third 2,

Index

135, 136, 143, 144, 146, 147, 150; Navy Cross 2, 150, 206; newsboy 12; pay as private 18; pension 193; physical scars 51; proselytizers, attitude toward 203; reputation of 3, 201–203; retired 193; scrounger 203; as sergeant 52, 201; as sergeant major 193; Silver Star Citation 207; story-teller 203; women 40, 46, 191, 203; wounded 139, 177
Daly, David (brother) 9, 11, 91
Daly, Ellen Donovan (mother) 7, 8, 9, 91, 193
Daly, John (father) 7–11
Daly, Julia (older sister) 9
Daly, Julia (younger sister) 9, 11
Daly, Mary (sister) 9, 11, 91, 193, 197
Daly, Timothy (brother) 9
Daniels, Josephus 69, 84, 87, 114, 118, 149, 150, 192
Dartiguenave, Philippe Sudre 76
Davis, Robert Beale, Jr. 74
Degoutte, Jean Marie Joseph 140, 145
USS *DeKalb* 107
Depue, David E. 182
"Devil Dogs" 141, 142, 155, 199
Devoe Manufacturing Co. 13
Diaz, Porfirio 56
Dickman, Joseph 144
Dieckmann, Edward 194, 201, 202
Distinguished Service Cross, created 144
Distinguished Service Medal, created 144
Dollar, Betsy 45, 46
USS *Dolphin* 57
Dominican Republic: Guayacanas 99, 100; Las Trencheras 98, 99; Santiago 96, 101
Doyen, Charles 104, 109, 111, 112
Draucker, James 201
Dunbeck, Charley 181, 184
Duncan, David 186
Dunlap, Robert H. 100
Duryea Starch Works 10

USS *Eagle* 75
Ellis, Earl 174
Ellison, Hildor 165, 187
Evans, Frank E. 133, 134, 202

Fagan, Louis E., Jr. 185
Falls, Charles B. 142
Feland, Logan 137, 154, 160, 161, 163, 170, 174, 191, 195

Fleming, Peter 42
Fletcher, Frank F. 58, 59, 61, 63–65, 67–69
USS *Florida* 58
Foch, Ferdinand 152, 156, 161, 186
Forrest, Arthur 182
Fortson, Eugene 94
4th Marine Brigade, table of organization 108
Francis, William A. 140
Fredericks, Russell 80
Funston, Frederick 68
Furlong, Harold 183

Gabral, Maximo 100
Gamewell, Mary 26
Garrett, Franklin 138
Gaynor, William Jay 191
Gibbons, Floyd 129, 130, 132–134, 144, 145, 192
Giles, Lancelot 43
Glen Cove, New York 7, 10, 200
Glowin, Joseph 100, 101
Gourmand, Henri 168
Grant, Ulysses S. 92
Greiger, John C. 118
Gross, Samuel 83, 84, 88

Haiti: Fort Capois 78, 81, 82; Fort Dipitie 80, 81, 84, 87, 88, 90; Fort Liberte 78, 81, 82; Fort Riviere 82–84, 88, 90
Hall, Newt Hamill 18, 24, 26, 33, 34, 38, 75
Hamilton, George W. 124, 125, 170, 171, 173–176, 184
USS *Hancock* 66, 96
Hanneken, Herman H. 86
Harbord, James G. 111, 117, 118, 123, 126–128, 135–138, 140, 145, 149, 154, 160, 195
Harding, Warren G. 195
Harriman, E.H. 194
Harriman, W. Averill 194
Harrington, Samuel M. 72
Hearst, William Randolph 15, 16
Heureux, Ulises 92
Hoffman, Charles F. *see* Janson, Ernest August
Holcomb, Thomas 106, 117, 120, 126–128, 135–137, 149, 150, 157, 162, 197
Hoover, Herbert 87
Houchins, Lyle C. 165
Hough, Frank 106
Huerta, Victoriano 56–58, 67, 68

230

Index

Hughes, John Arthur (Johnny the Hard) 60–62, 68, 69, 105, 120, 135, 136–138, 149, 150, 157, 160
Hunt, John L. 185
Hunt, LeRoy 173, 184, 186

Iams, Ross Lindsey 83, 84, 88

Jackson, George R. 170, 185
Janson, Ernest August (aka Charles F. Hoffman) 125, 146, 147, 194
Jiminez, Juan Isidro 92–94

Kane, Theodore P. 95
Kelly, John J. 148, 172
Kent, Theodore P. 75
Keyser, Ralph 138, 140, 155, 157, 160
King, Charles B. 28
Kipling, Rudyard 15
Kocak, Matej 148, 156

Larson, Henry 170, 171, 174, 175, 183
Leconte, Cincinnatus 73
Lee, Harry 131, 154, 159, 162, 164, 170, 183, 187, 191
Lejeune, John J. 66, 90, 149, 150, 160, 168, 170, 181, 191, 193, 199, 202
Lengel, Edward 109, 111
Liggett, Hunter 144, 180, 181
Loeb, William (Daly's brother-in-law) 91, 193
Long Island City, Queens, New York 11
Loomis, Casey V. 165
Ludendorff, Erich 113, 152

Maas, Gustavo 60, 62
USS *Machias* 91, 101
Madero, Francisco 56
Mahan, Alfred Thayer 15
Mahoney, James E. 54
USS *Maine* 15
Mangin, Charles 153
Manney, Henry E., Jr. 112
USS *Marietta* 56
Marshall, S.L.A. 109
Mayo, Henry T. 58, 85
McCalla, Bowman 21, 23
McCarren, Patrick H. 191
McClellan, Edwin N. 118
McCloy, John 63
McCord, Charles 45
McGraw, John 191, 192
McKinley, William 15, 48
McMurty, George C. 146

Messersmith, Robert E. 162, 170, 171, 174, 175, 181
Meyer, George 52
Miller, Adoph 80
USS *Minnesota* 53
USS *Mississippi* 51, 54
Mitchell, Joseph A. 32, 37
USS *Montana* 102, 103
Morgan, J.P. 11
Morrison, George E. 41, 43
Myers, John Twiggs 20, 21, 28, 30, 31, 38

USS *Nashville* 75
National City Bank of New York 72, 73
Navy Cross created 144
Neibar, Thomas C. 146
Neville, Wendell C. 58, 60, 63, 65, 66, 68, 104, 112, 125, 138, 149, 150, 154, 160, 163, 164, 170, 176, 191
USS *New Jersey* 96
USS *Newark* 18–20, 37, 39, 47

USS *Ohio* 53
O'Leary, Arthur J. 161, 170
USS *Oregon* 20
Oriente, Michael 73
Ostermann, Edward A. 80, 81, 88

USS *Panther* 50
Peirce, John "the granite king" 165
Peirce, Reginald Carman McKnight 165, 170, 187
Pendleton, Joseph H. 96–98, 101
Peralte, Charlemagne 85–87
Pershing, John J. 107, 111, 141, 146, 149, 150, 159, 160, 161, 167, 170, 179, 180, 186, 189
Peterson, Carl E. 37
USS *Prairie* 49, 51, 52, 55, 58–60, 63, 94
Pratt, Charles 11
Preston, Diana 42
Pruitt, John Henry 148, 172
Pulitzer, Joseph 15, 16
Puller, Lewis B. "Chesty" 199
Puryear, Bennet, Jr. 112

Quick, John H. 105, 202

Rameau, Pierre 77
Rendinell, Joseph 135
Renold, Arnold 45
Renstrom, Gustave L. 46
USS *Rhode Island* 96
Robinson, Robert Guy 149

Index

Roosevelt, Franklin Delano 76, 82, 83, 87, 104, 196
Roosevelt, Theodore 48, 51, 71, 92
Root, Elihu 67
Rush, William R. 61–63, 69

Sam, Vibrun Guillaume 73, 74
USS *San Francisco* 65
Schmidt, Hans 89
Sellers, James McB. 172, 202
Shearer, Maurice Edwin 106, 111, 112, 117, 135–137, 140, 149, 150, 154, 160, 162, 163, 170
Shepherd, Lemuel 178
Shuler, George 162, 165, 170, 171, 174, 176, 177, 184, 185
Sibley, Berton W. 117, 126–128, 131, 133, 135, 140, 149, 150, 157, 160, 165, 170
Silverthorn, Merwin H. 156
Simmons, Edwin H. 112, 134, 186
Simon, Francois, Antoine 73
Simpson, Bertram Lenox 43
Smith, Holland M. 96, 98, 112
Smith, Julian C. 101
USS *Springfield* 52
Stockham, Fred 138
Stowell, George 185
Summerall, Charles 180, 181
Sweetman, Jack 61, 64, 67, 69
Swink, Roy Cleveland 111, 162

Taft, William Howard 54
Talbot, Ralph 149
Tassin, Raymond 121
USS *Tennessee* 75
Theodore, Joseph Davilmar 73
Thomas, Gerald C. 158
Thomas, R.E. 30, 31
Thomason, John 172
Turnage, Allen H. 81, 202
Turner, R. 30, 31
Turrill, Julius 124, 125, 149, 150, 154, 160
Twain, Mark 14

Upham, Oscar 23, 34–37
Upshur, William P. 78, 80, 81, 88, 202
USS *Utah* 58, 63

Vasquez, Horacio 92
Villa, Pancho 56, 111

Walker, George Herbert 194
Waller, Littleton T. 75, 77, 78, 82, 88–90
Waller, Littleton T., Jr. 117
USS *Washington* 74
Wells, Clarke H. 85
Westermark, Axel 32
Whittlesey, Charles 146
Wilcox, Albyn A. 187
Williams, Ernest C. 162, 164, 170–172, 174, 176
Williams, Lloyd C. 122
Wilson, Henry Lane 56
Wilson, Woodrow 54, 56–59, 64, 68, 74, 93, 94, 104, 144, 191
Winans, Roswell 100, 101
Wise, Frederic M. 94, 117, 120, 136–139, 149, 150
Woodfill, Samuel 146
Woolworth, F.W. 11
Wynn, Joseph A. 196
Ypiranga 58, 63
Zamor, Oreste 73
Zapata, Emiliano 56

www.ingramcontent.com/pod-product-compliance
Ingram Content Group UK Ltd.
Pitfield, Milton Keynes, MK11 3LW, UK
UKHW011435100725
460636UK00016B/344